I Make

Horse   Calls

Living a Dream with Horses

Aloha,
Come ride along!
Dr Thibeault

Marcia A. Thibeault, DVM

I Make Horse Calls

Living a Dream with Horses

Copyright © 2008

Marcia A. Thibeault DVM

ALL RIGHTS RESERVED

The events described in this book are true, but the characters are composites of several people, and the names have been changed to protect their privacy.

ISBN 978-0-9817848-0-9

Library of Congress Control Number 2008905920

First Printing July 2008

Second Printing March 2009

Published in the USA by
Medicine Beau Ink
P. O. Box 1702
Georgetown, Kentucky 40324

For additional copies of I Make Horse Calls or More Horse Calls send $14.95 per copy plus $4.95 s&h to the above address or visit our website at www.imakehorsecalls.com.

A portion of the proceeds from sales of this book will be donated to create a scholarship for a student enrolled in the Colorado State University College of Veterinary Medicine.

Printed in the United States by Morris Publishing
3212 East Highway 30
Kearney, NE 68847
1-800-650-7888

This book is dedicated to my family.

My mother, Catherine, lives her life as an example of unconditional love. She shared her interest in science, thoroughness and lifelong pursuit of learning.

My Father, Irv, who taught me how to work with my hands.

My grandmother Kitty and Great-Grandfather, Tom, taught the value of dedication, hard work, and persistence.

Thanks to the talented horsemen and women, professors and veterinarians who helped me along the way, and the faithful, loving animals that shared my life.

Prologue

Since I first set eyes on a horse as a toddler, a bond was formed that would never break.

When I was a young child, peering out the back window of our car, if I spied a pony ride, I'd beg my parents to stop and let me ride. I'd gladly hand over the entire contents of my piggy bank to ride until my meager savings was gone.

The smell of the ponies, their glistening coats and long manes and tails, the clip-clop of their hooves, their beautiful brown eyes - the windows to the spirit within - all captured my soul.

As a teenager my bond with animals, especially horses, grew steadily stronger. I wanted to - I needed to - spend my life around these wonderful, inspiring creatures. And when I found people who shared my passion I let them into my inner circle, for it was a special kinship, inexplicable to those who lacked it.

No matter what obstacles lay in my way, nothing would deter me from that goal.

My life would be forever be enriched by horses. By caring for them my dreams came true.

I Make Horse Calls

Chapter 1 Her Dream Horse 3
Chapter 2 Clancy Comes Home 11
Chapter 3 Decision Day.. 15
Chapter 4 Right Time - Wrong Place 25
Chapter 5 Please Come.. 39
Chapter 6 Only Four More Hours 59
Chapter 7 Over Hill and Over Dale 71
Chapter 8 Buyer Beware 103
Chapter 9 Be Careful What You Wish For 115
Chapter 10 Jet and the Heavy Rescue Unit 121
Chapter 11 Nothing's Wrong 127
Chapter 12 A Holiday Tradition... 131
Chapter 13 Fort Fun.. 135
Chapter 14 Designated Fainters... 169
Chapter 15 Dead Man's Curve 179
Chapter 16 Rocky's Championship Fight 195

Chapter 1 Her Dream Horse

The gray Arabian gelding, Dream, bucked and frolicked on the end of the lunge line, demonstrating just how good he felt. With his compact, well-muscled frame and round body shape, he looked like a Lipizzaner from the Spanish Riding School in Vienna demonstrating "airs above the ground." This certainly made my job easier, as I had come to assess his health for Heather Marks, who wanted to buy him for use as a trail horse.

Heather watched my exam intently as wisps of auburn hair danced around her cheeks on the warm breeze, refusing confinement in the braid that cascaded past her shoulders. I heard the excitement in her voice when she scheduled the appointment to check Dream. She had been looking for a sure-footed, sensible horse to ride through the Rockies, and was certain she had found just the right one when she came across Dream. Arabians were bred to cross the desert, and their endurance is legendary.

Dream was full of energy, but after he blew off a little steam he relaxed into the rhythmic trot I needed to evaluate his gait. I was checking for lameness problems, looking for anything that would prevent him from carrying Heather over the rough mountainous terrain. Subtle lamenesses may only be apparent when the horse travels in one direction, so I examined Dream trotting both ways. He was fine to the left so I asked him to reverse, which he did obediently. As he struck off trotting I could see that he was sound when going to the right as well. I asked Dream to whoa, and he settled down and walked to me, pressing his velvety soft muzzle into my hand looking for treats.

I Make Horse Calls

I was impressed with this horse's cooperative nature. He was healthy and full of energy, galloping and bucking, yet he quickly responded, settling down and trotting rhythmically when I asked. During his physical examination he had stood calmly and patiently as I meticulously checked him over, touching practically every inch of his body.

When I slid my hand down Dream's front leg, he had willingly raised his foot to be examined. I put hoof testers on several sites on the frog and the sole, checking the health of the structures invisible beneath the surface. He showed no pain anywhere. I palpated each leg for scars, thickenings, swelling, or heat. His tendons were free of blemishes. His joints moved freely as I extended and flexed each joint separately. There was no arthritis to interfere with his movement.

Using my stethoscope I listened to Dream's heart, which had a regular rhythm and no murmurs. His lungs easily moved the large volumes of air he would need to perform efficiently at high altitude.

I checked his teeth. He was only six years old, as the seller had reported. That was a relief. I had seen dishonest sellers claim horses were in the prime of their lives when they were actually much older. I examined Dream's teeth for sharp points or missing teeth, as horses' dental problems can limit their usefulness and shorten their lives. Dream had received good dental care in the past. His teeth were fine.

I asked Christy, Dream's owner "Why are you selling him?"

"My husband is taking a job out of state, and we can't afford to keep him. We've been struggling financially until he found a new job, and the cost of moving is putting us in a bind. We just can't afford to take him with us."

I could hear the sadness in Christy's voice. I understood all too well, because I had to sell my first horse for the same reason. It was little consolation, but Heather was excited to find Dream and would give him a loving home. Maybe some reassuring words would put Christy's mind at ease.

"Well, Heather sure likes him. He's getting a good home."

"Yes, he is, but I'll miss him," she said as her eyes welled up with tears.

"I know you will. You've taken good care of him."

4

I Make Horse Calls

I remembered how I missed my first horse, never seeing him again after we moved. As a child, the pain of that loss was deep. My horse was more than my hobby - he was my friend.

Maybe as an adult, Christy would be less pained by his loss. Maybe not.

"Let's take him into the barn. I need to check his eyes in a dark place."

Christy took the gelding into a stall at the back of the barn while I got my ophthalmoscope and atropine to examine Dream's eyes. Once I had dilated his pupils, I could see clearly through his cornea and lens, and examined the retina at the back of the eye. Everything looked normal.

Every prepurchase exam is an opportunity to check a horse thoroughly to find any health problems which might interfere with the horse's ability to perform up to the buyer's expectations. Few horses are perfect, and the buyer needs to know the general condition of the horse's health, and be aware of any problems that might limit the performance or make the horse unsuitable for their needs. I felt an obligation to every horse, to make sure it wouldn't be pushed beyond its physical limits.

Sometimes sellers tell me I'm negative - that I never have anything good to say about their horse. That's not really true, because I always say *something* nice about every horse, whether it's the horse's temperament, conformation, or even its coat color. I'm a horse lover at heart, and can find at least one redeeming feature in every horse.

I remind sellers that their job is to tell the buyer how great the horse is - to point out all of its best qualities. My job is to objectively examine the horse - injecting a dose of reality into the horse buying process. My comments balance the sales pitch of the sellers, helping buyers get a realistic picture of the horse, so they can make the informed decision that's best for both horse and buyer.

Some clients decide to buy the horse, and then schedule the exam as an afterthought. Disappointment descends like a black cloud when I find a serious problem. Both buyer and seller become upset. Sometimes they buy the horse anyway, choosing with their hearts instead of their heads, and then deal with the problems as best they can.

I Make Horse Calls

Some of the stories are sad, like the grandfather who went to an auction and bought a young horse for his grandson, planning to train it and give the colt to the boy when he was old enough. A quick look at the horse's teeth showed that the horse was elderly, and was unlikely to still be alive by the time the grandson was old enough to ride.

At least today I didn't have any bad news for Heather. It's rare that I can't find anything wrong with a horse, but Dream was that exception - as close to perfect as any horse I've ever examined, and I checked him meticulously so I was confident in my findings.

As I finished the exam I was convinced that Dream would be perfect for Heather. Dream's gray coat was glossy and he was a little overweight, giving him what horsemen call bloom - that eye appeal buyers want. While beauty is said to be only skin deep, Dream's beauty went all the way through - no physical problems and a lovely attitude as well. I told Heather I could see no reason not to buy Dream.

I gathered up my instruments and filled out the health certificate so Dream could travel to his new stable.

"If you don't mind, would you tell me how much the asking price is on this horse?"

I don't like to pry, but my clients often ask me how much a horse is worth, and by doing prepurchase exams regularly and asking the selling price, I keep tabs on market conditions.

"I don't mind. Christy is asking $300. Do you think that's a fair price?"

Was she kidding? That was a steal!

"At that price you might get arrested for horse theft!"

I said goodbye to Heather. Her cabin was beyond the boundaries of my practice, so I wouldn't see her or Dream again. I wished her well.

I walked back to my Suburban to an enthusiastic greeting from Clancy, my Border collie, who was hanging so far out the open window she was in danger of falling out. She was trained to stay in the truck, although sometimes she would be hanging on to the running board by her toenails to avoid stepping on the grass.

"Move over, Clancy, you can't drive. Your legs are too short, and besides, you don't have a license. I need to get in."

I Make Horse Calls

I loved Clancy's zest for life, and enjoyed her company on my daily rounds. Leaning over her head I put the health certificates on the dashboard, trying to keep her kisses from slobbering up my sunglasses. Then I went around the truck to put away my instruments.

My father enjoyed carpentry, so together we built a custom wooden box for my medicines and instruments. It fit perfectly into the suburban, and held more than commercial vet boxes. Compartments were custom-fitted for each bottle of medicine and piece of equipment. Rubber mats kept things from sliding around and were easy to clean. Long drawers slid out the back, and short drawers and cabinets were accessible through the side doors. We installed a refrigerator for vaccines and antibiotics, and a tank of warm water for cleaning - everything I needed.

Clancy followed me inside the truck as I went around the outside, from cabinet to cabinet. She kept trying to lick my face as I put supplies in each drawer. Somehow she could slip her slender frame through the six inch gap between the box and the side of the truck. I tried to discourage her from walking there, as that gap contained splints and the hacksaw I used for cutting splints, which could cut her paws. I closed the rear door in front of her as I finished. Even more amazing was the fact that she could turn around in the small gap, and was at the driver's door again to meet me as I climbed in, weary from my long day's work.

Clancy knew the routine. This appointment was over and we'd be on the road awhile, so she settled onto the seat beside me, her head in my lap as I started the engine. The lane to Christy's farm was west of the first foothill, and so close to the neighboring ridge that the sun was gone from here for the day. I turned onto the familiar road and as I topped the first hill the prairie unrolled for miles in front of me. I looked across the city of Denver, and thought I could see all the way to Kansas. The eastern plains were bathed in the soft glow of the waning day.

Turning north I was rewarded every summer evening with a spectacular sunset behind the Rocky Mountains. The afternoon clouds dappled the sky, reflecting a glorious array of golds and reds. The heat of the day was giving way, and the long shadows and fading light made the foothills serene and beautiful.

I Make Horse Calls

Dusk is my favorite time of day, and I felt happy and satisfied. I loved my work and was glad to help. Dream was going to a good home, and Heather would have many happy years, enjoying the mountain trails from Dream's back. And maybe someday soon Christy would get a new horse.

Clancy stretched out on the seat beside me, content to sleep on the way home through familiar territory. She was quickly twitching her toes, chasing errant sheep through her dreams. Diligently guarding my truck while I worked was a serious job for a Border collie with a strong work ethic.

When I was a child, I had boarded my second horse, a gift from a friend, at a stable just down the road from Christy's ranch. The road was a dirt track then, but progress had turned it into four lanes of asphalt.

I grew up in the city, but my parents shared my interest in horses, as they had ridden together as teenagers. Mom drove me to the stable in the summer before she went to work and Dad picked me up on his way home. Until I was old enough to get a summer job, I traveled this road every day.

I began riding lessons at age six, and my parents insisted on English style lessons. From watching westerns on TV, I knew I wanted to be a cowboy, but any chance to be near horses was a chance I took.

When I was eleven my sister and I saved enough money to buy our first horse and saddle. My parents approved, if my sister and I paid half the costs of boarding the horse at a nearby stable. My sister baby-sat and I mowed lawns to pay our share, and my parents paid the veterinary and shoeing expenses. We bicycled to the stable every day in the summer, but in the fall we moved away and had to sell the horse. I knew exactly how Christy felt today.

When we returned a few years later, a friend loaned us one of her horses, which we boarded within walking distance of home. But when the stable owner moved his operation further out to Christy's neighborhood, I needed my parents to drive me.

The new stable had 300 acres, and both boarded and rented horses. I volunteered to brush and tack up the rental horses, leading the guests on trail rides. My favorite memories were Saturday nights in the summer, when the ranch would have steak fries at a site perched high on a steep hillside along the Front Range. Those sunset trail rides ended at a campfire with steaks sizzling over an open fire. At dusk we sat around the campfire watching the thunderheads build higher and higher in the eastern sky. The displays of lightning they spawned were spectacular, flashing for miles across the prairie sky. The clouds reflected the pink and golden sunlight back to us, but having endured my share of severe storms, I knew they loomed black and ominous over anyone caught beneath them.

As the years passed since those stormy summer evenings I had been privileged to train under renowned trainers and have success in the show ring. I taught riding and trained horses, then earned my biology degree and went to vet school.

But those summers as a child, enjoying the horses and the wide open spaces and racing my friends across the plains like cowboys in Western movies being chased by the Indians are memories I treasure.

The campfire site was still nestled into the hillside, but the city was encroaching across my memories. Pastures were replaced with subdivisions and shopping malls. Dirt roads were paved into highways, flooded by a never-ending stream of drivers in a hurry to get to their destinations without noticing the beauty or stopping to breathe in the fresh country air.

But the horse people responded by moving further out so the lifestyle continued, for those who sought it.

My practice was growing. Hopefully, someday, I could afford a small farm for Clancy and me.

Chapter   2 Clancy Comes Home

She stood trembling on the kitchen floor, her paws spread wide in an attempt to grip the slippery linoleum, her spindly legs precariously holding her body a few inches above the floor.

The tiny, black and white puppy was only eight weeks old, and this was her first excursion out of the grassy kennel. There she had been tearing around with her brothers and sister, running, jumping, and playing until they dropped to the cool grass to rest, with sides heaving and tongues unrolling with each breath.

But today was the day the puppies came inside to be sold. I was here to choose my favorite - to make it my very own. I adored puppies,

"I am only interested in a female," I told the young boy who owned the puppies.

"We have two," he replied.

He pointed to a large female puppy, with an extra thick white coat dotted with black streaks and freckles. She was boisterous and strong, not meek and shy like her little black sister. She had quickly gotten hold of the slippery footing and was chasing her brothers. The smaller female had found a place to hide from the bright lights of the house, and was creeping carefully toward the long flowered curtains that hung to the floor in the farthest corner of the kitchen.

I sat down on the floor amidst the pool of playful puppies.

The litter had two females and three males. The stronger male puppies were growing used to the slippery footing, and were exploring the kitchen and me.

I quickly made my decision. I told the young man, "I want the white one."

He hesitated.

I Make Horse Calls

"The white one is going to my uncle. I promised him a female from the litter, but Mickey is available."

He pointed to the bulge behind the curtains.

"We call the little one Mickey because she has three round black spots on her back, which remind us of Mickey Mouse ears."

The small female was the runt of the litter, and my last dog had been the runt. Although that puppy had grown into a marvelous dog, and we shared 13 loving years together, the dog's life was plagued with health problems that made my life a constant worry. I was hoping for carefree times to come. The recent loss of my old dog, after such a long time together, still weighed heavily on my heart. I was afraid to fall in love with a puppy that might be sick.

"I really want the white one...or I can just keep looking." I was disappointed the stronger female could not be mine.

I played with the puppies on the floor. The braver males were jumping at my face, begging for attention, falling flat in their clumsy attempts. But nothing would deny them a chance to explore this new person.

Choosing a puppy was a big decision for me. My dogs went everywhere with me - for rides in the car, for walks in the park, and visiting friends and family. They slept beside me, sharing my bed.

I had to choose just the right puppy.

"If you promised the white puppy to your uncle, I won't ask you to go back on your word. Promises can't be broken."

By now the litter had spread out across the room, with puppies under chairs, and puppies under tables, puppies scratching at the door, and puppies playing tag. Wrestling matches were breaking out everywhere.

"Well, my uncle never actually saw the white puppy. We just liked her best and thought he would too."

The puppies continued to investigate me. They nipped my fingers and crawled over my legs. The innocent perfume of puppy breath filled the kitchen. Even if I didn't take one home, seeing these energetic bundles of love eroded the sorrow of losing my old dog.

The white female was playing roughly with her brothers, battling with tooth and claw, showing how vigorous she was.

"I guess we could give Mickey to my uncle. He hasn't seen either pup, so he probably wouldn't mind."

I Make Horse Calls

I looked down in my lap. The small female pup had summoned the courage to venture unseen from her hiding place and was curled up asleep in my lap.

What could I do?

The puppy had chosen me.

It was meant to be.

"No" I whispered as I gave my heart to the little pup. "I'll take this one." My other dog was small, but wonderful. And if this puppy has chosen me, what more could I ask?

So I picked up the tiny puppy, who stiffened her body in fear of being lifted.

"If you felt unsafe and like to hide, I know just the place for you."

I unzipped my jacket, and invited the puppy inside. She eagerly climbed in and crawled around my waist until her nose was tucked into the small of my back. There she settled, safe and warm.

I paid the young man and drove home with the puppy snuggled pleasantly in my coat, knowing our lives together would be good.

I named her Clancy.

Chapter 3 Decision Day

As I sat on the edge of my bed, my toes trilled in anticipation. Pulling on my clean, dry, threadbare socks, I was eagerly anticipating a day of dry feet. Since my rubber boots split open a few weeks ago, my feet had been drenched by the morning dew sloshing around inside my boots. The duct tape I used to repair the gap quickly came off in the wet grass. My feet had been miserably cold and wet all day - my toes shriveled like pink raisins. Every morning my boots were still wet.

I had no money for new boots, but today I had a plan.

Through the early morning darkness I slid in my stocking feet down the cold hallway floor to the kitchen. Like a predator I searched cabinet after cabinet, until my eyes finally located my prey - a box of plastic sandwich bags.

Slipping a bag over each foot, I then slid my toes into the soggy boots. I gave my new footwear a test. It was a bit dicey navigating around the kitchen with my feet sliding sideways inside my boots, but the plastic bags kept my socks from absorbing the moisture from the boot linings.

Success!

I grabbed my windbreaker, and was out the door. Walking past my car, sitting silently under the morning dew, I grabbed my rusting bicycle from the shed and was off. Even though the four miles to the farm was completely flat, and the air at sea level was heavy with oxygen, it seemed unbelievably hard. I had cycled over the mountainous terrain of Colorado, in the thin mountain air, through two years of college, but even though the central Florida terrain was as flat as a pancake, this old bike never made the trip easily. After a month of pedaling the route every day, I did not seem to be getting more fit. I hoped the cause was the aged bicycle and not my aging body.

As I cycled along the marshland, the sun was pushing its way through the fog on the eastern horizon. Egrets were coming to life along the roadside, preparing for the day's vigil keeping the Brahman cattle free of insects. Swags of Spanish moss draped from the trees, and I knew huge vultures were skulking in the treetops, although it was still too dark to see them. I pedaled faster. I had to show them I was still alive. Buzzards only eat carrion, right?

Look alive, I told myself. Keep moving!

Perhaps today was the day to admit that my parents were right. To admit that I needed a college degree to survive financially in today's world. With my whole soul I wanted to spend my life with horses, but the financial challenges of working as a groom were insurmountable.

The reality was hitting home. I earned less than $1 an hour, plus a room for me and board for my horse, a horse that I needed to sell soon. Despite working 60 hours a week grooming show horses, I had little to show for it. In fact I had less than little…I had debt.

My wisdom teeth began to erupt, but there was no room for them. As a result, my back teeth were pushing my front teeth out of alignment. I would have to get them out sooner or later, and sooner would mean that I wouldn't need braces. The only problem was - I had no money.

I knew that money couldn't buy happiness, but poverty was certainly buying me misery. I didn't need to be rich to be happy, but food, clothing, and medical care shouldn't be luxuries when working hard from sunrise to sunset, six days a week.

My employer recommended an oral surgeon, who did a fine job, but charged me five weeks of my salary for 20 minutes of his time. I offered him the few dollars I received for my birthday as a down payment, and convinced him to accept ten payments equaling half of my salary for the next ten weeks. I needed a few dollars to buy groceries. He obliged, while telling me he was sending his daughter to Italy to study art for the summer.

I was *so* happy to help finance her trip abroad, while I struggled to afford groceries on $25 a week.

I Make Horse Calls

Today I was halfway through the 10 weeks, with no money for gas to drive to work, and certainly no money for new boots. I saved my gas money for the weekly trip to the grocery in town, and after cashing my paycheck at the bank I stopped by the dentist's office to pay my bill. With gas over 50 cents a gallon, I had to do all of my weekly errands on a gas budget of one dollar.

I had been buying my t-shirts at the surplus store for $3.00 and my sneakers at the grocery store for $4.00, and praying that my jeans wouldn't wear out. I didn't see how I could tighten my belt any more. The farm supplied me with a furnished room and electricity, but we had no phone. I had to bicycle to a nearby store to call home.

My co-workers and I found free hobbies for the rare days we had off between horse shows. Enjoying the beach was free, if we could afford the gas to get there. Tennis was free, and if we went at noon we could always find an open court. We were fit enough to play in the noonday sun, while the sane people stayed inside. In the cool of the evening the courts were too crowded for us to find a court.

Our tennis balls were so old and heavy that it felt like we were hitting rocks. I gave my financial situation serious consideration when my tennis partner requested $1.50 to split the cost of a can of new tennis balls and I was forced to say no. I couldn't spare even such a meager amount.

I cycled on. There was no traffic on these country roads in the early morning. I searched for a way to make a better future for myself as I pedaled onward through the fog.

I had to make a change in my life. Maybe I could find a better job in the business sector, and afford to board a horse at a nice stable, so I wouldn't lose all contact with the horse world. But jobs offered to women rarely paid enough to afford such a luxury. Women were still being funneled into traditional careers - teaching, nursing, interior design, or secretarial positions - none of which appealed to me. I had worked as a file clerk during high school and college, and came home late, numb with boredom.

Being poor was better than being bored.

My sister studied hard, wanting to be a doctor since childhood, and earned good grades in college. When the time came for her medical school interview, they denied her admittance, although they acknowledged that she was a competent student. They said it wasn't worth their time to train her, because she would take time off from practice to raise a family. Today such remarks would be considered sexual discrimination, but at the time, it was just the way things were.

But I didn't have my sister's strong background in science. I had barely been exposed to it.

I had gone to a rigorous Catholic school for elementary grades. English and math were emphasized, and spelling and math bees fostered my competitive spirit. We had classes in history and geography, but biology was not taught.

When I transferred to public school, I was intimidated by the classroom science lab, with black soapstone counters, drawers full of beakers and other strange equipment. The natural gas spigots at each desk made me afraid my classmates would set the building ablaze with their Bunsen burners. And I was years behind them in the sciences.

Because of my Father's job, I attended six schools before graduating from high school, and every school system had different graduation requirements. I was told I lacked credits in art, music, and home economics - subjects in which I am still deficient.

I couldn't take high school biology with the smartest students because I had to take choir. Anyone who has tolerated my singing, which I only do under duress, knows what a waste of time that was. I pity the poor choir director and any choir members who stood within earshot of me.

I couldn't take biology with the average students because I had to take home economics, learning to make tomato soup. I have always hated tomato soup.

Finally I was allowed to take biology with the football team. While many a high school girl might love sitting next to the varsity quarterback, I felt completely out of place sitting at a table for four, with three members of the football team. There were no scientific discussions at our table, only replays of their spectacular plays made during last week's game. I sat there in silence as they embellished their athletic feats. While I was an avid fan of professional football, working on Saturdays prevented me from going to the high school games.

I Make Horse Calls

The players were poor students, barely capable of finding their desks each day. To make matters worse, the teacher was rude and insulting, so I never liked biology.

The delay cost me the opportunity to take physiology and chemistry in high school. Chemistry sounded too hard anyway, and I wasn't sure exactly what physiology was, but I was sure it wasn't for me. I took physics and really enjoyed it.

I slowed my pace as an armadillo scurried across the road and was soon lost in the tall grass.

I enjoyed creative writing, but English majors become school teachers more often than they become authors. I had no younger siblings, so I was uncomfortable around children. And I sorely lacked patience. But then again, if I strangled an unruly student, I would get free meals and housing for life in the federal penitentiary and my financial worries would be over.

Although I liked physics, I couldn't imagine myself working as a physicist, locked in a windowless laboratory all day. I knew I'd go crazy if I couldn't be outside.

I studied anthropology at the university as a way to avoid the harder sciences. I was fascinated by the study of physical and cultural evolution of early man, but from my classmates' experiences I discovered that anthropologists remained unemployed after graduation, so many went to graduate school only to delay the inevitable.

Physical education was required and the college offered horseback riding. I was eager to spend time around horses and to improve my riding. There I met a wonderfully talented rider, a young man from Connecticut named Chip, with his eyes on vet school. He was a passionate instructor, who taught me to ride and show jumpers. He repeatedly pushed me to the limits of my courage and athletic abilities with difficult obstacles, but never let me get hurt. He trusted that I could do it, and somehow I always did. And I was proud to exceed my own expectations.

When I left college Chip put in a good word for me with influential people in the horse world, helping me on my way.

I truly loved my job - grooming horses, being outside all day, walking the horses out to their paddocks each morning as the fog hovered in the orange groves, bathing and grooming the horses until their coats gleamed in the sunlight, watching the young horses progress through their training until they were strong and confident jumpers bringing home top prizes at shows. I took pride in the good condition of the horses in my care. I also helped maintain the farm - the hedges were neatly trimmed and the barn was immaculate. It was a great place to work and a great place for a horse to live. It just wasn't so great come payday.

But today, as I cycled past the cow pastures of central Florida, I knew it was time for a change. My financial situation was dismal. I needed something else. But what else could I do?

With his degree, the oral surgeon billed his 20 minutes equal to 300 hours of my work. If his college diploma meant that his time was worth 900 times what my work was worth, I could see that I would have to use my brains to get ahead. Physical work was not my road to financial security.

It was disturbing to think that even my horse, Frank, made more money than I did! I was paid $7.50 for every *hour* he was used for a riding lesson, while I only made $7.00 a *day* as a groom. At least he had a good job, so I made him pay his own expenses.

When I left college I had set two goals for myself - to groom for a reputable barn within six months, and to ride for one within two years. I achieved the first goal quickly, but the latter goal remained elusive.

It was now nearly five years since I left college, years spent working at large stables where I handled many horses. I left Colorado to train in the east riding under American, French and British riders. I watched riders from all over the world compete at international shows, with drastically different breeds of horses and riding styles, and noticed the best riders accomplished the same goals with strikingly different methods. Observation of these horsemen opened my eyes to techniques that were worlds apart from what I had been taught. I assimilated this information with my own experience and found I now had the answers to many problems I would encounter training horses.

Over time I came to understand the horse industry and its people.

I Make Horse Calls

I returned to Colorado and took a riding instructor's course, becoming certified as an instructor, but lessons had to be canceled too often because of inclement weather. If I had an indoor arena I could teach evenings, as well as in the winter, and earn a dependable income. But I couldn't afford such an undertaking. Without a steady income, I could never qualify for a mortgage to buy a house, much less a farm.

And the clock was ticking. Mr. Right was not waiting in the wings, eager to sweep me off my feet and relieve me of my financial difficulties - eager to keep me in the manner to which I would like to become accustomed.

I hoped to get around the lack of an indoor arena by relocating to a warmer climate, so I moved to Florida when offered a job taking young thoroughbreds that had no success at the racetrack and teaching them to jump. But the job disappeared while I unpacked.

There were no jobs available in Florida in the winter. The population swelled with snowbirds - northerners escaping colder climates. I searched everywhere for work, but couldn't even find a job for the Christmas season, so I went back to grooming because it was the only job I could find. My salary as a working student four years ago was $25 per week plus a room, and this job offered only $50 per week plus a room. The farm already had an instructor so I couldn't supplement my income by teaching there, and I worked too many hours and traveled too often to shows to establish a clientele teaching off the farm. The manager told me there was no future in grooming. I was sad to reply that there didn't seem to be much of a present either.

I could only see two jobs in the horse industry that yielded regular paychecks - horseshoer and veterinarian - and horseshoeing was too much like work.

As I neared the farm, the sun was peeking through the fog, and the palm trees were casting long, faint shadows across the roadway.

My parents had urged me to enter pre-veterinary classes after high school, but I couldn't stand the thought of using healthy, unwanted animals to learn anatomy. Dissection of an animal that could have found a home as someone's pet was revolting. And at that time less than five percent of veterinary students were female. So the door to a veterinary career was slammed shut for women.

Why set my sights on vet school if I had no chance to get in?

No one in my family had gone into medicine. I had no female role models in medicine. My physician and the veterinarians that treated my animals were men. With my weak background in science, I had no confidence that I could pass the courses required for a veterinary degree.

Knowing of my plight, my sister sent me information on veterinary technician school. They accepted women, and the academic track would be easier than earning a doctorate degree. The pay for veterinary technicians probably wasn't enough to live on, but it would certainly be a step up. But did I want to spend that much time and effort for just a step up?

My college entrance exams had gone well, but I had no idea what my science aptitude was. But I was wasting my brain. I had to try something.

As I pedaled down the farm driveway, I scattered the flock of guinea hens that ran willy-nilly down the path ahead of me in panic. They never learned that turning off the drive, rather than trying to outrun me, was the secret to survival. It was the same scene every day. They'd run straight down the lane as fast as their spindly legs could carry their oversized bodies, tiny heads bobbing with every stride. Then suddenly, when they were nearly beneath my wheels, they'd turn aside, escaping imminent death. Surely this flock was the inspiration for the term bird-brained.

I pushed my bike across the grassy knoll to the side of the barn. Another work day was about to begin, and although I loved my job, I had to consider my future. I would never own a farm if I didn't make a change. And the time was now.

I stowed my bike in the feed room and grabbed a halter, taking the brown thoroughbred gelding out of his stall through the dew-soaked grass to the sandy paddock. The screeching peacocks brought the barn to life as the other grooms arrived for the day's work.

I Make Horse Calls

Breathing in the rich, earthy air of the farm, I closed the paddock gate. The gelding immediately dropped to his knees, and began to grunt as he rolled contentedly in the white sand. I walked back to the barn for my next horse, my toes pleasantly dry. Maybe I would solve more than one problem today.

I had to pursue my dream of a career with horses in another way.

While vet tech school might be the answer, why not aim for vet school? In the years that passed as I worked in the horse industry, the climate for women entering traditionally male-dominated professions was slowly changing. More freshman veterinary students were female. Perhaps going to vet school would be possible.

I had benefited in two ways from leaving college - I gained hands-on experience in the horse industry, and opportunities for women were opening up.

If my grades weren't good enough to get into vet school, then I could apply to vet technician school.

I had a plan and a back-up plan.

My horse, Frank, was already for sale, and if I sold my horse trailer, I could fund a few semesters of tuition at the state university - the most affordable option. With good grades, I had a chance. It was time to take that chance.

I would push myself academically as Chip had spurred me to success in the riding arena.

My great-grandfather, Tom Hogan, used to say "The best place to find a helping hand is at the end of your own arm." It was time to follow his advice.

I snapped a shank on the bay filly, pushed open her stall gate, and set out as the last wisps of fog were giving way to the intense sunshine of the new day.

I would make a brighter future for myself, transforming my life without losing my goal of working with horses.

I would become a horse vet!

Chapter   4 Right Time - Wrong Place

The ink was barely dry on my veterinary license. I had graduated two months ago, and passed all three national veterinary examinations and two state board exams.   The only positions advertised in equine practice were in southern California.   I landed a job in Los Angeles, working for Dr. Tillman.

While I had heard of California as being a place of great opportunity - the land of milk and honey - my mentor from vet school, Dr. Turner, called California "the land of the fruits and the nuts." We'd soon see who was right.

I had graduated from vet school at Colorado State University, and after visiting other schools, I knew I had attended one of the best schools for equine medicine and surgery. But I was surprised to learn that California horsemen held Colorado graduates in higher regard than California graduates from Davis. Davis is highly esteemed by the veterinary community.   So besides proving my worth as a newly licensed vet, I had to prove worthy of the respect of these critical strangers - clients who were comfortable with my experienced boss, but wary of anything new, including me.

But I soon found that my hiatus from college worked to my advantage in another, unexpected way. Being five years older than my classmates, the age showed on my sun-worn face, so my first clients never suspected I was a recent graduate.

Despite my education and years of working with horses, I had no experience in private veterinary practice, other than observing practice as a pre-vet student, or when watching the veterinarian treat my own horses. So I sought employment as an associate veterinarian, rather than starting out on my own. I hoped to learn valuable lessons from more experienced veterinarians, and ease into the rigors of private practice gently. Busy, older practitioners often mentor young graduates, while in return they receive an update on medical treatments and procedures, and an assistant willing to work for lower wages. It can be a win-win situation.

Private practices are much busier than university practices. At the university teaching hospital each patient is attended by a specialist veterinarian and also by a resident and an intern - fully qualified graduate veterinarians who are pursuing specialty degrees - as well as several junior and senior veterinary students. Private practices can't afford the luxury of such manpower. Dr. Tillman had only one part-time assistant for three vets.

As a new associate in the practice, I did not know any of the clients, or their horses. After hours the office was closed, and without a key I couldn't access the medical records. I was also learning my way around the crowded roads of Los Angeles, and was shocked to find horses tucked away on small dry lots in the canyons and in backyards in downtown Burbank.

While Dr. Tillman's practice did some routine care, there was so much emergency work that I felt like a firefighter plunged into an inferno. Practitioners who find themselves constantly on the run, going from emergency to emergency, are called "Fire-Engine Practitioners." In veterinary school we were advised to provide complete, comprehensive medical care for our patients, rather than just "putting out the fires" once they're burning.

Firefighters rely on teamwork, but I was completely on my own. Dr. Tillman didn't provide an assistant to hold horses for me while I struggled awkwardly with procedures that were still new to me. The vets in the practice were spread out across several counties, and as cell phones were still prohibitively expensive, there was no way to contact a more experienced colleague if I needed some advice.

Dr. Tillman's expectations were unrealistic. He thought I should float teeth on 50 horses a day. No one can do that many horses, and certainly not a new graduate! I backed my uncooperative patients into the corner of their stalls so they were safely confined. However, this left me standing in the lowest part of the stall, the wet spot, and my tall thoroughbred patients resisted my efforts by towering above me, easily keeping their teeth out of my reach.

At the end of my first week Dr. Tillman said he would be attending a medical seminar and I would be taking emergency call alone. Applying my knowledge to clinical situations hadn't yet become second nature. Trying so hard to do my best made the work mentally and physically draining. I looked forward to the chance to prove myself while dreading the thought that I might confront a situation I couldn't handle.

So that Friday evening, as I returned to my tiny motel room after a long day of appointments, I grabbed a burger at a drive-thru and ate in the car while stuck in traffic. I realized there was another possibility - maybe there would be no emergencies tonight. Maybe I could spend a quiet evening at home relaxing. Maybe not - the squawking pager changed my thinking just as I settled comfortably onto the bed with a veterinary journal. An emergency meant my respite was short-lived. Reading would have to wait.

A quick call to the answering service and I was connected to Maureen Thompson, who had a sick colt.

"Hello Maureen, this is Dr. Thibeault. How can I help you today?"

"Dr. Thibeault? Where's Dr. Tillman? I always use Dr. Tillman."

"Dr. Tillman is out of town at a medical conference. May I help you?"

"Well, I guess. I don't have any choice, do I?"

Thanks for the vote of confidence.

"My two year old paint colt, Apache, is acting really strange. I don't know what's wrong with him."

"What's he doing?" I asked, hoping it would be something easy to solve.

"He's not eating, and he's pawing, but it doesn't look like colic. He normally is playful, and bites me, but he's not acting playful now. Oh yeah, and he crosses his front legs when he walks."

Oh brother, what a bizarre list of symptoms! I didn't want to admit that I had absolutely no idea what was wrong with her colt, so I just replied that I'd be right out and I was soon on my way.

Traffic was always terrible in Los Angeles, but if it can get worse, Friday night rush hour would be the time. The sign at the edge of the city listed the population of LA as 13.4 million. Tonight most of them seemed to be in front of me, crawling home from work, eager to get started on their weekend activities. I recalled a comment attributed to Peter Lynch, investing guru of Fidelity, who, when told Americans are lazy and don't want to work, replied that if that was the case, then who were all these people clogging the roads at rush hour?

A quick check of the map showed no faster way to get to Maureen's so I thought about the traffic, as there seemed to be nothing I could do about it.

I was born in Baltimore, and although I only lived there a few years, it seemed that the local citizens rarely traveled, and were proud of it. A long trip for many of my neighbors was a trip to York, Pennsylvania, an out of state adventure which entailed a 30 minute drive up the highway. Many never traveled far in their lives, except perhaps a summer sojourn to the shore at Ocean City.

But people were different in the rural west. In Colorado my ranching friends thought nothing of driving 50 miles for a steak dinner or to square dance on Saturday night, and in California, people seemed to live in their cars, jamming the roadways around the clock.

Where were all these people going?

After serious deliberation and miles of inching along in stop-and-slow traffic, it occurred to me that when the pilgrims came to the new world, there must have been two different personality types. Some came seeking freedom and wishing to make a new start. After crossing the stormy north Atlantic in relatively small boats, they were glad to set foot on terra firma and never strayed far from port. Their descendents shared this characteristic. Others were explorers. They hit the ground running and soon went through the Cumberland Gap to Kentucky, canoeing up and down the rivers, going by wagon from St. Louis to points west, blazing the Santa Fe and Oregon Trails and searching for the Northwest Passage. When they hit the Pacific coast, they had nowhere else to go, and their descendants are driving in circles, looking for new frontiers to explore.

But Apache's puzzling case distracted me from my traffic woes. Going slowly had its benefits, since I had no idea what I'd do when I got to Maureen's. I could use the extra time to mull over the problem. I'd begin with a thorough physical exam and maybe the cause would become obvious.

In veterinary school there were a few catch phrases drilled into us. The first was "above all, do no harm." That seemed easy enough. The second was "make all of the symptoms or clinical signs fit one disease" if possible, because it's more likely that one disease is occurring, than that the animal has multiple problems. That wasn't looking so simple right now. The third phrase was "for every mistake you make for not knowing enough, you will make nine mistakes for not looking hard enough." My grandmother, Kitty Hogan, had remarked while I was just a toddler that one of the character traits that I possessed was a fierce determination, and she hoped I could find a way to channel this energy for a good cause. That determination would be tested today.

I vowed to be thorough...but what could be causing these bizarre symptoms?

Doubt crept in.

Did I really know enough to figure this case out?

Maureen's first complaint was that the colt was not eating. A whole raft of things can cause a horse to lose its appetite - pain, infection, spoiled feed, exhaustion, intestinal problems. That wasn't much help narrowing down the cause.

Her second complaint was that the colt was pawing. When a horse has colic, the pain in his belly keeps him from eating, and causes him to paw at his belly, lie down and roll. So lack of appetite and pawing fit colic.

The colt was not playful, which could be caused any illness or fever. That clue wasn't particularly helpful.

But then there was Apache's odd gait. When a colicky horse tries to lie down, he will prepare by tucking his hind legs up underneath himself. Sometimes the horse will change his mind and not lie down, leading the owner to observe a strange way of walking, but that wasn't quite what Maureen had described.

Young Quarter Horses and Paints are prone to a neurologic syndrome called "wobbles" where a pinching of the spinal cord in the neck causes horses to be ataxic or wobbly in their hind legs. The problem is more common in colts than fillies, and this colt was the right age, and breed, but Maureen described the colt as crossing his *front* legs. As far as I could remember, that *never* showed up in my classes at veterinary school!

Could this horse be a wobbler suffering from colic and an infection?

I Make Horse Calls

Probably not. Keep thinking.

I had my work cut out for me. But then, an encouraging thought entered my head. Even experienced veterinarians rely on special tests, like x-rays and blood screenings, and consulting with specialists on difficult cases, so maybe I wouldn't be completely incompetent if I couldn't figure this case out by myself.

Arriving at Maureen's address I drove up a dusty lane. Her horses lived on a dry, barren ridge. California was in the midst of a drought. There was not a blade of grass in sight, or a shade tree. The horses lived on small dirt patches, enclosed by pipe corral panels. I saw a middle-aged woman and a Paint colt in a small pen on the back of the ranch, away from the other horses. I parked the truck near the corral as she walked over to my truck. She did not look happy to see me.

"It's about time you got here. That's Apache. He's my favorite colt, and I'm worried sick about him."

Why is it always the owner's favorite horse that gets sick?

"I'm Dr. Thibeault. Let's see what the problem is."

I got out of the truck, slipped my stethoscope around my neck and stuffed a thermometer in my pocket.

I followed Maureen into the pen. First I walked around Apache, looking at his general condition and his surroundings. His small pen was clean, with no piles of manure. The fence was not damaged, as if he had been trapped in it, and the ground was smooth, not churned up from struggling. The water tank was clean and full. Apache watched me as I looked around.

He was a fine big colt, in good flesh and obviously well-cared for. Big colts are more likely to have wobbles.

Apache's coat was shiny, and his conformation showed his good breeding. He was standing with his head over a pile of sweet, green hay, but he was not eating. I laid my hand on him as a way of introducing myself to him. He did not feel hot to the touch. Apache raised his right hoof, and pawed at the pile of hay.

"Hey, boy. What's going on with you?" I said as I put my stethoscope over his heart, really wishing he could tell me. He stood still while I examined him.

Colic and respiratory infections are common illnesses in horses, so I checked for those ailments first. His pulse rate was slightly elevated, which is a nonspecific response to pain, excitement, or infection. His heart sounded normal, with no murmurs or rhythm problems. I listened to his gut sounds because colic will change gut activity, but they were normal, too.

So I knew it wasn't colic, but I needed to know what it was. My exam was ruling out problems, but wasn't helping me reach a diagnosis.

When I listened to Apache's lungs with my stethoscope, they were normal. He didn't have pneumonia. The lymph nodes under his jaw were not inflamed, and his temperature was only 100, so an upper respiratory infection was crossed off my list.

Poisonous plants grow in this region, and toxins cause liver damage that turns the whites of the eyes yellow. But Apache's dry lot was bare of vegetation. As he rolled his eyes warily at this strange new vet I could see the whites of his eyes were pearly white. Besides, poisonous plants usually taste bad, so well fed horses avoid them, and Apache was certainly well fed.

I examined the hay. There were no weeds - only good quality alfalfa and grasses. Poisonous plants were now eliminated as the cause of Apache's problem.

I now had a long list of things Apache didn't have, but I knew Maureen had called me to figure out what he *did* have. He was in no immediate danger, so I asked Maureen for more information about Apache.

"Which vaccines has he had?"

"Well, I'm about to graduate from vet tech school, so I have him on the best program. He received the full series of rhino, flu, sleeping sickness and tetanus vaccines as a foal, and regular boosters since then. I boostered him 60 days ago and deworm him every eight weeks. I muck out every day, and keep his water tank clean."

"Is he on any medications?"

"No."

Maureen took excellent care of Apache. Her treatments reduced Apache's risk of colic and infection. His problem wasn't a vaccination reaction, because 60 days had passed.

In years past, deworming medications were given only by veterinarians. A veterinarian would accurately measure the dose, and give it to the horse by running a tube up the horse's nose to the horse's stomach. The medications were fairly toxic, so accurate dosing was critical. Powders and pellets that could be put on feed were available, but horses often spit out the bad tasting medication, or refused to eat the medicated feed, so accurate dosing was nearly impossible.

Recently, safer dewormers were developed that were available over-the-counter. These were pre-measured individual doses in a paste that the owner could squirt on the horse's tongue. The paste was sticky and hard to spit out. Most of these medications were safe enough that minor miscalculations of the horse's weight wouldn't cause a problem. There were a few paste dewormers that were not as safe, but the side effect of those drugs was over-stimulation of the horse's intestines, and Apache's intestines were normal. So paste dewormers were ruled out as the problem.

I needed to keep looking.

"Is his manure normal?"

"Yes. I muck out his pen twice a day and everything was normal."

Perhaps Apache had injured his neck.

"Has he had an accident, or a fall?"

"No, not that I've seen. He has just been started under saddle, and he's very mellow."

If Apache had gotten caught in the corral panels, he should have some skin injuries and the panels usually bend as the horse struggles. The panels were straight, so I didn't see how he could injure himself here without it being obvious.

It was hard to find fault with Maureen's care of Apache.

"Are there any other sick horses on your farm?"

"No. They're all fine. And since he's a stallion he doesn't have contact with them anyway."

Maureen was well informed about equine management and gave Apache good care. I walked around the colt again, looking for any signs of swelling or trauma, but I found nothing.

I didn't have a clue what was making him sick, but I tried to hide my inexperience from Maureen.

Apache resumed pawing at the hay. He still didn't look distressed, like a horse suffering from colic, but he certainly wasn't normal. I think I was more distressed than Apache.

I Make Horse Calls

Why couldn't I begin my practice career with an easy, straight forward case?

I continued my exam, stalling for more time to think.

"Slip a halter on him, please. I'd like to watch him walk."

Maureen haltered him and dragged him around the small pen. He was slow and stiff, like he was 100 years old. But he wasn't really lame, like a horse with a hoof abscess or founder.

He was young, so why would he be so stiff? Arthritis was unlikely, as his conformation was good and he had never done hard work that would lead to injury. He had no old scars, indicating previous injury. When Maureen turned him in a circle, he crossed his front legs. He looked like an ocean liner being pushed sideways by a tugboat.

This was certainly no ordinary case of wobbles.

Strenuous exercise or getting cast - trapped against a fence or wall - can cause myositis or severe muscle cramping, which will make a horse move stiffly. Apache had no history of strenuous exercise, but maybe he had done something unseen. I was running out of options, so I palpated Apache's large muscles for myositis, but they were soft and pliable.

He didn't have myositis.

So now I had ruled out everything on my list – colic, infection, injury, wobbles. Where do I go from here? I hoped my frustration wasn't showing.

There should be only one answer and it was my job to find it. I kept looking, but it would help if I knew what I was looking for.

"I take such good care of him. I just don't know what happened to him. He was fine yesterday."

I didn't want to tell Maureen I was stumped but I finally had no choice. I wanted to appear competent even though I wasn't feeling very competent at the moment.

Sounding professional and positive I told Maureen "It's not obvious from the physical exam what's causing his problem. I want to run a panel of blood tests and check him for internal problems, including liver or kidney ailments. The results will be back tomorrow. He's comfortable, and it won't jeopardize his life to wait until morning for the results."

Maureen was angry.

"What do you mean you don't know what's wrong? If Dr. Tillman were here, he'd know! When is he coming back?"

Her anger fueled my frustration at not having an answer for her. Keeping up a professional demeanor was growing difficult.

"Dr. Tillman will be back tomorrow, but I wouldn't wait until then to draw blood, in case he takes a turn for the worse overnight."

"Well, if you think that's best, that's what we'll do, but my husband and I are going on vacation this weekend to Las Vegas. We were planning to leave early tomorrow morning, to drive through Death Valley before it gets hot. We'll cancel the trip if we have to, for Apache's sake."

Great! Now I'm going to be responsible for ruining this couple's vacation if I can't make a diagnosis right now! Well, I'll keep looking.

I leaned back against the corral panels and hung my elbow over the top rail. No matter how long it took I was determined to figure out what was bothering Apache. By observing his behavior, surely he would give me a clue.

I went over his medical history and my examination findings again in my head. All my management questions had been answered with no hint of the problem. The physical exam I gave was thorough, but yielded no useful clues. There were no other sick horses on the farm. There was no access to poisonous plants and the hay looked great. The water was clean. Apache had no bleeding, swellings, sore muscles, coughing, runny nose, diarrhea or sign of injury.

What was his problem?

Apache continued to paw. Just then I realized he hadn't moved from the spot where Maureen left him. In fact, he hadn't taken a single step since I arrived, except when she dragged him around by his halter, and then he moved reluctantly. I had an idea!

It may seem silly to say that horses have facial expressions, but Apache looked mad. I walked over to him and picked up a handful of hay raising it to his muzzle. He grabbed it out of my hands and began to eat!

Maureen gasped, "He's hungry!" She cracked a smile, knowing a healthy appetite was always a good sign.

Finally, I got one piece of the puzzle!

I Make Horse Calls

For some reason he wouldn't reach down to eat from the ground, but he was hungry and had a good appetite. That explained the pawing - he was hungry and mad that he couldn't reach his hay.

If Apache would eat, he definitely did not have colic or a major metabolic problem. If he wouldn't reach the ground, he probably had neck pain. Wobblers wobble as a result of a neck ailment, but usually are more bothered by hind limb balance problems than neck pain. Apache had no problems with balance in his hind limbs, but he must have a neck problem!

I ran my fingers over every inch of Apache's neck. There was no swelling or heat. When I touched the right side of his neck, he turned his head slightly to the right. When I touched the left side of his neck, he didn't move at all. When I touched a single spot on the left side of his neck, right over his spinal column, Apache rolled his eyes at me but never moved a muscle. I had an idea.

"What product did you use to deworm him?" I asked Maureen.

"I used the new shot dewormer. It's supposed to be the best dewormer on the market. And I know all about the complications of the shot wormer - that horses can die if contamination occurs from the shot. So I did a full surgical scrub on his neck before I gave the injection. That's *not* the problem."

That changed everything! If Maureen had told me that she gave Apache an injection, I would have checked the injection sites first. I hadn't suspected the injectable dewormer because it was a prescription drug - supposed to be used only by licensed veterinarians, not by owners.

This new shot dewormer could result in a fatal infection where the injection was given. Some vets added antibiotics to the injections, some clipped the injection site and rinsed it with alcohol or iodine, and others scrubbed it thoroughly.

The product had only been on the market for a few months, and millions of doses had been sold, but a few horses died following the injection. The product was so new that the cause of the deaths wasn't clearly understood yet. It would be pulled off the market before the year's end.

Horses that died from the injection had high fevers, but Apache's temperature was barely elevated. His neck pain was probably caused by the injection, but he had no infection. I tried to reassure Maureen that Apache didn't have a life-threatening infection.

"We're not dealing with an infection, because his temperature is almost normal."

I went over Apache's neck one more time. The spot on the left side of his neck had to be the key, but the sore spot was low on his neck, not where injections should be given.

"Maureen, exactly where did you give him the injection?"

She pointed to that very spot.

Maureen should have been trained to give injections properly as part of her veterinary technician courses. Apparently that was not the case.

I finally had the one cause that could account for all of this colt's abnormalities! I even surprised myself, as I had been seriously challenged by this case. I tried to hide my surprise, but my happiness was undeniable. I just needed to present my findings professionally to Maureen.

"Well, I have the diagnosis" I proudly proclaimed, "and you and your husband can go to Las Vegas! Apache will be fine!"

"Really, Dr. Thibeault! What's wrong with him?"

"You gave him the injection too close to his spinal cord. It caused internal swelling, which put pressure on the nerves coming from Apache's spine. His neck is so sore he can't stretch to reach the ground, but he will eat if you hold the hay up for him. His appetite is fine. He's pawing because he's mad. He's hungry, and the hay is just out of his reach. He won't nip at you because he's tensing his neck muscles as a splint to keep his neck still, and he would have to use his neck muscles to reach out to bite you. He crosses his front legs when he walks because he's keeping his neck straight to ease his pain."

I was relieved to reach a diagnosis.

Maureen flashed a wide smile, glad her colt would be fine. She wasn't the least bit apologetic for having caused his pain.

"You need to raise his hay and water to the level of his muzzle, so he can reach it. I'll give him some medicine for pain and swelling, and you can pack your bags!"

I drew up the medication and gave Apache his injection intravenously, so it would work right away, and filled a prescription so Maureen's son could keep Apache comfortable while she and her husband enjoyed their trip to Las Vegas.

Driving home that night I felt like a hero. Even the traffic couldn't spoil my mood. The confusing clinical signs Apache showed made it difficult to reach a diagnosis, but I was persistent. I silently thanked my professors for training me so well. Best of all, I was happy that Apache would be fine.

Those long nights I spent studying were paying off, and my Irish determination was being put to good use!

Chapter 5 Please Come

After living in a small farmhouse in Colorado during vet school, living in Los Angeles was like being dropped abruptly onto another planet. As an ambulatory vet, I spent my days driving through a city constantly snarled by traffic. I treated horses unnaturally confined in small stalls behind huge houses - houses with concrete front yards full of cars, RVs, and jet-skis on trailers, and concrete back yards full of swimming pools and two stall barns. The horses ate hay cubes because there was no room to store bales. My equine patients were confined to stalls, with no access to turnout, no chance to socialize in herds, and no grass to eat. Most were even denied the luxury of standing in the sun. It was worlds away from the equestrian lifestyle that captured my heart on those summer evening steak fries in the Rockies.

My life was as far removed from nature as the lives of my patients. My personal life was unexpectedly difficult. When I first arrived, I stayed at an inexpensive motel - a national chain I had found acceptable when I patronized them elsewhere. However, even though the motel was near the practice, I soon found it to be a poor choice for me.

I hoped I would not be there long as I searched everywhere for affordable housing - local real estate agents, newspaper ads, driving through neighborhoods reading "for rent" signs on telephone poles, stopping at the grocery stores to check their bulletin boards. The California housing market was tight, and there was no room for me. I put my belongings in storage to return the rented moving trailer.

My Mom came along to help me get settled, but had to return to work before I found a place to rent. She helped me unload my furniture into the storage locker. I knew if I ever found a place to live

I would have to move it from the storage locker to my new place by myself, as I had no friends in California.

The hotel room cost $300 per month *more* than my paycheck, and the storage locker was an additional expense. Food was now optional, but most days I was too busy to feel hungry. So despite working seven days a week, and being on call every night, I was getting further and further into debt. And my student loans would be coming due in a few months. I had not expected to be poorer now that I was a veterinarian than I was as a groom.

The transition to practicing veterinarian was more difficult because I did not have my reference books available. They were in boxes somewhere in my storage locker. I knew it was expensive to live in California, but had I known it cost so much for housing I would have negotiated a higher salary. But my self-confidence was so low I didn't dare ask for more money now, so soon after being hired.

Not only was the hotel room dirty, but the day I moved in there was a young man on the parking lot begging for money to buy gas to drive home, saying he had run out of gas. I doubted his story, but gave him $10 anyway. The next day it became apparent that he begged there every day. He could see when I was alone, and I worried that he would vandalize my car if I didn't pay him, but I had no money to pay him again.

One morning I came out of my room and found that someone had gotten sick in the stairwell, and I had to step over the mess to get to work. It was time to find another motel. I found one a few miles out of town. It was a longer commute, in ten lanes of snarled traffic every morning, but the hotel was clean and I felt safe.

My search for a home continued. The cheapest house I found for rent cost double what my house in Fort Collins had cost, and was in a bad neighborhood where I would be uncomfortable living alone and going out in the middle of the night. It was unaffordable on my salary anyway. There was no reason to look at any more houses.

I focused on apartments, although an apartment in Los Angeles was a long way from my goal of owning a farm someday. I needed patience.

Because I had my dog with me, and most apartments wouldn't take dogs, my choices were limited. I had to find a place that I could afford alone, because I didn't have a roommate. I finally learned of a place in Burbank that took dogs. In fact, they even took horses, having a stable under the parking lot behind the apartments. It seemed strange to have horses underground, but this was Los Angeles.

There was a waiting list, but in a few weeks a studio apartment became available. It was a difficult transition from a three bedroom house on seven acres to one room with a bath, and the rent was the same. With a busy street in front, a swimming pool out back, and hundreds of strangers living in my building, the little room yielded no peaceful respite from the stress of LA traffic and work.

I got a few hours off to move my furniture, but had to keep paying for the storage locker for another month until I could find someone to move the heavier furniture. Luckily our practice assistant and her husband helped me.

I was so grateful to be relieved of the storage fees. Now I could afford food. I was rich!

Life in the apartment was like living in a furniture store. One single room contained my bedroom, dining room, and living room furniture, my extensive collection of veterinary books and bookshelves, and a desk. I had no place to hook up my washer and dryer so I threw a table cloth over them and pretended they were furniture. My rocking chair couldn't rock and my recliner couldn't recline because there was no room. I practically had to walk across the furniture to reach my tiny twin bed in the back corner.

My professional life fared no better. I was delayed by traffic every day, arriving late to my appointments, to angry greetings from clients whose emotions only fueled my own frustration. They were upset that their horses would be tended by a stranger instead of Dr. Tillman, and I was upset that they were upset. I needed to be a psychologist as well as a veterinarian.

And Dr. Tillman and I weren't getting along all that well either. The mentoring I had hoped for didn't happen. In front of the clients he acted like I was brilliant, but behind their backs he treated me like I was an idiot.

I Make Horse Calls

Dr. Tillman rarely asked my opinion, but when he did, if it differed from his, he immediately dismissed it, saying "I've been doing it this way for years!"

Why did he even bother to ask?

Still I tried to make our arrangement work. On my new graduate salary I worked seven days a week - a regular list of appointments, emergencies almost every night, polo games on Friday and Saturday nights, horse shows on the weekends, and a backlog of surgeries on the Sundays when there were no shows.

As his assistant, I didn't challenge Dr. Tillman's medical decisions. Instead, I politely tried to share with him new treatments and medications. He used a common colic drug that research had proven to be useless. I didn't want to use it because I felt bad charging a client for a worthless drug while denying the horse a better treatment option. The newer medication had strong scientific proof of its benefits. I knew he wouldn't believe me, so I brought him the research paper detailing the benefits of the drug. He used the paper as a coaster for his coffee mug for a few weeks, but never read it. When I finally retrieved the article, it was ruined.

He never did try the drug, saying it was too expensive. Compared to what my vet at home had been charging me, Dr. Tillman's prices were exorbitant, and should have easily covered the cost of this drug. No matter the price, I felt patients should be getting the best available treatment, and I couldn't give it to them if the practice wouldn't stock the drug.

I asked him one day why he became a vet, and he told me the sad story of a dog he had as a child. The dog became sick and died, and he wanted to know how the dog could have been saved.

But over the years, the compassion in him disappeared. He may have been overwhelmed by the long hours, the costs of running the practice, paying his mortgage, and saving for his children's college. He seemed to have lost his focus, still working long hours every day, but without the spark he needed to be his best. I tried to find a way to help him re-ignite that spark, to no avail.

Dr. Tillman endangered my health by insisting that I hold x-ray plates for him bare-handed, without protective lead gloves and aprons, and without cassette holders, which would protect from the radiation. I was so shocked that I did it once, but I never did it again,

I Make Horse Calls

demanding that protective gear be supplied. I hated being confrontational but I stood my ground to protect myself, and he begrudgingly complied.

The practice did not provide the nurturing environment I needed to become the best practitioner I could be. Instead, I was forced to do procedures the way the practice owner had done them for decades, even when those procedures contradicted proper modern techniques.

I would scrub for surgery, put on sterile gloves, and then have to answer the telephone. What would I say to the caller except "call back, we're in surgery?" If I touched the phone, I would have to re-scrub and re-glove before coming back into surgery, to keep from contaminating our patient. We had an answering service to handle the calls when we were busy. Why didn't he use it?

I was concerned about losing the good habits I'd learned in school. If I did things his way for very long, his habits would surely replace the education I just paid for so dearly - paid with my time, my energy, and my money.

Dr. Tillman also forbade me from socializing with clients. With the hours I worked, there was no time to meet new friends outside of work.

I felt very alone.

I couldn't use my education to its fullest advantage. It was hard to stand by and see the horses receive second rate treatment, and I couldn't change that, despite my efforts. I could barely afford my studio apartment and there was no way to turn it into a comfortable home without selling most of the furnishings I'd hoped would decorate my farmhouse someday. Traffic was unbearable and every day I dealt with clients who expected Dr. Tillman, not me. This created a lot of negativity, on top of the strain of trying to make the transition to being responsible for the health of my patients.

These factors had me searching for another job. I gave Dr. Tillman notice, and planned my return to Colorado.

On my last day an unruly mare fractured my foot, so there was no way I could move while hobbling on crutches. I called one of my dear classmates, Tom Welsh, to help me move. Tom had finished his schooling, but was awaiting the results of his board exams before he could practice. The timing was perfect.

43

I Make Horse Calls

I didn't think I'd make a good first impression hobbling around on crutches, and no jobs were advertised in Colorado, so I set my sights on getting licensed in other states with large numbers of horses. I took state exams in Virginia and Maryland, and searched for jobs there.

I interviewed for a job in Maryland, and it had many perks that the California job lacked. It had well equipped, full size vet trucks, and assistants to go on calls. They could introduce me to the clients and report the horse's medical history as we drove to the farms. They could help me learn the roads and kept the truck stocked. They restrained horses during examinations. In addition, the practice owner did all of the night work unless he was out of town, then I would have to split emergency calls with the other associate.

It seemed like a dream job compared to Dr. Tillman's practice, but when I went on rounds with the vet he sutured a deep wound on a foal that had been injured five days before, and had been kept waiting all that time for help. How could the vet make an injured horse wait that long, as the summer flies festered the open wound?

The practice didn't offer the quality of medicine I wanted for my clients, so I refused the job offer.

After much soul searching, weighing my assets and limitations, I decided to go out on my own. I lacked experience, but my education was solid, I understood horses and horsemen, and I sincerely cared for the horses. I would never make a horse wait days for emergency care and I would never lose a patient because I didn't care.

I had to find the right location and settle for ambulatory practice - going from farm to farm treating horses out of the dependable old truck I had driven to vet school - until I could afford to build a clinic.

Even if I could never save enough money for a clinic, I knew it was the right choice for me.

I came home to my parents' house in Mountain View, a small farming community east of the front range of the Rocky Mountains. It seemed the ideal place for my practice because it was only an hour's drive from the veterinary hospital at Colorado State University. Being a recent graduate, I knew the staff and would ask

I Make Horse Calls

for their help on difficult cases to assure my clients received the best care even if I was in over my head. And being near Denver meant there were many potential clients for my practice.

From a hill near the house on a clear day I could see Pike's Peak to the south and Long's Peak to the north, a spectacular span of over 100 miles. The beautiful blue skies provided a fitting backdrop for the dramatic mountain splendor, and a welcome change from the smoggy skies of Los Angeles. The move did my soul good.

The mountains were close enough to enjoy when time would allow, but the climate in Mountain View was far milder than the mountain weather. A nearby state park was home to bald eagles and great blue herons, and coyotes and foxes were regularly seen in the open meadows around the park's reservoir. Mountain View was a good place to settle down, away from the bustle of Denver. But my clients would come from several counties, forcing me to drive through the city often on my rounds. Denver's two million residents all seemed to be on the road in front of me when I was in a hurry, but the roads seemed nearly deserted when I remembered the traffic in Los Angeles.

Unfortunately, I had just missed the advertising deadline for the local phone book, and had a year to wait before the next publication. I had no clinic location where I could hang a sign. I lived in the city, and would do all of my vet work at the client's farms. I knew that finding clients wasn't going to be easy, and I had to win their confidence on my first visit or I may never get a second chance.

I went around town introducing myself to small animal vets. I knew they didn't treat horses so they wouldn't see me as a competitor, but as an ally in providing health care for animals. I gave them my business card, and told them to please give my number to anyone who called in search of a horse vet.

I contacted my friends who owned horses, and told them I would be available if their regular vets were not. A few chose me over their previous vet, but it was going to take time to build a clientele.

So I waited.
And waited.
And waited.

45

I Make Horse Calls

In early February, on a cold, snowy night, I got my first client. My pager went off at 3 AM, jarring me from a deep slumber. I didn't keep a phone near my bed, because I'm not at my best when I'm half-asleep. After my pager wakes me I climb out of bed and walk across the cold floor to the kitchen phone, and retrieve the client's information from the answering service. By then I'm awake enough to converse somewhat intelligently.

This morning's call was from Mrs. Vincent Carson. Their miniature mare, Spirit, was having difficulty delivering her foal. They knew the mare was in trouble. Vince was in the barn, trying to help the mare, but he didn't know what to do. They had been calling vets listed in the phone book, but no one would come. Finally they contacted a vet who had my card and she gave them my number.

"Will you come?"

"Yes. I'll be right there."

"Oh, thank goodness!"

I could hear the relief in her voice as she gave me directions.

The farm was 15 miles away, across town, and I knew I had to hurry. I also knew that I don't think clearly when I'm freezing. It seems like my IQ drops with the temperature, so I took a few extra seconds to put on as many clothes as I could possibly wear and still move. I'd need to have my wits about me tonight.

Clancy was jumping at the back door as I fumbled with the knob.

"Get back, Clancy, so I can open it!" I shouted at her. She obediently ran back two steps and waited for me. I opened the door as she stood quivering at the ready, and when I said "okay" she bolted through. The blast of cold air hit my face and the swirling snow stung my eyes. It was as cold as a winter night in the Rockies could be. And having just climbed out of my warm bed, the cold was a shock to my system, which was fighting off sleep.

Clancy bounded over the drifts ahead of me as my boots plowed a trough through the deep snow. The garage door lock was full of ice, but I finally jammed the key in.

Clancy jumped in the truck and I climbed in behind her. I pushed the garage door opener as I started the engine. I was happy every time the old truck sprang to life. I watched in my mirror until the door was fully open. My truck was tall, and I didn't want to hit the door. Once it was clear, I threw the truck in reverse and backed out of the garage.

THWACK.

What was that??

Pieces of wood hung menacingly from the door frame. In my haste, I was too close to the side of the garage door frame, tearing the moulding off the doorway with my mirror as I backed out. Hopefully that was not an omen of things to come.

Oh, well. My parents were sunbathing on the beach in Florida, avoiding the harsh Colorado winter. I was handy with a saw and hammer, and I could fix the damage before they came home so I'd never have to explain it.

The good thing about going out in the middle of a cold winter's night, if there is a good thing, is that there's never any traffic. My mind could focus on my patient as I planned a course of action.

Difficult births, called dystocias, are the most critical emergencies in equine practice. Mares can die after being in labor only a short while. It was imperative that I get to the Carsons' quickly. Mrs. Carson said they had called other veterinarians, so I knew the mare had been in trouble for a long time. I hoped I wasn't too late. The mare might even die before I could get there.

As I drove, I dwelled on the fact that I had never actually delivered a foal, or a calf, or even puppies before. The only foaling I had even *seen* before this night was when my own mare foaled. I was just 14 years old, and the old mare suffered the worst complication of foaling - she bled to death right before my eyes. I stood by helplessly as she suffered a horrible death. There was no vet to help her despite the fact that she foaled at 9 AM, on a warm, sunny Thursday in June, and that three horse vets had a practice only a few miles away - on the same road as the barn. I listened as the barn manager called the vet every 30 minutes, begging for help, and they kept promising to send someone right away. If they hadn't promised to come, we would have called someone else. It took my mare six hours to die, and it took the vet six hours to arrive. I still remember walking out of the barn that day after she died, and seeing the vet's truck pulling into the driveway. I was so sad - and so angry.

The visions of that day are forever burned into my memory and I vowed to never let a horse or client go through an experience like that if it was up to me. I know I won't be able to save all of my patients, but I promise to get to the farm as soon as I can. In case I'm faced with more than one emergency, I carry the phone numbers of nearby vets so I can refer any client needing immediate help. No client or horse should ever have to go through what my mare and I did on that horrible day.

Needless to say, I was nervous driving to the Carsons'.

In vet school we had an obstetrics exercise to practice deliveries. The lab was warm and well lit, and the exercises were performed right after lunch. It was now cold and dark, and the middle of a snowy, winter night. Adrenaline was fueling my efforts tonight.

During the lab exercise no lives hung in the balance, and instructors were there to guide us. I'd have no help tonight, just a worried owner looking over my shoulder, watching my every move.

The lab didn't have a live mare to kick us, just a metal frame to simulate the birth canal, and an aborted calf fetus that couldn't resist our manipulations.

Why couldn't my first very own client just have a simple problem, like a wire cut? I was good at suturing wounds.

Oh well, I passed the lab. I was prepared. I knew what to do tonight. I just had to do it.

Foals are in charge of getting themselves positioned for birth. If the foal was in the wrong position, it might already be dead. If the foal was alive, it might not fit through the birth canal due to a deformity, meaning that the mare might need a Cesarean section. On the other hand, maybe I would be lucky. Maybe the foal would just have a leg positioned in the wrong place, and changing the foal's position would result in a quick delivery. Or maybe I would be really lucky, and the mare would have worked out the problem before I arrived and delivered a healthy foal on her own. Sometimes that happens.

I made good time getting to the farm. Despite the stormy conditions, the highway department's snow plows had made the roads passable.

Pulling into the driveway I was pleased to see the golden glow of lights coming from the barn windows. Many hobby horse owners in Colorado don't have barns, and fewer still have electricity in the barns, so on a night like tonight, Vince's barn could well be a lifesaver.

A female figure was watching me through the kitchen window, and she soon appeared in my headlights as I slowed to greet her. She ran down the drive to meet me and motioned me to park by the paddock gate. She clutched her long coat tightly around her as the wind whipped her dark hair in swirls around her bare head.

I rolled down the truck window.

"Hi. I'm Dr. Thibeault."

"I'm Mrs. Carson. Thanks so much for coming. Vince has Spirit in the barn. Go on down, and please hurry."

I gathered my supplies from the truck, and asked about the mare's medical history as I followed Mrs. Carson into the barn.

"Tell me about your mare."

"She is only two years old, and this is her first pregnancy. We've been calling everybody!"

As my eyes adjusted to the dim light in the barn, I spied Vince - an imposing man from his height and his bulk, but his kindly face was riddled with worry. He stood helplessly outside Spirit's stall, looming over the small figure lying in the straw. At two years of age, she was just a filly herself, and very young to be giving birth.

As he extended his huge hand to shake mine he said, with a mixture of gratitude and anger, "Thanks for coming. I'm Vince Carson. Called every vet in the phone book. Couldn't get anybody to come. What's wrong with these people?"

He held the gate for me as I entered Spirit's stall.

"Well, Mr. Carson, most vets only work on small animals these days. The phone book lists all of the vets together, so it's not easy to tell who treats horses. I'm sorry you had to work so hard to find me. How long has she been in labor?"

I could already see there would be no joyous celebration tonight. The birthing membranes, which supply oxygen to the foal, had
already passed. The foal would be dead. But maybe I could save the dam, if I could get the foal out quickly.

I went to work, listening to the filly's heart and lungs, and checking her gums for color as Vince filled me in.

I Make Horse Calls

"I don't know. I didn't think she was due yet. I put a birth monitor on Countessa, our paint mare, and it went off at 12:30. When we came out to check on her, she was fine, but Spirit was down, in labor. We didn't see her water break, but it had to be before 12:30."

Birth monitors transmit a signal to an alarm in the house when a mare lies on her side. The alarm eliminates the need to run to the barn every 30 minutes to check on pregnant mares. It was a lucky coincidence that Countessa decided to take a deep slumber when Spirit was in labor. Without the alarm there would have been no warning that Spirit was in trouble. She would have died.

But it was now 3:45 AM. The filly had been in labor too long. The Carsons were familiar with cattle, but not with horses. They knew that cows can be in labor for hours, and still give birth to healthy calves, but they didn't know that mares usually deliver their foals in about 20 minutes once the water breaks. The mare must deliver the foal quickly, because the membranes that supply the foal's oxygen in the womb come loose from the mare in about two hours, meaning any foal not delivered on time will suffocate. We were long past the deadline.

Vince didn't know the foal was dead. I would have to tell him.

Spirit's life was in danger. Difficult deliveries can cause internal injuries, resulting in the death of the mare. There is so much to do, in so little time, and I was already too late to save one of my two patients. I didn't have time to compose my thoughts - to think of a gentle way to tell Vince his foal was dead. I had to deliver this foal right away to save Spirit.

She was lying in a clean bed of straw, but was so weak. Her pulse was racing, her membranes were pale, and she was too tired to push anymore. She was going into shock. I had to act fast. Two years old is young to be foaling, but tonight it might just save this filly's life to have youth on her side.

As I prepared to clean her up, I peeled off my heavy coat and pushed up my sleeves. I thought of James Herriot's book, <u>All Creatures Great and Small</u>. In the first chapter Dr. Herriot is stripped to the waist, lying on the wet, cobblestone barn floor delivering an oversized calf as the snow is blowing through the doorway and settling on his bare back.

I Make Horse Calls

I, too, would be lying on the ground, trying to deliver my small patient, but I was *not* James Herriot. I was going to stay as warm as possible when delivering this foal. I was glad the straw was clean and the barn was dry.

I slipped on plastic obstetrical sleeves, applied lubricant, and reached inside the mare. I found the foal's tail and rump in the birth canal. It was a breech presentation. I would have to reposition the foal so it would fit through the birth canal.

In a normal delivery the foal comes out front feet first, like a diver going off the diving board. This foal tried to be born tail first, which meant all four legs were pointing forward, towards the mare's nose, making the hips too wide to come through the birth canal.

I unwrapped a pair of sterile obstetric chains and peeled off my heavy sweater. I could work fine in my turtleneck.

The foal was a normal size. I had enough room to work and the mare was too tired to push against me. Slipping an obstetric chain around the first tiny hind hoof, I pushed the foal forward in the womb with one hand and cupped my other hand over the hoof to protect the mare's womb. I brought the hooves, one at a time, into the birth canal. As soon as the foal was properly positioned, a little pull on the chains cause the foal to slide right out.

The foal's gums were blue, and it had no pulse, no respirations. It was clearly dead. It had died hours ago.

"Is it breathing?" asked Vince.

"No," I said as I checked its heart and lungs with my stethoscope just to be sure. The silence was deadly.

"The foal lost its oxygen supply when the membranes came out. It's been gone a while. I'm sorry."

"Are you sure?"

"Yes...I'm sure."

I wished there was a better way to tell him.

Mrs. Carson turned away and walked into the darkness at the end of the barn. I could hear her muffled sobs, but couldn't comfort her. I had to attend to the mare as Vince stood stoically by, watching my every move.

Spirit was lying still, and seemed to be resting easier, now that the foal was out, but she needed my help. She had been through a very difficult delivery and was completely spent. Shock was the number one problem now. As I stepped out of the barn into the cold winter wind to get IV fluids from my truck, I asked Mrs. Carson for a bucket of hot water from the house. I had to warm the fluids before I gave them to Spirit, so they would not stress her heart.

Mrs. Carson silently went to the house and soon returned with a steaming bucket of water. I placed the bottles in the bucket while I prepared the mare. Spirit didn't flinch when I pushed the catheter into her vein, she just watched me. I reached into the bucket of warm water to grab the first bottle of fluids. The warm water felt good on my cold hands, although I was surprisingly comfortable, considering the storm outside had driven the temperature near zero. I began running a solution of glucose, electrolytes and fluids into her vein to help her recover her strength. I handed the bottle to Vince.

"Please hold this above her heart while I recheck her."

He took the bottle without speaking.

In some dystocias, the foal will have a leg in a position that will damage the mare's womb when the mare pushes. At least with a breech presentation, Spirit should be uninjured, and should be able to foal again. I put on fresh gloves and thoroughly examined her reproductive tract. Her womb was okay.

As I examined the mare internally, my eyes wandered around the barn. I saw six small stalls with miniature horses watching the proceedings with interest. But as I gazed to the dark recesses of the barn, my eyes rested on a strange creature, the likes of which I had never seen before. In vet school they taught us many breeds of domestic animals, from dogs to cats, pigs to cattle, sheep to horses, and goats, but I had never seen anything quite like this creature. Its huge eyes peered out at me from the darkness of the corner stall. It was some exotic bovine, with horns as long as a Texas longhorn, but the horns went up, not straight out to the side. The creature was liver colored, with white spots. And it was big! There was a sturdy gate between it and me, so I'd inquire about it later.

I finally had time to talk to the Carsons, to help them through this difficult time.

"I'm sorry about your foal. But at least Spirit is not injured, so she should deliver a healthy foal for you next year, if we can get her stabilized."

I Make Horse Calls

I could see the disappointment on Vince's face. Eleven months of anticipation ended in tragedy instead of joy. It shouldn't be this way. "We had high hopes for this foal. Spirit was Champion Filly at the National Western Stock Show, and she's our first miniature. She would have produced our best foal this year."

"I'm sorry."

He didn't realize how lucky he would be if we could save Spirit. He could only focus on his loss.

Vince had not consulted with a vet for prenatal care, so no one was alerted to Spirit's impending delivery. If only he had sought vet care throughout Spirit's pregnancy, he could have known how to recognize dystocia earlier and would have known who to call tonight. They could have avoided the delay that cost this foal its life. And Spirit would have had the advantage of prenatal care, including vaccinations and the special diet that would help her produce a healthy foal.

Losing this foal re-enforced my belief in the value of education. The Carsons were a caring couple. They would have done a better job, if only they knew how. They would have been spared the frightening experience of calling clinic after clinic searching for help as their foal was dying. I decided to dedicate myself to educating amateur breeders to recognize foaling trouble quickly.

But how could I educate someone I've never met?

I'd work on that problem later.

I was too late to save Spirit's foal, but the Carsons had another pregnant mare, Countessa. Perhaps I could help her. Foaling difficulties are rare in mares - rare, but too often fatal.

The Carsons pasture bred their mares - turning their stallion loose with the mares for several months. They did not know the breeding dates for their mares. With no breeding dates, they could only guess at delivery dates. So the pregnancy monitor on Countessa had saved Spirit's life, because it gave me time to treat her.

"If you'd like some information to help you with your other mares, get a copy of <u>Blessed Are the Broodmares</u> by Dr. Phyllis Lose. It's a great book for mare owners, and will answer many of your questions."

"We will, but will you come when Countessa foals?"

"Of course. But tomorrow I'll give her a pregnancy check-up, and go over her vaccination and deworming schedule with you."

"Thanks, Doc."

While I finished giving Spirit fluids, and pain medication to keep her comfortable, I gave the Carsons information about how to monitor Countessa's udder to be alerted to impending delivery.

"The formation of wax on the mare's teats often appears within 72 hours before delivery. It is not a very accurate indicator, but without breeding dates, it's the best we can do."

"We'll watch her carefully," Vince vowed.

I packed up my medical supplies and put on my stack of warm clothes. Then I saw a heater in the corner of the barn. I was too busy to notice it until now. That's why I was too hot for all of those clothes! It was 60 degrees in the barn. Poor James Herriot was never so lucky!

It seemed bitterly cold as I walked to my truck for the last time. The stress of handling a case I'd never done before, for new clients, and the fatigue of being up most of the night in the cold made matters worse. The sadness of losing the foal, and seeing the Carsons' disappointment, put a damper on my spirits.

The sun was just beginning to scale the horizon as I packed my truck to leave.

I was proud that I could save the mare while the Carsons were understandably saddened by the heartbreaking loss of their foal. But I had to concentrate on helping the Carsons in the future, and not dwell on the fact that I could not change the past.

"I'll be back later today to check on Spirit. Leave her in the barn until then, and leave another horse inside to keep her company."

"Thanks Doc."

I bid the Carson's good-by and climbed into my truck. Clancy was glad to see me, as I had been in the barn for four hours while she waited in the cold truck. Her friendliness was comforting, as I struggled with the realization that I failed to save the life of my very first patient. But I had saved her dam.

Soon I was on my way, driving home in morning rush hour traffic. As I drove, I tried to figure out a way to prevent clients from experiencing the delays that the Carsons had suffered through.

I Make Horse Calls

When the new telephone directory was published, I would place an ad large enough to include a picture of a horse. It would be expensive, and I could ill afford it, but people like the Carsons wouldn't have to search so hard if they could see a picture. My ad would stand out, so a client with an emergency, but without a regular veterinarian, could find me in a hurry. While physicians no longer make house calls, equine veterinarians still do. So I would let clients know, by including in my ad, in bold print "**I Make Horse Calls.**" That should help.

Before climbing into bed I called Dr. Wight. He answered his phone every morning before rounds, so I knew I could catch him. He was an equine veterinarian from the next county, and graduated from vet school ten years before I did. He was kind enough to mentor me. He shared his years of practice experience with me, and I shared my more current veterinary education with him. I was grateful for his guidance.

I told him about Spirit - what I found on my examinations, and the treatments I had given. What I did not know was how to monitor her progress. Should she bounce right back, or be off feed and depressed for a few days?

Dr. Wight was positive and encouraging. He told me I had treated her properly, and the mare should be looking better in 48 hours. If not, I should re-examine her to make sure I hadn't missed anything. I thanked Dr. Wight and got some sleep.

Returning to the Carsons' farm after only a few hours sleep, I was anxious to check on Spirit. I was both proud to have saved my first patient, and nervous that I might have missed some hidden problem - like a small uterine tear or a bowel injury from the foal's kicking.

As I pulled into the farm, revealed for the first time in the daylight, I saw some of Vince's minis in the paddock, and the strange bovine standing placidly beside them. Seeing it in the daylight made me certain it was bovine, but the likes of which I had never seen before.

"Hi, Vince. How's Spirit?"

"Good to see ya again, Doc. Spirit is doing better."

"By the way, what breed of cattle is that?"

"Oh, she's a Watusi, from Africa. Isn't she cool?"

"Well, she's certainly unique."

We walked through the paddock into the barn, but I kept an eye on those horns. While the cow was contentedly chewing, I certainly didn't want to do anything to upset her. I could only envision myself skewered on one of those horns if she took a dislike to me.

Spirit indeed was doing better. She was standing in her stall eating, although not with much enthusiasm. She was sore and tired, but was looking brighter. I was glad to see her on her feet and proceeded to examine her. She was doing well.

"Continue with the pain medications, and give her a bland diet. Leave her in the barn so she doesn't get chased around by the other horses, but leave one horse inside with her so she's not alone. Don't turn her out until she acts like she really wants to go out. Do you have any questions?"

"Naw, I was just pretty upset last night that you couldn't save the foal, but this morning I called some of my friends in the miniature horse club, and they told me I was lucky you could save Spirit - that mares can't deliver breech foals without help. They told me that you saved Spirit's life - that she would have died without your help. So I really appreciate what you did for us. I didn't know cattle and horses were so different. I want to thank you again for coming last night."

"You're welcome, Vince."

"And I'll know what to expect next time. I'm going to find a copy of that book today."

We gave Countessa her exam, and Vince and I were both relieved that he shouldn't have the same problem again, as I would be on stand-by as her due date approached.

Vince and I stayed in contact by phone, and Spirit made steady progress. In three days, Vince reported that she was pawing at the stall door, and went for a nice romp with the other mares when given the chance.

I did all of the medical work for Vince's horses from that time on. It was a great boost to my confidence as a fledgling veterinarian that my first client chose me to do his future work after one visit. I had earned his trust.

I soon began getting calls from miniature horse owners all over the county. Vince referred everyone in the miniature horse club to me. I eventually had 60 miniatures in my care, which must have been nearly all of the minis in the county.

And Vince was a caring owner and a quick learner. He never made the same mistake twice, so his horses benefited from his growing expertise.

In the spring when I saw Vince, he complimented me on my figure.

"Hey, Doc. You've lost a lot of weight since last winter. You look great!"

"Well, actually, that was just the five layers of clothing I wore because it was so cold. My weight hasn't changed."

He continues to compliment me on my weight loss but I now say nothing, graciously accepting any compliments without argument, even if they aren't deserved.

And I never told Vince that he was my first client and Spirit was my first delivery.

Some things are better left unsaid.

Chapter   6 Only Four More Hours

Introducing myself to small animal veterinarians landed a few referrals like the Carsons, but my practice was growing too slowly to keep ahead of the expenses. I needed another way to build the client base that would keep my practice afloat while I waited for the new telephone directory to be published.

The rules that prohibited veterinarians from advertising were relaxing, but it was not acceptable to advertise aggressively. Because I lived in the city and practiced in the country, a sign in front of my house would be useless.

When I was approached by Horse Helpers, a local humane organization that assisted the state veterinarian's office in caring for impounded, neglected horses, I jumped at the chance to volunteer. I donated veterinary services, and served on their board of directors. There I met a young couple who published a regional newsletter for horse owners. They asked me to write a monthly column on horse care, and I immediately accepted this unpaid position. It was just the kind of exposure I needed. I wrote articles on all aspects of equine management and veterinary care. I explained the value of good conformation, preventative medicine, equine behavior, how the anatomy and physiology of the horse affects management choices, and other topics of interest to horsemen.

These columns were well received, so I approached the publisher of our local newspaper, the Mountain View Gazette, and soon was writing a regular column there as well. One day they sent a staff photographer to shoot me with my horse, Rocky. When I saw my picture at the top of my column, I was thrilled. Soon I was writing for a third publication. While the exposure was good, only a small number of new clients were attracted. Despite these volunteer efforts, I still needed more clients.

Although I did have some professional horsemen in my practice, most of my clients were amateur horsemen who made their living in other fields. They loved their animals, but didn't grow up around horses, so they lacked the guidance of parents or equine professionals to help them along the way. The questions that my clients asked me revealed a fundamental ignorance of basic horse management. I needed a way to educate these horse owners before problems occurred, but I often did not meet them until their horses had medical problems. I wanted to change that, for the sake of both the horses and their owners. Losing Spirit's foal was always on my mind.

I began offering free seminars on horse management. I advertised the seminars through the publications that carried my columns and invited my few clients, asking them to bring their friends, and the volunteers at Horse Helpers. Invitations went out to stables, riding clubs and breed associations.

To interest as many potential clients as possible, I needed a topic that would appeal to every horse owner, regardless of breed or riding discipline. I wanted to reach breeders who didn't even ride, so I chose first aid. Barbed wire injured many horses in the area. Sometimes what the client had done, or neglected to do, to the horse before I arrived made the injury worse, rather than better.

I treated so many injured horses that I had to agree with one of my clients, Todd Palmer, when he told me "Horses are born tryin' to die, and it's our job to slow 'em down."

There are medical supplies available over the counter, and first aid kits are sold by tack shops and catalogs, but my clients didn't know what to do with the kits after they bought them. So I put together a presentation showing how veterinarians approached wound care and gave the attendees an opportunity to buy first aid kits that contained the same medications that I use to treat wounds. I didn't include prescription medications, only over-the-counter wound disinfectants and ointments for common injuries. Each kit included an instruction sheet with the horse's normal vital signs and a list of the kit's contents. Clients could take the list to the phone when calling their vet. If the vet got an adequate description of the wound, and knew what materials the client had on hand, it would be easier to give specific instructions for any emergency. Every vet in the area would benefit from having educated clients.

I assembled these kits at home in front of the television. One day I saw a special presentation on Public Television about the restoration of the antique carousel in Kit Carson County, Colorado. I was fascinated by the history of this marvelous machine, and learned that Colorado had a group of enthusiasts called the Colorado Carousel Society, and I soon joined them so I could visit this historic landmark. Such began a life-long quest to ride all of the antique carousels in the country as I traveled to attend the educational seminars that were required to maintain my vet license.

At the first aid seminars I taught clients how to describe the injury when calling their vet, how to clean a wound without further contaminating it, and how to properly apply a variety of bandages for different parts of the body. With this knowledge, clients could give vital information to their veterinarian over the phone. The vet was then better able to decide if the clients could handle the situation themselves with the supplies they had available, or if an appointment was necessary. Clients learned how to protect a major injury from becoming even worse while awaiting the arrival of their vet. The kits would be available only to people who attended the seminar after they were trained how to use them. When owners completed the seminar, they had both the knowledge and the supplies to make a difference in their horses' health.

The seminars worked like magic. At the end of every seminar at least one person asked me to become their veterinarian. They liked the fact that I treated them with respect, and included them in the health care team caring for their horse. Over time, I did more than 100 of these seminars, and built a substantial client base, all by freely sharing my veterinary knowledge with horse owners.

In time, I had given the first aid seminar so often that I could give it in my sleep, so I developed presentations on conformation, shoeing, parasitology, care of the pregnant mare, and other topics of interest to my clients. Later I invited veterinary experts from the university to speak to my clients. I loved the interaction with these horse owners, as they were always interested in caring for their horses and learning new things.

I Make Horse Calls

As word spread about these seminars, I was asked to travel outside my practice area to speak. Even though I couldn't get new clients this way, if a seminar could be scheduled during my slower months, I accepted the invitations and charged a nominal fee to cover expenses.

I worked hard to earn my veterinary degree, but not everyone who had the talent to become a veterinarian had the opportunity because the class size was limited. I felt obligated to share my education. It was a way to give back to the horse owning community that supported veterinarians.

One such request to speak came from a trail riding club at Sandy Mesa, a small, rural community located on the other side of the continental divide from Denver. Riders from several nearby states were expected to attend the regional meeting. Sandy Mesa was far from my practice, but I agreed to go because the meeting would be in January, during my slow season. Although the club offered to pay for my hotel room, I asked them to schedule my presentation right after lunch on Saturday, so I could drive over and back in one day. That would minimize the time I was away from my practice, allowing me to be on call Friday night. There was no one to cover emergencies when I was gone, and like a nervous mother hen, I didn't want to leave my patients unattended for long.

Because it was winter and I had to cross two mountain passes to get to Sandy Mesa, I kept a close eye on the weather reports as the date of the seminar approached. As luck would have it, a storm was due to arrive on Friday. It was a long way to Sandy Mesa, and if I waited until morning to leave and was delayed by the storm, I might miss my presentation time altogether. I decided to travel on Friday night. I called the club secretary and asked if the hotel room was still available. It was.

My Mother would be accompanying me on this trip, leaving Dad and Clancy to take care of each other. Mom loved to travel, whether it was a trip to the mall or across the country. If a train, plane, or boat was leaving, she'd be on it. Between Mom and Clancy, there was always a crowd waiting for me at the door when I put on my coat.

Mom began going on late night emergency calls with me early in my veterinary career. On the way to emergencies the adrenalin kept me alert, but the exhaustion and let-down that occur once the emergency is over sometimes made it hard to stay awake on the way home. Her main job was to keep me awake, but her curiosity made her a great sounding board, so I began discussing my cases and treatment plans with her as I drove.

When she retired from her accounting position she accompanied me on my daily rounds. She yearned to become a physician, but advanced education was beyond her family's financial means. Yet she never pushed me into medicine. She stayed in the background, letting me decide my own future. Once I became a vet, however, she was fascinated by my cases.

She learned about my medicines when she inventoried the supplies in my truck. She made a list of every item in my truck so she could find it when she served as my "go-for." She soon learned the uses of each drug, and how I categorized the truck for efficiency. I was adamant with my assistants that every drug be returned to exactly the same location from which it had been retrieved. When doing emergency work after dark, I had to be able to find everything quickly to provide prompt treatment.

Mom learned to pronounce the tongue-twisting names of the medicines and common equine ailments. Soon she was getting medicines and syringes from my truck once I made the diagnosis, but I never had her fill the syringes. I checked each bottle to be certain she had brought the right drug, ensuring safety for my patients. She soon worked flawlessly around the truck, and began retrieving the correct supplies without being told, once she heard my diagnosis.

Her job as an accountant had required strict accuracy and good penmanship, recording by hand a myriad of numbers in neat, orderly columns every day. I, however, possess the poor penmanship skills for which doctors are famous. My penmanship teacher in first grade must have known that I would become a doctor, and I'm sure my feeble attempts at recreating the beautiful cursive strokes of my mother exasperated her to no end. Mom soon was writing all of my medical records and bills.

Her life was forever changed by the Great Depression, which occurred when she was a child. Hard-working families lost their savings, their jobs and their homes. She vividly remembered the bread lines, and beggars who came to the house asking for food.

I Make Horse Calls

Although her family had little to spare, no one was turned away. Anyone hungry enough to beg for food was given a sandwich and allowed to sit on the front porch to eat it.

My parents didn't talk much about how they struggled during the depression, but only spoke about how much others had suffered. But she and Dad lived their lives in a way to minimize harm should another depression occur. They worked full time, and opened a savings account, paying the family first. They only bought what they could afford. A tight budget kept expenses under control, and the family only went into debt to purchase a home. They paid their mortgage faithfully, so one day they would own a home from which no bank could ever evict them. They would never take the equity out of their home.

Mom went to work right after graduating from high school to support her family. She had earned a college scholarship, but there were no night jobs, so she worked by day and attended class by night. She paid her own tuition, as her scholarship would not pay for night courses. She chose accounting school, and was the only woman in her class.

Dad was the oldest son, and dropped out of high school to support his family, but Mom insisted that he return for his diploma. She and Dad shared a strong work ethic, which enabled both my sister and me to stay in school long enough to earn advanced degrees.

From my parents I learned to work hard, and I paid a good portion of my college expenses. I sold my horse, horse trailer, saddle and boots to pay tuition. I worked three jobs to pay my way. I felt so fortunate to land those jobs, and to have things to sell. But without the additional support of my parents, becoming a veterinarian would have been impossible for me. I will be forever grateful for the sacrifices they made.

My parents taught me to always do my best and accept the outcome, whatever it may be. I could have no regrets if I gave every project my all.

They taught me that I could have almost anything I wanted if I worked hard enough, but also let me know that I was unlikely to get everything I wanted - I had to prioritize. Once I set my eyes on vet school, everything else became secondary as I worked toward that dream. I learned to focus.

I Make Horse Calls

When my Mother first accompanied me on my rounds, she was afraid of horses. She was even afraid of my own gentle horses, but she followed directions well, and soon learned to handle herself safely around most of my patients. If I was working on a dangerous horse I made her stay in the truck, where she filled out the medical records.

While veterinary practice is interesting and can be challenging, it is often quite routine. I see the same diseases over and over again, and explain my findings to the client every time. I help each client understand the cause of the horse's problem and its treatment. Sometimes I feel like a broken record, as I may see the same ailment several times in one day, but I try to remind myself that this is the first time the owner has seen this problem, so they deserve a thorough explanation. My Mother heard my spiels so often that she could recite them verbatim. If a client waited until I was out of earshot, and then asked my Mom questions about the horse's condition, she always gave the right answer. But I had to stop her, because rendering a medical opinion without a veterinary license is a violation of the Veterinary Practice Act!

As a result of her competence giving medical advice, I nicknamed her Dr. Mom. Her genuine smile and sparkling eyes opened the door to friendship, and once my clients experienced her heartfelt compassion and unconditional love, she won them over. They welcomed her warmly. If my clients saw me arriving alone, they would be concerned if Dr. Mom was ill. They were relieved to hear that if she wasn't with me, she and my Father were relaxing on a sunny beach somewhere in a warm climate.

Friday was a slow day at the practice, and the storm came in right on time. Heavy, wet snow was coming down furiously, and beginning to pile up. We ate an early dinner so we could get started. It might take all night, but we would just keep going until we reached Sandy Mesa.

We loaded the first aid kits and handouts into the truck, and were on our way by six PM. The wet, heavy snow flakes settled on the windshield like lace doilies. Soon the snow was piled high on the glass, except for the path cleared by the wipers. The snow was packing down below the blades, which could no longer complete their full sweep. We would need four-wheel drive to get through the storm tonight.

We started on smaller country roads, but soon approached the interstate. We were only a few miles from home when we saw an accident. A four-wheel drive was upside down in the ditch. When I'm the first person on the scene of an accident, I always stop to render medical assistance, but an ambulance was already there, so we went on.

"That's not a good sign," said Dr. Mom as a little worry crept across her brow.

"No, it's not. I think we're gonna be glad we left tonight, so we can take it slow. It's only half a mile to the interstate, and that should be plowed." I tried to sound confident.

It had been snowing for hours, and since the storm had been predicted the snowplows were out in force, removing snow and putting sand on the main roads.

In a few minutes I drove up the ramp onto the interstate. Around the second curve was a sign, Sandy Mesa - 240 miles. The highway crews had done their job and the road was well sanded and free of ice. As we began the steep climb, I could feel the tires get traction. The posted speed limit was 60 miles per hour, and it looked like clear sailing from here. I settled deeply into the driver's seat and began to relax.

Dividing 240 miles by 60 miles per hour, I told Dr. Mom, "We should be there in about four hours. That'll put us into the hotel around 10:30. We can get a good night's sleep and be rested for tomorrow's presentation. This was a much better choice than driving in the morning, hurrying and worrying that we might be late."

She agreed.

We traveled safely onward through the storm. It was snowing, but here the storm was not fierce enough to seriously impair visibility. This storm was caused by upslope conditions, where the storm formed on the prairie and was pushed westward up the eastern face of the Rockies. When that happens, the storm may not cross over the mountain tops, and the valleys west of the Front Range may be dry. We might drive out of the snow before we got to Sandy Mesa.

I Make Horse Calls

We really treasured these trips, and each other's company. My mother shared a strong relationship with her mother, and I am glad this trend carried into my generation. I feel so lucky to be so close to her.

Dr. Mom and I discussed how well the practice was growing and talked about our trips to the annual continuing education meetings each December. Seeing the Christmas lights decorating the houses and public places, and the respite from practice, always put us in the Christmas spirit by the time we arrived home from the meetings.

We chose to drive to the meetings, rather than fly, so we could take side trips, and we allowed an extra day to visit local attractions near the meeting sites.

We enjoyed watching the historic re-enactors display their age-old crafts at Williamsburg and wandered the halls of the Smithsonian learning about America's past - from steam engines to space travel.

On a stormy, windswept December evening in Salem, Massachusetts we followed the local Christmas walk, winding our way in and out of small shops along the coast, being warmly greeted by shopkeepers with hot spiced cider, homemade cookies, and peppermint candies at every stop.

In San Antonio, we rode the barge along the River Walk, decked out in Christmas lights serenaded by spirited carolers.

Every day during the New Orleans meeting was punctuated by Beignets at the Café du Monde while watching steamboats move up and down the Mississippi River.

We visited Old Town in San Diego and enjoyed the carousel that featured large dogs - friendly carvings of Saint Bernards that seemed to invite us to ride. Our longest side trip was driving the length of the Pacific Coast from San Diego to Seattle, riding antique carousels along the way.

We came home from Seattle through Montana, and as we drove south across Wyoming I saw in my rearview mirror, the fiercest winter storm, like an angry ocean wave thousands of feet high, bearing down on us from the north. I was outrunning it, but when the highway turned east at Casper, we were overtaken by it. We sought refuge in Douglas to wait out the storm when the highway was closed. Dr. Mom and I were lucky to have a warm place to stay.

Tonight's storm was intensifying as we gained altitude. Soon it was snowing so hard that visibility was shrinking. To be safe, I slowed to 50 miles per hour. We passed another sign for Sandy Mesa – 200 miles. When I did the mental calculations, I again announced, "At this rate, we'll be there in four more hours."

Dr. Mom laughed.

As I drove on in silence, I thought about how hard my parents worked to give me the opportunity to go to college, and how upset they were when I dropped out. But years passed before I understood why. I hadn't lived through the Great Depression. I felt certain I could return to college any time I wanted. I was ignorant of how much my parents yearned for the very thing that I seemed to be throwing away. But I was searching for my future. I had to turn my childhood passion for horses into a sustainable career, and my first attempts at college didn't seem to be leading there, or anywhere else.

My experiences in the horse industry led me back to college to pursue my veterinary degree, and my parents were thrilled. My Dad volunteered to be my clinic's "official puppy petter" after I graduated. He was disappointed when I told him I would only be working on horses, but I always made sure we had a dog at home. Dr. Mom got her medical education at my side, and even in her sixties was still an eager student. I loved sharing my life with her.

The snow was coming down so hard that we couldn't see any house lights along the roadside. I drove confidently up the approach and through the Eisenhower tunnel but had to creep down the steep grade into Dillon. Conditions were different on the backside of the mountain - the road was icy and I was having trouble getting traction. But we made it safely down. As I came out of Frisco, heading up Vail pass, conditions improved slightly but the snow on the road was getting so deep that I could only maintain 40 miles per hour. I wasn't sure even that was slow enough. We soon came to another highway sign - Sandy Mesa 160 miles.

Doing the math again, I told Mom "Only four more hours."

This time she didn't laugh.

I Make Horse Calls

I crept over Vail pass. The road crew had been unable to clear the heavy snow that was now coming down unbelievably hard.

The truck felt like our cocoon. There didn't seem to be anything outside but sheets of white snow shrouding the darkness beyond. We couldn't see out the side windows. All of the truck's windows were covered with snow, except the ever shrinking path where the wipers kept the windshield clear. I rolled down my side window and grabbed the wiper and banged it on the windshield, knocking the snow from it. I brushed my hand down the side of the windshield and over the rear view mirror to increase my field of view. Dr Mom did the same on her side.

When the occasional car would pass me, I'd follow its tail lights because I couldn't see the road anymore. I was hoping the drivers were locals who knew the road. But even that plan was short-lived. It was snowing so hard that their tail lights were soon lost in the darkness. And there was almost no one else on the road tonight. Maybe they were smarter than I was. But the road was not slippery here. There was no ice, only packed snow. Traction was good.

As I came down the backside of Vail pass, into the town of Vail, I couldn't believe my eyes. There were no car tracks visible in the snow on the road – and this was Interstate 70! Was the road closed? Sometimes the highway patrol will close a road if it considers the road to be impassable, but I'd expect to see a state trooper guiding drivers to safety. There were no cars anywhere. I was still on the highway. At least I *thought* I was still on the highway.

My speed through Vail was so slow there was no use calculating our arrival time. If there were any signs telling us how far it was to Sandy Mesa, I couldn't see them. We were on a never-ending journey.

I might have pulled over to seek refuge in Vail if I could have seen signs for lodging. The reflectors marking the side of the road had also disappeared in the storm, as had the exit signs, so I kept going.

The road flattened as we drove down the canyon, through Vail Valley. A few miles west of Vail I could begin to see the road better. The snow had slacked off and visibility was getting better. Plows had cleared the snow. The roadway looked darker, a sign that it was warmer and the snow was melting. I could now distinguish the driving lanes from the shoulder, so I increased my speed.

I Make Horse Calls

Maybe we would reach our destination after all.

In a few more miles, the snow on the road was melted, and the wet, black road and lane markings were visible. The salt applied by the road crews and warmer conditions cleared the roads.

The snow turned to rain by the time we got to Glenwood Springs, and a few miles after that it stopped raining.

I got the truck up to highway speed, and was glad to arrive in Sandy Mesa in one piece. I didn't check my watch. I didn't want to know how late it was.

The temperature in Sandy Mesa was mild and the night sky was clear. The stars shone brightly over the small town. It hadn't even rained here, much less snowed. Everything was dry. It was unbelievably warm as I climbed stiffly out of the truck to register at the hotel.

My snow-capped truck was quite a contrast to the dry vehicles parked nearby. The snow, piled high on the roof, was melting, dripping into a lake that was forming under my truck. It looked like an oversized slice of spice cake with whipped cream frosting.

As some of the hotel guests walked across the parking lot from the nearby restaurant, clad in shorts and short sleeved shirts, they were gawking at my truck.

The old saying," if you don't like the weather, just wait five minutes" is a good one, but in the mountains where upslope storms occur, I've noticed that, "If you don't like the weather, just drive five miles."

Exhausted, we checked into the hotel. I was glad my presentation was after lunch. I'd enjoy sleeping late, knowing the drive was behind me.

The seminar went well. I met some wonderful horse people, and contributed a portion of the proceeds from the sale of the first aid kits to help the club buy helmets for their young riders.

The return trip was blissfully uneventful, but now, whenever Dr. Mom and I travel, and either one of us asks how long it is to our destination, we often joke "only four more hours!"

Chapter 7 Over Hill and Over Dale

I stood on my pedals, pulling hard against the handlebars to overcome the strong pull gravity had on my back wheel. My muscles were aching and my throat was parched, but I was nearly at the crest. In the three years since I'd returned to college in Boulder, I'd traveled this route so many times, always attacking these hills, trying to go faster every time.

Bicycling was a great way to relieve the stresses caused by trying to get good grades in every class, especially those classes that seemed useless to me but were required for admission to vet school.

Only a few more strokes and I'd be at the top.

I powered my way through.

As I topped the crest, I shifted to high gear and grabbed my water bottle. I gulped a few swallows as I accelerated, and soon I was enjoying flying down the back of the hill, pedaling fast to gain momentum for the next climb.

I was glad to be completing my biology degree - a degree that got off to a rocky start with trouble at the admissions office.

"What do you mean 'admissions are closed?' I just got this acceptance letter in today's mail." I shook the letter at the clerk whose eyes and nose stuck out the cracked door to the back office.

The letter said I had been accepted to the University of Colorado undergraduate degree program and I had to send in my deposit by August 15th, or whenever admissions closed. The letter arrived in my mailbox only an hour ago. I had driven straight to the registrar's office with my check. How could she tell me admissions were closed? It was only June.

I Make Horse Calls

"We reached our quota of students at noon."

I checked the large clock in the lobby, and it was 12:08. How could I have missed the deadline by eight minutes? Eight minutes that would cost me a year of waiting. I already had two years of college behind me, but the pre-vet studies required three years of chemistry. And vet school took four years. If I was one of the rare students who got in on my first try, my journey of seven years had just become eight years, all because I was eight minutes too late for a deadline that was impossible to make.

"Oh please, please let me in!" I begged.

When I arrived home from Florida the pre-vet program at Colorado State was already full - closed to new students, as was the University of Colorado, but former students in good standing were still being accepted at CU. I filled out the paperwork and mailed it in. I checked my mailbox everyday for the letter. When it came I jumped in my car and sped straight to the registrar's office. To have missed this year's class by eight minutes was unbearable.

"Please. It'll cost me a whole year! And there was nothing I could do to get here any sooner!"

The clerk snatched the letter and deposit from my hand saying "Okay, you're in," and closed the door in my face.

I was both stunned and elated.

"Thank you," I mumbled to the closed door.

The first hurdle on the way to vet school was behind me, the first of many.

I accelerated over the next hill on my route and counted my blessings to distract me from the strain.

I was so fortunate to be able to attend college. It was a luxury for me, when I consider how my parents struggled to afford college.

Selling my horse, Frank, and my horse trailer provided money for college expenses. I continued working on the Florida farm through the end of the show season. I bid farewell to my employer in March and headed home for the mountains of Colorado, enjoying an extended cross-country vacation on the way.

First I went south to the tip of Key West, and then drove the Atlantic coastline to Canada as spring advanced with me.

I Make Horse Calls

I saw dogwoods blooming in the Carolinas, and I visited friends in Virginia and Maryland, allowing spring's northward journey to overtake me as I dawdled. My Sheltie and I walked the beaches from Key West to Cape Cod. I traversed southern Canada until I was above Minneapolis, and then drove south to see my sister. My suburban, decked out with a mattress and sleeping bag, was my home, as I saved money for school.

When I got to Mountain View I reconnected with my friends who had horses and found a job at a local tack shop. I had enjoyed my free time, but vet school would be expensive. The shop owner grew hay on his farm, and raised sheep and Border collies; he needed someone to keep his shop open during baling season. The pay wasn't much, but was a fortune compared to my grooming salary. When he said I could have weekends off, I accepted his offer. I had not had a weekend off in five years, and had not had a Saturday off since I turned 16.

After working with him for four hours, he left me on my own. I waited on his few customers, repaired horse blankets, polished silver tack, and made foal halters. With nothing else to do, I spent the rest of the summer in the back room watching TV and crocheting between customers. I felt guilty, but I didn't know what else to do.

My first stint at college had started out well. I was an honor student and made the Dean's list the first year, but things turned sour the second year.

During finals week I got an infection and was too sick to attend class. I visited the campus hospital and got my medical condition documented, then met with my professors, according to University policy. I had studied hard and was prepared for my exams. If I had been able to take exams when I recovered I would have gotten A's in the classes and remained on the Honor Roll, but the professors insisted that I take the finals on schedule. I did, but I was too sick to understand the questions. In the end, I dropped two letter grades in two classes, ruining my grade point average irreparably.

I was so disgusted that educated people, scholars with PhDs, would treat an eager student so unfairly. I didn't want to spend my life working with people like that and I was no longer interested in higher education. I dropped out.

I left college to pursue my passion for horses. I learned about the horse industry, but I needed an education to support myself, and I was anxious to get started. The veterinarians I had met were well-educated, friendly, approachable and compassionate. I felt a kinship with them that I never felt with my professors.

When I decided to become a veterinarian, I returned to college with more zeal than ever. I declared my major as biology and I now had a tangible goal - vet school admission. My plan to accomplish that goal was to devote myself fully to that end. The biology courses would capture my interest, and the biology faculty was amazing and inspiring.

I downshifted for my last climb on the Foothills Highway. As I crested the hill I could see the large yellow barn of Foothills Farm, pushed against the dry windswept slope that ran down from the pine forest above. It was here while a freshman nearly ten years ago that I boarded my filly, and rode her over the hills bareback after classes. My world was in chaos then, as my young friends where shipped to Vietnam to fight a war that Americans didn't support. Too many of them came back wounded, mentally and physically, or didn't come back at all.

And the country was torn apart over the war. When four protesting students at Kent State were killed during a protest, the campus in Boulder erupted.

I couldn't make sense of the world I was about to enter as an adult.

My refuge was the stable, where I tried to make sense of things. Time spent here - with these gentle, willing and beautiful animals, gave me a break from the hot political climate on campus - gave me time to clear my head.

Foothills Farm was where I met Chip, the riding instructor whose youthful enthusiasm and talent sparked my interest in pursuing a life working with show horses. Chip helped me make connections with respected trainers when I left college. The jobs didn't pay well, but the education I got regarding the horse industry was invaluable.

I Make Horse Calls

And it was here that I became aware of how commonly jumpers and race horses suffer from lameness problems. I wanted to know more about the problems I saw then, and I had returned to the university in Boulder to do just that.

Boulder is a small, high-tech town in a beautiful mountain setting. Driving into town on the turnpike, going over the last steep hill, yields a breathtaking view of Flagstaff Mountain and Boulder, sitting at the foot of Boulder Canyon. On a summer's eve the haze serenely shrouding the mountains gives the scene a beautiful, surrealistic cast, making it hard to believe the scene is not just some artist's idealized version of mountain majesty. The dry, clean air and high altitude makes the region a magnet for avid runners and cyclists. But Boulder is plagued by wind.

Frank Shorter, the Olympic marathon runner, owned a shop in Boulder, and I hoped one day to see him running around town. I carefully scrutinized every male runner I saw during my first year in Boulder, to no avail. I finally quit looking.

Some Boulder residents took the healthy lifestyle a bit far. The "in" thing to do is to be well-educated and thin, eating only organic foods and exercising vigorously. I agree with the concept, but after eating some of the whole grain breads offered at the more trendy restaurants in town, I found myself picking seeds out of my teeth all afternoon. And exercise hovers somewhere between a religion and an addiction for some of the population. A friend bought expensive jogging shorts and shoes, and then took jogging lessons. I didn't get it. I always thought jogging was simple - right, left, right, left - repeat. Why would anyone need lessons?

Cycling to class on my old bike was a challenge because the classrooms were uphill from my dorm and I needed to adapt to the thin air which was lacking in oxygen. I struggled against gravity and the wind every day, but it never got any easier. I worried that there might be something wrong with me because I didn't seem to be getting any fitter despite training over the same route intently every day.

My part-time jobs left me a little better off financially, so I offered my friend Peter a few dollars to tune up the old bike for me. Peter was a part-time bicycle mechanic and my racquetball and tennis partner. I was overjoyed when Peter told me the bike's wheel bearings were rusted into a solid mass.

It wasn't me after all! It was the bike.

So I sold it and bought a brand new, shiny gold Motobecane Super Mirage. I justified the expense, thinking that, if all went according to plan, I would be cycling around a college campus for the next seven years, plus I could ride the bike to work off campus. An old ankle injury made it painful to run, but I could comfortably cycle for aerobic workouts. It would be a good investment in my health.

My gleaming new bike was unbelievably lightweight. It flew effortlessly down hills, and climbing was *so* much easier. It had a cherished spot in my dorm room, not left outside in a rack where it would be exposed to the elements or theft. This had to be my means of transportation for many years to come.

The first day I rode this speedy wonder I was astounded at how fast and how far I could go. Struggling against those rusty bearings had indeed made me quite fit, and now I sprinted like a rabbit, reaping the benefits of those many tortoise-like trips. I bicycled east on Baseline Road, and in 30 minutes arrived in the next town. My new bike could fly! The terrain was slightly downhill, but this new bike was so fast I felt powerful. I spent the day jumping horses with friends, and in the late afternoon headed home. While I was enjoying the companionship, a fierce wind came up. I jokingly asked my friends to check on me, and if I hadn't reached my dorm in two hours, to send out a posse to find me.

I bade my friends goodbye and headed uphill and upwind, to campus. The wind was fierce - blowing off the mountain with a vengeance - and blowing right into my face.

I had to pedal downhill to maintain momentum, pedal furiously on the flat just to keep going and walk on the uphill sections. If I stayed in the saddle the wind pushed me backwards.

The wind was so strong it took my breath away. I couldn't breathe when I faced into it. I had to turn my head to the side.

Struggling against the wind I quickly grew tired. I stopped under a massive, aging cottonwood tree to catch my breath. Its multiple, broad gray trunks sheltered me from the wind. But soon I found myself in danger sitting at the leeward base of the tree. Decaying branches were being sheared off by the unrelenting force of the brutal winds and cracking onto the ground all around me. It was time to move on.

After a few more miles I grew too tired to continue. I stopped again, this time finding shelter behind a thick hedge. I sat on the grass at the side of the road, gasping for air, muscles burning. The wind was so totally overpowering that it blew through the hedge and toppled my bicycle.

I had to get on my way again. The weakening daylight of late autumn meant the temperature was dropping and the wind tore the heat from my body. As the second hour elapsed, I kept looking over my shoulder for my friends, but no one came. I kept moving, as the road had a narrow shoulder. It was growing dark and my bike had no lights, so I would be invisible when night fell. The wind would die down at sunset, but it would be too dangerous to be on this winding country road after dark.

When I finally arrived at the dorm exhausted, I collapsed on the floor as soon as I got in the door. My roommate thought I was dying. My battle home had lasted two and a half hours, five times as long as the ride out.

The next day I read in the local newspaper that the National Center for Atmospheric Research, located within sight of my room, had noted unusually high sustained winds and a record gust of 152 miles per hour that day. I clipped and saved the article.

No wonder I was so tired!

I soon planned out a comfortable cross wind route, bicycling north and south, up the Foothills Highway to Nelson Road three times a week. The first ten miles had several major hills and valleys, but no loss of altitude. It was a great place for interval training - a strenuous climb, followed by easier pedaling down a short hill while I recovered, and then the next hill was upon me.

Then I would turn east for the downhill section of the loop, pedaling effortlessly for miles in top gear. While it was exhilarating to fly down these country roads, I knew I would pay the price later, climbing back to campus. So discretion ruled my route decisions. Before I turned downhill I always checked the wind, as downhill also meant downwind. A late return could cause me to miss class or work.

I soon adjusted my schedule to bicycle in the morning because the winds tend to come up in the afternoon. The loop, which

I Make Horse Calls

took me three hours on my first attempt, could now be done in less than two hours - wind willing. I had learned when to stand above the saddle to climb each hill. If I stood too soon, I'd tire before I reached the top. If I waited too long, I lost momentum and slowed to a crawl.

My fierce, competitive streak surfaced if I spied a cyclist on the road ahead of me - I had to catch him. With my slick new bike, I was soon passing most solo cyclists, but when I would encounter male cyclists in black Lycra shorts riding in packs, I knew there was no use pursuing them. They were just too fast.

I would return red-faced and exhausted from each day's ride and collapse on the cool concrete floor of my dorm room. But it was a great stress-reliever, and both body and soul felt cleansed after each ride.

I turned right on Nelson Road and selected the largest gear. The wind was calm today, and there were miles of downhill roads ahead. I was going to enjoy every inch of them. This was as easy as finding a job when I moved to Boulder.

To my delight, the friend who got me the summer job called again. She worked at a saddlery in Boulder, and they needed someone to work Saturdays. Since I was experienced, they offered me the job. I jumped at the chance, as I had classes all week and Saturday jobs were hard to find in college towns.

Why was I so lucky to get a good job without even looking?

Shortly after I began working at the saddle shop a young lady came in, looked me up and down, and said, "Shouldn't you be in Minneapolis in grad school?"

I replied that she must know my sister, who was doing just that. It turned out that she was a friend of my sister. She needed a riding instructor to help her with a difficult hunter. I referred her to the best local barn, but she refused. I referred her to a friend of mine, but she again refused. She was still at the store at closing time, refusing to leave until I agreed to teach her.

I have no idea why she chose me. She didn't even know me.

I got another student at a neighboring farm. The money was good, although not dependable due to the weather. But teaching paid better than my other jobs. I used this money for clothing. No more rubber boots with holes for me!

I Make Horse Calls

This seemed too good to be true.

The first time I visited the pre-vet adviser's office with questions about my schedule he tried to hire me as caretaker of his colony of research cats. The job entailed examining the animals, medicating the sick ones, feeding them, and cleaning litter pans. I am allergic to cats, so I kindly refused.

He offered money, but I had a job.

He offered letters of recommendation for vet school. I graciously refused. I had other options. I knew veterinarians who would write letters for me, and their recommendations would carry more clout with the vet school admissions board.

He offered a research project which would lead to graduation with honors. I accepted. My damaged GPA needed all the help I could give it.

Why was I so lucky to be handed this opportunity?

The pieces of the puzzle were falling into place. I worked in the cat colony four nights a week, sold saddles on Saturday, and taught riding lessons on Tuesday afternoons, weather permitting. The sale of Frank and the trailer paid tuition. My jobs, with extra hours in the summer, paid for my dorm room, meals, and books.

It was a comfortable balance. On Tuesdays and Saturdays I was the expert - teaching people to ride and fitting riders for saddles and clothing, answering all of their questions. Evenings were spent enjoying the company of two dozen cats, as long as I protected myself from allergens. The rest of my time was spent as a student, asking the questions and expanding my knowledge. And I took a step closer to my goal every day.

Life was good.

My mild allergy worsened. I had to take steps to keep from further sensitizing myself to cat allergens. I wore a lab coat, mask, and a set of shoes and slacks which I left in the lab. With my rubber gloves, I looked more like I was entering an EPA Superfund cleanup site than taking care of cats, but I had to do it. Any break in my protective gear would have me sneezing and teary-eyed for the rest of the day. I would have to take out my contacts, and I couldn't study if I couldn't see.

On a regular basis I had to give the cats a laxative for hairballs. I thought this would be difficult, but I was mistaken. The

I Make Horse Calls

student who shared my job showed me how. The medicine came in a tube, like toothpaste. All I had to do was take off my gloves and sit on the floor with two inches of paste on each finger. The cats thought it was so yummy that I was quickly mobbed by a dozen friendly cats, fighting for the opportunity to lick my fingers clean. I repeated the process until all of the cats were treated.

I then went directly to the shower and laundry.

I had envisioned the lives of research animals to be terrible, but these cats were well cared for. They had each other for companionship, and plenty of room to move around. They were fed and the room was cleaned daily. A special air purifier was installed to prevent respiratory diseases. Pregnant cats had a separate nursery, where they could tend their kittens away from the pride. And timid cats had roomy cages where they could hide from the others. At Christmas I was puzzled by small, dark red blobs I found on the shelves, until one of the researchers told me he had bought fresh liver as treats for the cats. Some of the older females were adopted by the researchers, and lived out their golden years as barn cats.

The walls held shelves at different heights, so cats could climb and play, peering down from above. They could also regulate their temperature by choosing how high to sit. We provided cardboard boxes so the cats never had to sleep on the cool concrete floor. One day I found all 28 cats stuffed into one small cardboard box. Various appendages were sticking out of this myriad of cat fur, arms and legs, tails and ears, all crammed together. I noticed the room was cooler than usual. The heating system had malfunctioned, and the cats were conserving body heat. The mass of cat fur separated into individual forms once the furnace was repaired.

In spite of my efforts, my allergies worsened and I found myself sneezing in the presence of the researchers and other students who worked with the colony. I had become allergic to people who touched cats.

I was sad to be too allergic to have cats at home.

But I kept working. Nothing would deter me from my goal.

I turned south on the Longmont Diagonal. The road was always busy, but the shoulders were wide and smooth, and the traffic was fairly tolerant of cyclists, as there were so many of us in Boulder.

I Make Horse Calls

I lived on campus, because dorm housing was the most affordable. I had met some good people in college - people who would become life-long friends.

My roommate the first year was Eleanor. She was a serious student, majoring in oceanography. Why she chose a campus 1000 miles from the nearest ocean was beyond me, but I was glad she did. She was a great roommate.

Wendy, who lived in the next room, would have been a terrible roommate for me. She came into our room one day wearing a t-shirt that said "When's day?" and it exemplified her usual mental state. She told us her major was Italian, so I asked what she was going to do with her degree after graduation. Was she going to teach Italian, or become an interpreter?

She was apparently disgusted that I could ask such a stupid question. Of course she wasn't going to do anything with her degree. She was studying Italian so when she went abroad during her junior year she could ski the Alps while conversing fluently with all of the young Italian Romeos.

Of course! What was I thinking? Perish the thought that she should have come to college for an education!

I lived in a block of dorm rooms that had been set aside for older students who were returning to college after a few years working. One afternoon a group of students sat around my room, talking about jobs we had held.

Bob had led tours of the local brewery, where he got all the free beer he could drink. It turned out to be a lot of beer. But when Bob returned to the university, he pursued a career in business with gusto. He dressed the part of an up and coming attorney, and I couldn't help but notice his perfectly polished shoes. I wondered how he could keep his shoes so gleaming and scuff-free when I looked at my manure-encrusted paddock boots.

So I considered Bob's daily routine. He dressed in his dorm room, walked down the carpeted hallway and emerged onto the concrete sidewalk that led to the asphalt parking lot. Once in his car, his beautiful shoes rested on the carpet until they were delivered to the enclosed parking garage in the office tower where Bob spent his internship. Traversing the interior walkway, Bob entered the office where his shoes made their way through another carpeted hallway to spend the day under his desk. Bob's shoes never touched the earth.

In contrast, my boots were often heavy with brown clay from walking through the fields, as I savored the refreshing aroma of the earth awakening after a shower.

But Bob was as happy in his element as I was in mine.

George had worked construction. Wendy had worked in the jewelry business, and Amanda had worked in a dress boutique, but only for one day. I had been working for nine years, so I was dumbfounded when Amanda told us she quit at lunchtime because handling the money made her hands dirty. She went home to cleanup.

Amanda had come to college in search of a husband. In her quest she returned to her dorm room every day at lunchtime to re-apply her make-up and re-style her hair. If handling money made her hands so dirty she had to quit, I wondered how she would deal with childbirth and diapers.

One evening, as Amanda was preparing for a date and I was heading out to clean cat litter pans she remarked how lucky I was, that I never had any dates so I didn't have to worry about my appearance.

Thanks a lot, Amanda.

I was so grateful to be paired with Eleanor.

Eleanor had short blonde hair, close cropped to her head because it was so curly. She wore half-glasses that hung on a tiny decorative chain around her neck. And she came to college for an education, as I did. El worked hard earning top grades in her classes.

But I was afraid I might lose her the day she had to get certified in SCUBA diving. She had been training in the indoor pool on campus, but the certification test was given in a mountain lake. On the early spring day when the test was given the lake was filled with ice cold water that only hours before had been snow gracing the mountainside. Her lips were blue and she was shivering uncontrollably when she got back to the dorm, but some hot tea brought her back to life.

Eleanor was a great student, but had little tolerance for students who disturbed her study. One afternoon I came home from teaching riding and Eleanor was on her bed trying to study, but she was fuming mad. It seemed that our neighbor upstairs had been bouncing a basketball off his floor - our ceiling - all afternoon.

The dorm alternated men and women on each floor, so we knew it would be a man doing the dribbling. But El didn't care. She finally couldn't stand it any longer, and stormed out the door. She stomped up the metal stairs next to our room, and I heard her pounding on the door overhead. I knew she was going to give that guy a piece of her mind.

Then all became quiet, and when she reappeared at our door, the angry expression was gone. She actually looked a little sheepish. When I asked what happened she told me that when the door opened, behind it was a 6'8" burly brute who snarled "Whaddya want?"

Always being able to think on her feet she wiped the anger off her face and like a perky coed asked "Can I borrow a cup of sugar?"

What a gal!

When she shared my calculus class, she was happy to be an environmental biology major, because that meant she didn't have to take a second semester of calculus.

I was sad to lose my study partner, but shared her joy when she burned her notes and sold her text book after finals. She offered me a little sympathy as she saw me struggling through the second semester, but she was so happy not to join me that I know she was smiling inside.

Little did El know that her first job working for the National Oceanographic and Atmospheric Administration would be contingent upon her passing another semester of calculus.

So after graduation she stayed on campus for the summer semester, hired a tutor and managed to eke out a passing grade in the course. I had a chuckle when I offered her my notes, but I really felt sorry for her. The course was brutal, and to give up her summer to take it was doubly annoying.

I approached the north edge of Boulder. Traffic was always heavy in this section, so I wheeled off the main drag and took a side street with a designated bicycle lane. I was comfortable knowing the safest routes around town, but returning to college after living five years on the farm had been daunting.

I Make Horse Calls

My nerves were rattled as the first day of class approached. I had to get top grades or my time and money would be wasted. If I hadn't chosen vet school, I had considered becoming a horse show photographer, and had enough money to buy a good camera and a small trailer that I could convert into a darkroom. But if I spent the money on tuition and then didn't get into vet school, there would be no money for a photography business.

I had chosen my future. Now I had to make it happen. There was only enough money for one choice.

The list of pre-vet courses was daunting. I was learning that vet school was not an occupation for animal lovers, but rather a calling for scientists who loved animals. And my ability to handle difficult science classes was about to be tested.

I consulted with the pre-vet adviser, puzzled that CU had two biology departments. He explained that one trained environmentalists and one was for pre-med students. I had already registered for environmental biology because it didn't require chemistry as a prerequisite, and the other course did. I was in the wrong class, but it was too late to change. I transferred to the right department in January and never looked back.

The more biology I studied, the more I liked it. Cell biology revealed the essence of life itself. If I didn't get into vet school, I'd have a career in biology. I had found myself. I spent countless hours studying biology, but didn't consider it hard work because it was so captivating. And I could study it anywhere - in the student cafeteria, sitting on the floor in the hallway of the classroom building - anywhere.

But it seemed that chemistry was going to be my recurring Nemesis.

Reading the fine print in the college catalog I saw that, because I lacked high school chemistry, I was required to take an introductory course in chemistry, which would push my completion time to four years.

I decided to skip it, and signed up for freshman chemistry - inorganic.

Hundreds of students packed into the huge auditorium on the first day of class. Looking around, I knew chemistry was the class that defeated so many pre-med students. I vowed to work hard and not become one of the defeated.

The first day in lab, when the instructor said "Take out an Erlenmeyer flask" I wished he would speak English. I glanced sideways at my classmates and followed their lead. I was so grateful when they gave us a manual with pictures of the items in our drawers. I worked hard, and soon I caught up to my classmates, almost.

First year chemistry was difficult, but manageable, until I made a mistake in lab. We had to analyze a sample of ore to determine the amount of iron it contained. I did all of the exercises, which dragged on for five weeks, but forgot to record the sample number on the first day. This would be a serious mistake for a professional chemist, but I was only a freshman chemistry student, taking my first ever chemistry class.

When I turned in my results to the lab instructor I admitted my mistake. I knew he could determine which sample I had by process of elimination. Grades were based on the accuracy of the assay, so I expected to be docked some points, but my work was good. We ran each stage of the test twice and my results varied by less than one percent. My assays were consistent.

The graduate student said that my mistake was a grievous one, and that I would receive a zero for the 50 point exercise.

A zero!

Now there was no way I could get an A in the course.

I thought he was unfair, but what could I do? I did make a mistake, but I thought it shouldn't negate more than a month's worth of work. I was taught to respect my elders, and all people in authority, so I did not challenge him. But I was angry enough to tell him that if I made the same mistake again, I'd just take five weeks off, rather than slaving away in the lab if he felt there was nothing to be learned by performing the exercise.

I didn't have the courage to discuss the matter with the professor, but I thought I'd blow a gasket when I learned the next year that other students who made the same mistake were only docked ten points while I lost 50. By then it was too late to file a grievance.

Second year chemistry, organic chemistry, was much more difficult, and is the course that separates the doctors from the business majors. Admissions boards scrutinize organic grades closely because mastering organic chemistry is like mastering the art of diagnosis. About half of the students who were in class the first day of freshman year were missing from the ranks by the first day of sophomore year.

I struggled, studying organic for hours every single day.

The chemistry department assigned graduate students to work at a help desk one hour a week, answering students' questions. Since there were 25 graduate students, it was open 25 hours per week.

We handled dangerous acids and bases in organic lab, so each lab session began with a quiz to demonstrate that we were prepared for the exercises.

I wanted to get perfect scores on my quizzes, and thought it wise to visit the help desk a few times over the semester. I checked to see when my lab instructor would be there, and visited the room only during those hours so he would know what a serious student I was. He was very young, having received his bachelor's degree in chemistry while still a teenager.

It paid off, because at the end of the semester, I had a 97% in lab. With my lecture grade bordering between an A and a B, my lab grade would push me over the top. I had earned an A in the hardest pre-med course. It would be the crowning glory on my transcript.

As finals approached, the lab instructor asked each student to meet with him to discuss their grades. I saw no need to meet with him because 97% is always an A, but I complied.

He reviewed my quiz results, and agreed that I had earned a 97%, but said that he was giving me a C.

I was absolutely dumbfounded!

How could 97% be a C, under any circumstances?

He told me that I needed his help to get the 97%. He said other students got good grades without using the help room. He was lowering my grade because I went to the help room.

Wasn't that what the help room was for - help?

I was fuming.

The little twerp had no idea if the other students visited the help room during the hours when he wasn't there and I told him so politely.

He had no reply.

I Make Horse Calls

I not so politely told him that I thought the idea was to walk out of college with an education, not walk in the door with one! A student should not be penalized for seeking help from an instructor. That's what education is about!

He was crazy!

I stormed out the door so upset I couldn't see straight, and the reasons I left college years earlier came flooding back. What was wrong with these people? Organic chemistry is hard enough without having anyone arbitrarily lower my grade on a personal whim! I had earned an A in lab!

I had been studying furiously for the final when an A was within my grasp. Now that opportunity was gone. With a C in lab I didn't have to study any more, because even a 70% on the final would still give me a B for the course.

I had no recourse, so I accepted his grade and went on. I was not going to let myself be diverted from my goal, but I was in shock that my GPA was in the hands of a graduate student who denied me the rewards of my efforts.

The second semester I came back more determined than ever. I refused to visit the help room ever again. If I couldn't count on the people whom I had already paid to teach me, I'd hire an outside tutor. So I diverted half of my riding lesson income to hire a chemistry tutor, Rob, and it was money well spent. There was no reason to devote three years of my life - my effort, and all of my financial assets - trying to get into vet school, unless I did everything in my power to succeed.

Before I hired Rob, if I couldn't answer a homework problem, I would work on it for hours in frustration. Now that I had Rob, if I couldn't do a problem, I just put it on a list to take to Rob during our weekly sessions. Sometimes the list was long, but there were usually only one or two concepts that I didn't understand. Once Rob explained them, I could solve all the problems. And he was always available for a few minutes before each test to answer any last minute problems.

Rob saved my sanity.

I mastered organic chemistry.

I had no regrets.

I Make Horse Calls

Organic chemistry had not defeated me, although I felt a bit battered.

I studied so hard, that after the school year was over, after I had finished my organic chemistry final, some friends threw a birthday party for me. When I got up to excuse myself early, saying I had to go study organic, Eleanor reminded me that I was done with that course - forever.

I often meet people who tell me they wanted to be vets, but dropped out because chemistry was so hard. They imply that because I passed it must have been easy for me. Nothing could be further from the truth. I worked hard every day to master those courses, and I rarely, if ever, use anything I was taught in them.

But Biochemistry was different. I actually enjoyed it. Understanding the functions within the cell laid the foundation for understanding what goes wrong when the body is attacked by diseases, and how drugs help cure illnesses.

By the end of the third year 450 of the 600 students had dropped out of chemistry. I was proud to have survived. The hard work paid off, as I was ranked in the top half of the dwindling class.

Calculus was the most difficult and useless course for me. Only one semester was required for admission to vet school, but two semesters were required for my degree and vet school admissions would look at all of my grades, so I had to do well.

The first semester was taught by an impeccably dressed and well-organized professor from Austria. He was quite fluent in English, but his heavy accent made his lectures difficult to understand. I never quite grasped Calculus I, but I passed.

I was not so enamored with the professor who taught Calculus II. He was always dirty and disorganized. He rode his bike to class and when it was raining, he had a wet stripe down his back because his bike had no fenders. He always seemed in need of a shower, and I found it hard to respect him. He assigned homework every single night - he would never assign it in advance. I had to schedule homework around my jobs, so if I knew my assignments in advance, I could better manage my tight schedule. But he wouldn't budge.

I Make Horse Calls

If I was studying calculus in my room, I found that I would use any excuse to interrupt my work - like dusting under the bed or washing the windows - tasks preferable to studying calculus. I hated calculus.

So I searched out a place without distractions. I found just the place in the upper stacks in Norlin library. There were tiny desks with dim lights dispersed throughout the attic of the dark and musty collection. I rarely saw other students in this remote location and the ones I did see shared that same, desperate look I'm sure I had when studying calculus.

I got to the library when it opened early Sunday morning and stayed all day. Every Sunday of the semester was devoted entirely to calculus. I did the homework so many times that if I looked at the problem I knew the answer. I had planned merely to learn the steps to the solutions, but I had reviewed the material so many times that by the end of the semester I had memorized both the steps and the answers to nearly all of the problems in our text.

But I still didn't understand Calculus, and finals were approaching.

To help us we were assigned recitations sections - small groups of students that met weekly with graduate students, but mine was a kook. He spent his days calculating the velocity of a dust mote orbiting the earth. How useful!

One of his assignments nearly killed me. I tried to solve the problem, and found the answer to be a fraction, with zero as the denominator. That made it an imaginary number, and we didn't deal with imaginary numbers in this course, so clearly I had made a mistake. I put the problem aside and re-read the chapter and my notes covering this topic. I again tried the problem, and came up with the same answer. I then re-read the chapter, reworked all of the sample problems at the end of the chapter, and checked my answers against the key, so I knew I had done them correctly. I then tried to solve the problem again, and again came up with the same answer.

It was growing cold and dark, and my eight hours were up. I was exhausted and completely defeated.

Was this going to be the class that stood between me and my dream?

Could I not conquer this course? I had sincere doubts.

I Make Horse Calls

What made me think I could be a vet, anyway?

At the next recitation, when the grad student said "I hope you didn't spend much time on the problem, because I wrote it while I was watching TV, and the answer was an imaginary number," I wanted to strangle him. He was laughing, but my confidence had been so thoroughly destroyed that I found no humor in the situation.

And I had a lot of anger. Even though I worked for the pre-vet adviser, he failed to tell me that I could have taken this course pass/fail and not had to worry about my grade. My classmates told me about it after the deadline had passed. It was my adviser's obligation to tell me and the fact that I was also his employee doubled my anger. If I cleaned up cat litter pans for him, the least he could do was his job!

And why did I have to take this stupid class, anyway? Calculus seemed to have little to do with medicine. In 160 hours of lecture the professor only gave us one application of calculus to medicine - we now had the formula to calculate the rate of blood flow of blood cells slowed down by friction with the vessel wall, versus the rate of flow of cells in the middle of the blood vessel.

I've never needed that formula.

For every exam I felt the same way. I had studied so hard that I was bleary-eyed and my head ached. I was sick of the class and sick of the studying. Just give me the stupid test. Put me out of my misery. If I was going to fail, just get it over and I'll move on. I can always find a job flipping burgers at the local fast food joint. Why did I want to be a vet, anyway?

My worst fears were realized on the day of the final exam. When the instructor handed me the test I looked at the first question and thought I was in the wrong class.

The question was "Derive all of the formulas for calculating the surface area of a sphere."

Had I been taught that?

Had I been taught *anything* that would prepare me to answer that question?

And it got worse from there. There were 17 pages of problems, none of which I could even begin to solve. I wrote down a few formulas and quickly left the room. My paper was nearly blank and I felt like I must be the stupidest person in the world. I hurried out of the room, embarrassed and angry.

I sat stunned in the hallway outside the classroom. How could I have worked so hard - attending every class, doing every assignment, passing every calculus exam for ten months, and found myself totally unprepared for the final? Obviously I hadn't learned anything. The final was proof of that. This ridiculous course wasn't even required for vet school, but any bad grade on my transcript would be a black mark. And 90% of vet school applicants were rejected, so this might just assure me a spot in that 90%.

I felt numb and unable to move.

When the classroom door opened and another student came out of the final, I was shaken out of my daze. He walked up to me and said "You must be really smart to have finished so soon!"

Smart?

"No, I was too stupid to have anything to say."

"Well, that was the hardest test I've ever taken," he tried vainly to reassure me.

I dejectedly walked back to the dorm.

The next day, as I was driving across campus, I stopped at a stop sign just as my calculus instructor was pushing his bicycle across the crosswalk right in front of my car.

If there wasn't a penalty for homicide...

Banish the thought!

When my final course grade came and was a C, I felt a little better. It was my lowest grade since returning to school, but it could have been worse. However I had done my best. I could not have possibly studied any harder, so there were no regrets.

I had completed my general graduation requirements five years ago, so I could concentrate on the science classes that would directly apply to my chosen career. Or at least that was what I thought.

Vet school required a course in public speaking. I had always been terrified to speak in front of a group of people, but if I had to do it to get into vet school, I would. And I would somehow get an A. I wouldn't let any course stand between me and my dream.

It turned out that CU did not offer a course in public speaking.

I Make Horse Calls

I was overjoyed.

My joy was short-lived. The university substituted a class in communications. The communications professor raised my hackles when he denounced people who study the hard sciences - biology and chemistry - as boring and lacking a sense of humor and praised those who study the soft sciences - psychology and sociology.

He spent the bulk of the semester delving into cocktail party conversations and bathroom graffiti.

It was a total waste of my time and energy, but I got my A and kept going.

I took another step toward my goal.

By my second year back, when I had enough credits to be a senior, I was allowed to move into a private studio apartment on campus. Eleanor had graduated, so it was ideal. I no longer got stressed when a customer stayed late at the tack shop, because I was not missing a meal in the dorm. I now had a small kitchen where I cooked my own meals.

The vet school interview contained questions on current affairs, so I prepared by listening to the news every night as I relaxed in the bathtub, recovering from bicycling and cleaning the cat room. I usually had my dinner cooking in the oven while I was soaking. Multi-tasking on my back amidst the lavender scented bubbles was my daily reprieve from the stresses of pre-vet life.

I neared campus and had to look out for pedestrians. Students rarely used the sidewalks or crosswalks, and could leap out in front of me faster than a startled deer out of the woods. They were much more dangerous than cars.

When I graduated from high school I didn't want to go to college in-state, thinking a small private college out of state would suit me better, but CU turned out to be the perfect match. Its huge size allowed it to have a wide range of course offerings, and extra-curricular cultural activities were plentiful. And CU was one of the top schools in the nation for Biology. It was a stroke of blind luck.

While I needed three years of chemistry for vet school, I only needed two more years of college credits to complete my degree, so I had time to take electives. And the university had eased its policy on pass/fail classes. The intention was to allow students who needed to get good grades for graduate school to reach beyond their primary focus of interest without risking their GPAs.

I took full advantage of this new policy, taking geology and environmental biology, and biology of the cancer cell. Dr. David Chiszar taught three courses in animal behavior. I loved every minute of his enthralling lectures. One course allowed students to go behind the scenes at the Denver Zoo, feeding the orphaned animals.

And I took courses in physical education, playing racquetball and getting fit for the coming ski season. The university had a marvelous recreation center - a weight room, basketball, racquetball, squash and tennis courts, an ice rink, a lap pool and a diving pool.

Boulder was so windy that if I could find time during the day to play tennis, I would find my serve blown off track into the court of my neighboring players. The recreation center was open late into the night, so after a hard day of lectures, work and study, I could let off some steam and enjoy a game of racquetball on days when it was too snowy to cycle.

The center also provided intramural sports. I played co-ed flag football in the fall and co-ed ice broomball in the winter.

Ice broomball is a crazy game, where students in sneakers chaotically chase a rubber ball around a slippery ice rink, whacking at it with brooms trying to score goals. Each team seemed to have one serious male hockey competitor, and unfortunately I was caught up in a collision between them and the ice. The rec center provided helmets, but no pads.

I never knew bruises could turn coal black.

I went back to bicycling. It was safer dodging cars than dodging hockey players.

The university offered two conditioning courses - modern dance for women, and co-ed conditioning for skiing. Envisioning myself leaping across the dance floor in a leotard did not conjure up images of grace and elegance, so I chose ski conditioning. The course was five weeks of physical training, a two week break, and then five weeks of ski lessons at a nearby resort, including transportation, all for an affordable fee. It sounded great!

When I arrived for the first class in Folsom field - the university's football stadium - I wasn't so confident of my decision. The instructor was a young male - a fit, cross-country ski racer.

I Make Horse Calls

Marathon runners and Nordic ski racers have to be so fit to compete at top levels that on campus they were called pneumopods - lungs with feet. This was not a good sign - to take a fitness class from a pneumopod.

And I was surrounded by 18-year-old men in shorts, with bulging thigh muscles. I was seven years older, and my thighs were bulging too, but I couldn't call it muscle.

I was in trouble.

But I wanted to get more fit, so I persisted.

The first day we were given physical fitness tests to establish our baseline fitness levels. I had grown up when President Kennedy's Council on Physical Fitness required public school students to undergo periodic fitness testing. I had an active childhood, and held some records at my school, so I was eager to demonstrate my fitness.

Grooming horses for five years had developed my upper body strength, but since this class prepared us for skiing, the focus was on core and leg strength. I hoped my cycling had helped my cardiovascular endurance.

The fitness test began with sit-ups.

Sit-ups had never been my forte, but I tried to be optimistic.

My partner held my feet down as I began, but my optimism quickly vanished, as I found myself red faced and gasping for air after only a few sit-ups. My abdominal muscles were on fire. I began hoping the test would end before I had a heart attack, but it went on long after I wished it would stop. By the end of the test I had managed 32 sit-ups. That wasn't so good.

The next test was the phantom chair. We had to bend our legs to 90 degrees while standing, holding the pose of down hill ski racers. In no time at all I found myself flat on the grass, my phantom chair had collapsed.

The third test was to run up the bleacher seats to the top of the stadium. It would have been hard enough to run up the stairs, but the bleachers were spaced twice as far apart, and I was shorter than my male classmates, so every step was a reach for me. The gap seemed to grow wider and wider as I tired near the top. I expected to fall backwards down the stands at any moment, but miraculously I didn't. I was exhausted and light-headed when I reached the top of the stadium, and clung tightly to the railing to keep from collapsing.

94

I Make Horse Calls

We completed the fitness test with a 400 meter run on the flat. Since breaking my ankle years earlier, I had given up jogging, and switched to cycling, which was far less painful. But I would show no weakness. Unfortunately, my lack of speed and endurance was obvious as I was nearly the last student to cross the line, but I gave it my best. It was a disaster.

I had my work cut out for me.

It was going to be a long five weeks.

Maybe I wouldn't look so bad in a leotard after all. At least I would be alive!

Grades were based on improvement, so I would have to work out every day in addition to stepping up my cycling. The final fitness test was only 30 days away.

The next day my abdominal muscles ached so badly that I could barely breathe much less practice sit-ups. I tried every day, but two weeks passed before I could do any. With only three weeks left, I began doing sit-ups every chance I got, squeezing several training sessions into every day. By the end of the course I was doing 80 a day, split into sets. I was working hard and seeing results.

At least my legs didn't ache after the test. Either I was fit from cycling, or I had run too slowly to put any strain on them.

I ran the stadium stairs on alternate days. It was safer than running the bleachers, and would build the same muscles and coordination. I would run up one flight, and recover while I walked across to the next flight, walked down, then walked across to the next flight by which time I was ready to run up. My goal was to get fit enough to run the entire stadium once.

I thought I was doing well until one day I watched a wiry lady in her 50s running the stairs while I was struggling on the stadium floor with my phantom chairs. She ran up one flight, and then ran down the same one before running to the next flight and scaling it quickly. She ran all the stairs in the stadium, and then ran all of the flights again on her way back. She had just done four times my goal, and was twice my age.

When I saw her start another set without stopping, I collapsed in amazement on the turf. I knew that Boulder was a Mecca for runners, but she was incredible. Another pneumopod!

I Make Horse Calls

When the day came for the final test, I knew I was much fitter. I was eager to demonstrate how hard I had worked. Passing this course would be a snap.

Cycling longer distances and more days per week had improved my endurance and my body was adjusting to the altitude. I could hold the phantom chair position twice as long. My stomach no longer ached when I did sit-ups, and I could do more - so many more. I had not practiced running on the flat, but climbing the stadium stairs had strengthened my legs and I was leaner. Even if I did not improve my running score, I should still pass because I had improved so much in the other three areas. I was eager to begin the test - to show how hard I had worked and how much I had improved.

The test began with sit-ups, and my partner held my feet as I began cranking them out.

1, 2, 3 - I had a smile on my face, no strain here.

10, 11, 12 - Boy, am I fit now?! I can do this forever.

18, 19, 20 - Not even getting winded.

26, 27, 28 - Muscles not aching.

33, 34, 35 - Look at me go!

"Time's up!" the instructor shouted.

Time's up?

What do you mean, "Time's up?"

I didn't know there was a time limit.

But I'm not done!

I could go on forever!

Really! Let me show you. I'm a lot fitter!

My partner recorded my score as I sat on the grass in disbelief.

I could be in trouble. With a starting score of 32 and an ending score of 35, I looked like a slacker - like I hadn't done anything.

I hadn't practiced doing sit-ups *quickly*.

I was panic stricken. Even though this class was pass/fail, would the instructor think I hadn't done my homework and fail me? That would damage my GPA and might ruin my chances of getting into vet school - and all because of a stupid PE class I took for fun.

The rest of the test was a blur. I sat in the phantom chair until my legs refused to hold me up any longer. I ran the bleachers without fear of falling through the cracks, and ran my heart out around the football field. But I was still worried about my score.

Then I heard other students bragging about their scores, about how they took it easy on their first tests so they'd look great now. Why hadn't I thought of that? My improvement looked minimal by comparison.

At the end of the test, because there was a two week break before skiing began, the instructor invited the class to continue training with him. He had been running too hard and developed shin splints, so he would maintain his fitness by bicycling.

This was my chance to show him I was fit. On the flat I could spin forever. Over hilly terrain, if the spacing between hills was far enough that I could recover on the downhill sections, I rode for hours. Most of the roads around Boulder were hilly and I trained at least three days a week. I just wasn't a good climber when faced with long, unrelenting canyon climbs or mountain switchbacks.

I rose to the challenge and I signed up for the ride - 18-year-olds or not.

Before the first ride, grades came out. The instructor had taken pity on his oldest pupil and I passed. I now had nothing to prove, but I went on the first ride to redeem myself.

On the day we were to meet for cycling, I was the only student who showed up.

I might be in trouble.

When he asked where I'd like to go, I suggested riding the Foothills Highway to Nelson Road and back. Twenty miles was far enough to show him I was fit. And it was a familiar route. I knew the hills, and had mastered them.

He said no. He wanted to go up Flagstaff Mountain.

Flagstaff Mountain!

Was he crazy?

It was a steep grade from campus just to reach the foot of the mountain, followed by an unrelenting climb, up switchback after switchback, in the thin alpine air. There were no down hill sections.

Now I knew I was in trouble.

I couldn't lose face by refusing, and there was no way to slink away unnoticed from a party of two, so of course I agreed and mustered up a weak smile.

I Make Horse Calls

He didn't have a bicycle, so he borrowed one. Thank goodness it was a cheap bike that was too small for him. Months of training on my speedy Motobecane gave me a chance to keep up, and I needed every advantage I could find.

When he stood up to attack the climb for the first time, his knees hit the shift knobs, unexpectedly changing gears and breaking his rhythm. It kept happening, thank goodness, so I was able to climb beside him. It was agonizing, but I kept going.

I was grateful when a mule deer buck bounded across the road. I stopped to admire it. Maybe he wouldn't notice me gasping for air. He stopped too.

After a brief rest we set off again. Legs aching and throats parched, we continued, rounding curve after curve, laboriously creeping, climbing our way to the top.

When we finally reached the summit I felt like the Queen of the Mountain with the world at my feet. A crisp, autumn breeze was blowing off the mountain as we savored our victory over gravity. The view was spectacular. Red stone buildings capped with tile roofs dotted the campus landscape, set off by the spectacular fall foliage. The entire city was laid out before us, and the plains stretched to obscurity on the eastern horizon.

I had amazed myself.

I didn't think I'd ever climb Flagstaff. I had heard other cyclists and runners talk about making the climb, but I would never have tried on my own. It was a daunting climb. I would have quit today if any other students had shown up and I could have escaped anonymously. But circumstances forced me to accept the challenge, and the pride of this unexpected accomplishment filled me to overflowing.

We couldn't stay long at the top, as I had to work this afternoon, so I climbed on my bike for the descent.

Now the fun should begin - payback for the hard work. It would be marvelous, flying effortlessly down the mountainside, the wind in my face.

For some reason, I glanced at my brakes before starting down. Peter had graduated, so another friend, Ralph, replaced my brake pads. I rarely used my brakes because my training runs were over rolling terrain, where momentum from the downhill run is used climbing the next uphill section and the country roads have no stop lights and little cross traffic. So it was only now that I noticed the pads were put in the brackets backwards. That meant that undue pressure on the brakes would cause the pads to slip out, leaving me with no brakes.

Flagstaff Mountain was steep and the descent would stress my brakes to the max. And it was a long, long way down, with narrow, winding switchbacks one after another. I'd have a word with Ralph - if I lived.

We started off, and my instructor was quickly out of sight ahead of me. I went as slowly as I could. I applied my brakes non-stop, hoping not to build up enough speed to break the pads loose. But I was soon out of control, careening down the mountainside. I was agile enough to make the turns. I just hoped there wouldn't be any cars in my way.

I kept telling myself that if there was no traffic I'd be okay.

With each switchback I gained momentum. Faster and faster I went. The seat was too high for me to drag my feet, but I'd have tried anything to slow down. There were no runaway bike ramps. I was on my own.

Then, as I came around a hairpin turn I saw it - dark, ominous, and odorous - looming just ahead at the next curve. A mere hundred feet away, a garbage truck was consuming my entire lane.

And I was going *way* too fast to stay behind it.

I had a split second to decide what to do. The shoulder of the road was only 12 inches wide. There was no way I could slip through on that side. At my rate of speed I wouldn't make the sharp turn. I'd shoot off the mountainside into the wide open spaces, dashing myself to pieces on the rocks below.

I could blindly pass on the left, but I couldn't see around the curve for oncoming traffic. I was going so fast that meeting a car head-on would leave me mortally splattered like a bug on the grill.

But I had to make a choice. I swore I would not die an ignominious death by crashing into the back of a garbage truck, my body catapulting into the pile of rubbish as my bicycle fell silently off the precipice. When the crusher was lowered, my body would be scooped up and compressed into the stinking mass, making my passing go unnoticed.

I Make Horse Calls

I refused to spend eternity buried in the local landfill.

I swerved into the left lane, hoping not to meet a car head on rounding the curve and closed my eyes…

Nothing happened. Apparently no cars were coming.

The rest of the trip was pleasantly uneventful, except for the loud pounding of my heart within my chest.

When I reached the bottom, I could see the instructor was annoyed that it took me so long to get down.

I was so glad to be alive I didn't care.

We cycled back to campus together, but I decided to train on my own until ski season started.

Reaching the dorm I dismounted and hoisted the bicycle over my shoulder to climb the stairs to my room.

To graduate with honors I needed a research project. I was assigned to map the cells of the kitten's retina, and to compare it to a map of the adult cat. I worked on the project for a year locating every cell in a dozen retinas. I bent over the microscope long into the night until I was bleary-eyed.

When I had gathered the data, I wrote a thesis and had to present my findings at a seminar, first in a session open to the public, and then to a closed door question-and-answer session with the Honors Board.

I was still terrified to speak in public, and this presentation to the Honors Committee would hold the key to my future. Graduation with honors could bolster my ailing GPA. If the Honors Committee was impressed with my presentation, I might graduate cum laude or higher, getting a leg up on the competition for vet school. My presentation had to be stellar.

So the night before my presentation I practiced my lecture on a few of my classmates. That was one of the smartest decisions I ever made, because then I knew my presentation was awful beyond description. I would have completely fallen on my face if I had not known in advance how bad it was.

I stayed up all night and wrote cue cards for every point. When the time came, my presentation went smoothly. I was grateful for my friends' patience.

I Make Horse Calls

The Honors Committee awarded me magna cum laude. I was thrilled.

As I leaned my bike against my bookshelf I looked at the books containing all of the coursework I had been taught. At the start of each new course the information seemed incomprehensible, but somehow the professors explained the material and I gradually came to understand biology. And it only made me hungry for more.

I headed for the bubble bath.

I had to take the Graduate Record Exam, an entrance exam given to students who plan to pursue advanced degrees. It helps admissions committees rank college programs - determining how students at one college compare in overall knowledge to students at other colleges. It gives the selection committee something besides grade point average to use when determining a student's competence. I was grateful for any opportunity to demonstrate expertise beyond my GPA.

I flew quickly through the five hour exam because my professors had taught me everything that was on the test. There were no surprises. It was now clear to me that CU deserved its ranking as one of the top biology programs in the country.

When the results were in, I scored well in molecular biology because it was my major. And the electives I took in environmental biology helped my score on that section. I give all of the credit to CU. The professors had prepared me well.

When I was in high school and first chose CU, it was a shot in the dark, but it turned into a stroke of good fortune. I was so glad I had gone to CU. Perhaps the fact that CSU was closed to new students when I applied was a good thing after all.

My time at CU was over. Graduation day came. Three-quarters of the pre-med students who sat beside me that first day had dropped out or changed majors, and only two students had graduated with higher honors.

Even I was impressed when I looked at my diploma - Bachelor of Arts magna cum laude in Molecular, Cellular, and Developmental Biology.

I Make Horse Calls

It sounded so important, but inside I was the same person who bicycled to the barn in Florida that foggy dawn three years ago.

I had a diploma, but I was only halfway to my goal.

Graduating with Honors and scoring well on the GRE might just be enough to convince the vet school admissions committee that I was worthy of an opportunity to enroll. Surely I would get in. Besides performing community service and observing veterinary practice in the summer, I had trained horses and dogs, managed a stable, cared for a colony of cats, done original research, written a thesis, and taken almost every science course in the universe, earning an A in every biology course.

I had all of the pieces of the puzzle in place.

Even if I was never accepted into vet school, I could have no regrets. I had done my best.

I felt a deep satisfaction from overcoming the challenges of this rigorous curriculum. And no one could ever take my honors diploma away. I earned it!

The day after graduation, as I walked to the stadium to turn in my keys, a tall, slender man with thick, dark, wavy hair ran past and smiled pleasantly at me - a warm, familiar smile, like I knew him.

I smiled back, but kept walking. I didn't know him.

As I opened the door to the maintenance office I stopped dead in my tracks.

It was Frank Shorter.

I Make Horse Calls

Chapter 8 Buyer Beware

It was a glorious spring day. In fact, today was Memorial Day, the day set aside to honor those who gave their lives in the defense of freedom. As the daughter of a veteran who fought in World War II, I took this day quite seriously, and gave thanks for the sacrifices so many soldiers made to ensure our freedom.

Memorial Day was also the official start of summer. This time of year heralds the end of spring - a season occupied with foalings, annual vaccinations, and health certificates and Coggins' testing the show horses. I had prepared my patients for the summer onslaught of young riders out of school all day, living on horseback.

I was sitting at my sister's house, under a shade tree, cool drink in hand, burgers sizzling on the backyard grill, when my pager went off. They reminded us in veterinary school not to growl when the pager goes off, that being paged meant being needed, and was vital to the stability of any private practice. However, considering that any true emergency would keep me busy until the barbecue was over, I really did feel like growling.

The call was from Sherry Orton. I did not have a client named Sherry Orton. This was an opportunity to gain a new client. As soon as I heard the panic in her voice, I forgot about the party, and only thought about how I could help her and her horse.

"Dr. Thibeault, thank you for returning my call. My new horse, Destiny, is really sick. I think she's dying. I'm so worried about her. I haven't had her long, and I don't know what to do. I found her lying in the field, and when we got her up, she tried to lie down again. My neighbor says she has colic, and if she lies down she'll die! She said I have to walk her, but I've been walking her for thirty minutes and she isn't getting any better."

I Make Horse Calls

"Well, Sherry. The first thing you need to know is that most horses that get colic recover completely, so she'll probably be fine. I'll be out to treat her right away. But you don't need to walk her if she's not rolling. It's just not true that horses with colic die because they go down. Just keep her out of trouble. Put her in an open, grassy or sandy area. If she will lie quietly, just stay with her. Put a long rope or lunge line on her so you can keep her away from fences or anything that might hurt her, but if she gets worse you don't want to be too close to her. If she throws herself down, don't let her land on you. Give me directions to your farm, and I'll be right there."

As I said goodbye to my partying companions and sped to Sherry's house, I tried to get over the disappointment of missing yet another family get-together, and look on the bright side. My classmates in college who wanted to practice on horses far outnumbered the equine positions available. Many gave up their dreams, settling for jobs in small animal practices. I was lucky to be able to have an exclusively equine practice. Money was tight, and developing a loyal clientele was taking time, but I loved my job.

Sherry's house was not far away. Her directions led me to a newly painted tan house, with a classic wooden red barn out back. The gambrel roof and white trim made her small farm picture perfect. As I entered the neatly groomed farmyard, Sherry and her bay filly were in the white fenced paddock.

Sherry was a tiny thing. Her wavy blond hair was pulled back into a pony tail. She looked like she was just a child, yet she was married. I would be surprised if she weighed 90 pounds. At least she had selected a horse that was her size, as Destiny was barely 15 hands.

Destiny was fidgeting, but she was on her feet. She didn't seem to be in distress, unlike her owner. The look on Sherry's face told me that she was sure Destiny was dying.

I quickly grabbed my stethoscope and examined the filly.

Sometimes a joke can relax a nervous owner. One of my professors told me that colic is a true emergency because 95% of them recover on their own, and if I didn't treat the horse before it recovered I wouldn't get credit for curing it. But Sherry didn't look like she was in a joking mood, so I kept that thought to myself.

I Make Horse Calls

I put the stethoscope over Destiny's heart, as heart rate is one of the most important factors in determining the severity of colic. With one stethoscope earpiece in my right ear, I turned my left ear to Sherry to get a quick medical history.

"How old is she?"

"She's just two."

"How long have you had her?"

"Only a few weeks. Oh, I'm so worried! Can you help her?"

"Yes, I can. Has she colicked before?"

"No."

The filly's pulse was 48 beats per minute, a good sign. While she was clearly in pain, she shouldn't need surgery. Severe cases of colic have faster pulse rates, sometimes above 100 beats per minute.

I moved through my exam quickly. Destiny fidgeted and pawed, but did not throw herself on the ground.

Destiny's gums were pink, and when I pressed on her gums to blanch the blood from her membranes, they quickly turned pink again, showing that her heart was working okay. Even though colic is the number one killer of horses, Destiny's colic was a mild case. She would be fine.

"Well, I've just begun my exam, but there is good news already. Her pulse is barely elevated, so this is not a serious case. She won't need surgery. I can treat her here. She'll be fine."

"But she's in so much pain. Are you sure she's not dying?

"I'm sure. She's definitely hurting, but I can ease her pain as soon as I'm done with her exam."

I listened to her intestinal sounds to determine if her gut was functioning. Lack of gut sounds indicates a more serious colic. Her intestines were rumbling non-stop, like a hungry teenager. She was also raising her tail and passing gas. Destiny had gas colic. Good. Gas colics were easy to treat.

I re-assured Sherry that Destiny would be fine.

I filled a syringe with strong medication to get Destiny's pain under control, and added a second medication to keep her comfortable through the night. The medications would both relieve her pain and help her stand quietly for the rest of my exam. I gave the medications intravenously so relief would come quickly. Shortly after I removed the needle from her vein, Destiny's head began to drop and she started to relax as her pain was eased. As Destiny lowered her head, the strained look soon disappeared from her face, and Sherry started to relax as well.

I needed more information from Sherry regarding the filly's medical history. As I put on a plastic obstetric sleeve and lubed my arm to enter the filly's rectum for an internal examination, Sherry told me that she had owned a horse as a teenager, and then had given it up before she married because money was tight.

"George and I've been working full time since we got married. We're getting ahead financially. We bought this house with a barn and acreage, and this spring decided we could afford a horse. I've always loved Paint horses, and when I saw the advertisement for a paint filly, I had to rush right out and see her. It was love at first sight, so we bought her on the spot. I call her Destiny. Isn't she beautiful?"

"Uh, yes... she sure is. But are you sure she's a Paint?"

The most distinguishing feature of Paint horses is their coat color, boldly splashed with white. Breeders call this white color "chrome" and the more chrome the better. This filly was a plain bay, with no white at all. She had a chocolate brown body, black mane, tail and legs. There was not a single white hair anywhere on Destiny.

"Oh, yes, I even have the registration papers to prove it. But, she's registered for breeding only."

"Oh."

In other words, the filly descended from a Paint sire and dam, but didn't have enough white to be eligible for competition in the show ring. Sherry bought the filly, gambling that she could breed the mare, and wait a year, hoping that Destiny might produce a foal with chrome that would be eligible to show.

Oh brother!

I found no obstructions, tumors, or twists. The internal exam showed no abnormalities besides loops of intestine distended with gas. My suspicions were confirmed - it was gas colic.

"Well, as I suspected, she has gas colic. She should be feeling good soon."

"Oh I hope so!"

"What is her training history?"

"She is not broke to ride, yet."

I Make Horse Calls

"What about her medical history?"

"The seller said she's had all of her shots."

In my experience when someone says "all of her shots" it means they can't actually name any of the vaccinations the horse has received. If owners are knowledgeable regarding vaccines, they list the vaccines by brand or disease.

"Exactly what vaccinations has she had?"

"Let me run into the house and get the information the seller gave me over the phone."

While Sherry was gone, I re-checked Destiny. Her pulse was still in the 40s, but her gut sounds had slowed to near normal. She was responding well to the medications.

Sherry came out of the house with a pad of paper in her hand.

"Here are the notes I took when the seller was telling me about Destiny's."

The notes showed that the filly had received the bare minimum - a vaccination against tetanus, sleeping sickness and influenza last year, and deworming for internal parasites every six months. While this might keep her from dying of tetanus, it certainly wasn't going to keep her healthy. It was time to see if Sherry really cared for this filly.

"Sherry we need to put her on a better medical program. Her care has been minimal. Her illness today might have been prevented. She needs to be vaccinated against common illnesses, and I'd start now.

"And treating her for parasites twice a year is not enough. She'll pass eggs in her manure a few weeks after she is treated, so dose her every six weeks. Her main source of infection is her own manure, so we should treat often enough to keep the manure free of parasites. It only costs a few dollars more per year - much less than it costs to treat colic, and she won't have to suffer so. Horses that are treated only twice a year pass 15 million parasite eggs every day in their manure and the eggs survive in the paddock for years."

"Fifteen million? Yuck!" Sherry looked appalled.

"Yes. That's what research has shown."

When I checked Destiny's gums I noticed that her teeth showed abnormal wear. She also had enlarged muscles on the bottom of her neck.

"Is this mare a cribber - chewing wood, or windsucking?"

"Yes, she's a cribber. But how'd you know?"

"Her teeth are worn down, and her neck muscles are bulging, meaning she is a windsucker."

Cribbers chew wood, while windsuckers grab onto fences and walls with their front teeth, and grunt as they inhale. Destiny was a windsucker, which is an addiction in horses. Even if surgery is done to remove nerves and muscles that allow windsucking, the addiction often persists. Windsuckers seem more prone to colic. It is an unsoundness and may prevent horses from performing to their full potential.

Unfortunately, Sherry did not ask for a pre-purchase exam before buying Destiny, so not only did she get an "unpainted Paint," she got one with major health problems. How I wish I had met Sherry before she bought Destiny! I could have helped her avoid some of the heartache that I would have seen coming. I feared this filly's destiny might not be all that Sherry envisioned.

However, once a young girl falls in love with a horse, I know better than to try and change her mind. My job was to provide Destiny with the best health care possible from now on.

"She has a mild case of colic, and we can get her through this bout. But you have a lot of work to do to keep it from happening again, and it is likely to happen again a few times in spite of our efforts. She's got two strikes against her with the windsucking and the parasites, but you really seem to love her. If you want to try to keep her as healthy as possible, I can show you how."

Destiny's head was beginning to come up, and she was looking around more alertly.

"Yes, I want to keep her healthy, but I don't know how. I thought she was healthy, until today. And now you've got me really scared."

"Don't be scared. I'll show you how to care for her - diet, exercise, vaccinations, dewormings - everything you need to know to keep her healthy, and you'll be amazed at how she'll respond."

"Great!"

"Do you have any grass hay?"

"I've got grass and alfalfa."

"Good. Get some grass hay for her now. She's ready to eat a little. Grass hay is better when her stomach is upset."

Sherry brought out some beautiful timothy hay and Destiny began to nibble at it, another sign that the crisis was behind her.

"Oh look! She's eating! She wouldn't touch her hay when I called you."

Sherry was elated.

I love treating mild colics. When the owners call, the horse looks terrible and the owner thinks it's dying. With a dose of analgesic, the horse's pain is controlled, and the horse is back to its old self in a matter of minutes. The client thinks it's a miracle, and I have to agree. I feel like a hero. Even after treating so many colics over the years, watching the horse resume eating is extremely satisfying.

"When was she last wormed?"

"In January."

"That was four months ago. You can start next weekend. I'll leave you some safe and effective dewormers that you can give her once a month to kill the parasites. And muck out your paddock. It's full of parasite eggs, so get rid of it before she gets re-infected. Then muck out every day. The worming program and paddock maintenance will break the cycle of re-infestation. Most colics are caused by parasite damage to the intestines and stomach, so breaking the cycle is the single most important thing you can do for Destiny. You'll see a real difference in her in a few months.

"It'll take time for her to heal. That means that no matter how good her care is now, she will probably colic again before she heals. Don't get discouraged. Most of the horses feel better in a few weeks and really begin to bloom in a few months.

"To limit her windsucking, get a cribbing collar. It'll be uncomfortable if she tries to windsuck, but she can eat and drink just fine. Put it on her and leave it on. Don't start feeling sorry for her and take it off, or we'll be back here treating her again. It may rub off a little hair, but that won't kill her like colic can.

"Because grass hay has fewer calories than alfalfa, you can feed more of it, so it will keep her busy, leaving less time to crib. Plus, a full stomach is satisfying, so she may feel less of an urge to crib. Turn her out for exercise as much as possible, and begin

109

training her to lunge or drive, so she has a job to do. Cribbing is more common in bored horses, so if you keep her occupied she'll be healthier."

"Boy, it sounds like I'm going to be busy, Doc T.," Sherry replied, "but I'm glad to know I can help her. I really do love her."

"I'll be back next week to check on her, and to begin her vaccinations. If you have any questions, call me right away."

I went to my truck for some information sheets on horse care and prepared a medical record and after-care instructions. As I figured the bill, Sherry's husband, George, came out of the house. George delivered bread for a bakery. He asked if I'd like some fresh bread. That was an offer too good to refuse. Dr. Mom loved cinnamon raisin bread, so George gave me two loaves for her. I knew it wasn't a coincidence that George appeared with a gift at the very moment I was figuring the charges. George was no dummy, and neither was Sherry.

As I was cleaning up my equipment I felt good, knowing that this filly had Sherry to give her a fighting chance at a healthy life. She certainly had a bad start, but things were looking up. Working as a team I hoped we could turn this filly's health around, but she might break Sherry's heart. Not all neglected horses survive and the compassionate owners that rescue them are devastated when they die.

I was unsure if Destiny would be as good to Sherry. She was ineligible for shows, had a major health problem and was not trained to ride. Sherry had really bitten off a lot for a beginner. Ignorance is bliss, they say. I hoped Sherry was up to the challenge!

As I was preparing to leave, Sherry gave me her heartfelt thanks for helping Destiny.

"Would you like to see my other horse? I rescued him from starvation, so he's not perfect like Destiny."

Oh, brother!

As I followed Sherry into the barn she told me when she and George went to buy Destiny, she caught sight of a thin, neglected thoroughbred colt in the adjoining field. She begged George to let her buy him so she could save him, and George grudgingly agreed.

The weanling was a pathetic looking creature, standing by himself at the back of the barn. He was a Thoroughbred, but he was so stunted that he was only a shadow of what he should have been.

I Make Horse Calls

His chestnut coat was dry and dull. He had a runny nose. His legs were so frail they were hardly able to hold him up. His belly was grossly distended, further signs of malnutrition and internal parasites. His hooves were overgrown and misshapen, placing undue stress on his tendons, and his knees were crooked. He hardly had the energy to drag himself around his stall.

"I call him Spunky!" Sherry proudly proclaimed.

Oh, brother! A paint filly with no white, a cribber, full of parasites, and if that wasn't bad enough, Sherry also had a starving, nearly lifeless colt she thought was "Spunky!"

What was she thinking?

I've always had a soft spot in my heart for Thoroughbreds, and it broke my heart to see one in such poor condition. But Spunky was less than a year old, so with proper care and nourishment, including special care of his hooves, he still had a chance for a good life. And Sherry would be Spunky's ally.

"How old is he?"

"Four months."

"Do you have a medical history on him? Has he ever been dewormed or vaccinated? Has he ever had his feet trimmed?"

"The seller wouldn't tell me anything about him."

Great!

I looked around the stall. His stools were soft, but he didn't have diarrhea. That was good. At least he was utilizing some of his feed. Sherry said she was feeding him grass hay, but I did not see any in the manger.

"Is his appetite good?"

"Yes! He eats everything I give him. I give him less than Destiny because he is smaller."

The good news is that he was eating everything she gave him. The bad news was that she wasn't feeding him enough. I never understand why horse owners don't feed their horses more when they are painfully thin and eating everything in sight. It seems like common sense to me.

"Then give him more. Keep grass hay in his manger 24 hours a day."

"Oh, I thought that would be too much for him."

I Make Horse Calls

"Well, it would have been when you first brought him home, but now that he's used to your hay you can increase it. Horses evolved to graze all day long in the wild. The best way to manage horses is to provide as natural an environment as possible. Thoroughbreds are hot-blooded and need more feed than a cooler-blooded horse like Destiny. Plus, he's still growing, and he's thin."

Sherry was anxious to learn, so I continued.

"Put one flake of alfalfa in his diet every morning and next week add another flake at dinner time. Increase it slowly, until his diet is about half alfalfa. Alfalfa has more calories, vitamins, protein and the minerals his bones need to grow strong. Spunky has a lot of growing to catch up on."

"Get a grain mix, and feed him one pound twice a day for the first week. Then add another pound per day each week until you get him up to six pounds per day. I'll recheck him and we'll adjust his diet as he grows."

"Be sure to follow this schedule or you'll make him sick. You don't need two sick horses."

"That's for sure!"

"If you give him too much alfalfa or grain too fast, he may get diarrhea. If that happens, just reduce the alfalfa and grain, and then add it back slowly in a few days. I'll leave you a mineral supplement with the proper balance of minerals for strong bones.

"I'll deworm him today, and start his vaccinations next week when I come back to check on Destiny. His dull coat and lack of muscle tell me that his diet has been too low in protein, and the parasites have taken their toll, so he won't respond very well to the vaccinations. He'll need booster vaccinations later to be sure he is protected."

I left Sherry the phone number of a good horseshoer, and wished her luck with her horses. She was going to need it!

A week later I was back to check on Destiny and Spunky. Destiny had shown no further signs of colic, and was doing well. The cribbing collar and exercise program had decreased her windsucking, but nothing would make it go away. If we made everything else in her life as perfect as possible, maybe the windsucking wouldn't cause her so much trouble. I vaccinated her and completed Sherry's medical card listing what had been done to each horse.

Owners are ultimately responsible for the health of their animals, with the veterinarian acting as an educated advisor, helping them make good decisions regarding health care options. To assist owners I give them a condensed copy of their horse's medical history and treatments, so if the horse travels to a trainer or to be bred, the record can go with the horse, leaving no question about the horse's health status.

"Here's a copy of all her treatments. Keep this card in case she gets ill and you have to call another vet to treat her."

"We're not calling any other vet."

"I mean, in case I'm sick or out of town."

"You don't have my permission to be sick or go out of town."

"Right. Well, let's check on Spunky."

Sherry went to the stable and put a halter on Spunky. She led him down the dark breezeway, into the sunlight. She could hardly handle him. He was rearing and trying to bolt away, dragging Sherry through the narrow passageway to the paddock. Somehow Sherry managed to get him to the paddock and release him. Spunky tore around the paddock, racing at breakneck speed. His poor muscle tone made him look like he would topple over at any moment, but his thoroughbred spirit made him run.

"He sure feels better, doesn't he Sherry?"

"Yes, but he doesn't *look* any better! He's still just skin and bones. His coat is so dull, I feel like I have to hide him in the barn if anyone comes to visit."

"You have to be patient. It will take time to put on weight, and build muscle, stamina and coordination. He is using his new found calories to do things we can't see, like build blood proteins, and put fat in his bone marrow. It'll take months for him to flesh out. As he grows, he will gain weight but still look thin because he'll be growing taller. Just keep him eating well, and he'll take care of the rest. His coat will shine up this fall when he sheds his summer coat and grows a new one for winter. Don't expect much until then."

"He's getting hard to handle."

"As soon as he is healthy enough, we'll castrate him. That'll make him more manageable. Right now he is still weak, and the anesthetic and surgery are too risky. In the meantime, turn him out as much as you can. The more exercise he gets, the easier he'll be to handle. He is too young for any forced exercise, like driving or lunging, but turnout is crucial for his development.

"Are you familiar with the books or videos by Dr. Robert Miller?" I asked Sherry.

"No."

"Well, he's done a lot of work with young horses. Most of his work centers on foals, but Spunky is young, and some of Dr. Miller's techniques will help. They'll just take a little longer at his age. Stop by the clinic when you get a chance. I have a lending library for my clients, and some of Dr. Miller's videos may help you with Spunky."

I could see that Spunky was already too much horse for Sherry to handle if he wasn't being turned out regularly, and the problems would only worsen as Spunky grew stronger. Sherry would need a trainer to help her. This young colt wasn't suitable for her in the long term, but if she could save him, perhaps we could find him a good home. At least he was feeling better. Sherry's kindness gave him a chance at a bright future.

After Spunky let off some steam, we caught him and began his vaccinations.

Driving home, I could see the differences Sherry and I, working as a team, were making in the lives of her horses.

It was a good feeling

Chapter 9 Be Careful What You Wish For

My friend Sandy, an equine insurance agent, knew that when I began my veterinary practice I needed new clients, so she gave my name to her customers when they needed veterinary services. I appreciated her confidence in me, as she was an experienced horsewoman.

One day she called me about a customer of hers who needed an insurance exam for his horse. The man lived near Mountain View, so I agreed to do the exam, which Sandy needed in order to insure the horse. The man didn't often use veterinary services, so he had no regular veterinarian to call.

I got his number and called Tom Filbert.

"Mr. Filbert, this is Dr. Thibeault. Sandy told me you need an insurance exam on your gelding."

"Yes, I do. Thanks for calling. I keep him in a pasture just north of town. Can you meet me at my office downtown tomorrow, and follow me out there?"

"I'd rather meet you at the pasture, if you can give me directions."

"It's pretty hard to find, and you'd probably get lost, so I'd prefer it if you could follow me out there."

I didn't want to waste my time to drive downtown, park my truck, walk to his office, wait for him to finish his work, follow him to his car, drive two cars out of town to the pasture, wait while he opens the gate, wait while he finds a halter and wait some more while he walks out into the pasture to catch the horse. A 20 minute insurance exam could turn into a half-day ordeal.

I am blessed with a wonderful sense of direction which I must have inherited from my Father, as my Mother can't find her way back to the car at the shopping mall. It comes in handy since I spend my days driving from farm to farm, relying on my clients' directions. My daily rounds criss-crossed several counties, and I was still learning some of the smaller back roads.

Dr. Mom likes to tell the story of when she drove my older sister and me across the country to join my Father, who had gone ahead to a new job. I was only six years old and barely tall enough to see out the car window. Our first stop was on Saturday night. Early the next morning, Mom drove us to church. When she came out of the church parking lot, she turned away from the hotel where we needed to return to check out. I asked where she was taking us, and she said "Back to the hotel." I told her she had turned the wrong way, and, of course, because I was only six, she ignored me. After driving the wrong way for several miles, and noticing that nothing looked familiar, my Mother turned around. She has a good nature, and after a few similar experiences she has decided that if there's any question which way to go, she'll follow my suggestion.

While most of my clients give good instructions, some are completely devoid of a sense of direction. They give instructions to go left or right at various intersections, which of course depends on which way I approach the intersection. Even though I may have a schedule of appointments written in my log book each morning, emergencies often disrupt that schedule, so I never know where I'll be when I head to my next appointment. As a result, I much prefer directions telling me to go east or west.

In Mountain View, with the mountains to the west, it's easy to know which way I'm heading. At least, *I* think it's easy.

My tolerance was pushed to the limit one hot, dry August day when a new client apparently didn't know where she lived. When giving directions to her farm, she apologized saying she was from Missouri so she didn't know which way was west. I'm sure they have west in Missouri! She was so confused she repeatedly sent me on wild goose chases, driving down ribbons of dusty, washboard roads that laced their way through fields covered in sun bleached stubble following the wheat harvest. I followed her directions in futility while the searing, summer sun poured through the windshield. From each wrong destination I called her again, only to learn that I was no closer. In desperation she told me to go to the gas station in town and ask the clerk, because he knew her and gave good directions.

116

I Make Horse Calls

Could she really have no idea where she lived? How did she get home from work?

As a last resort I stormed into town through the choking dust and got directions. I resented spending so much time just to find her farm, but was grateful for the clerk's help, without which I never would have found it. I grabbed a cold drink before setting out on what thankfully would be the last leg of my journey, knowing I would spend the rest of the day apologizing to clients as I arrived late for their appointments.

She must have been distantly related to another client of mine who, when I asked her to meet me at the north end of the barn, said "there's no north inside."

Since I didn't know Mr. Filbert, I wasn't sure why he wanted me to follow him. Maybe he wanted me to meet him at his office because he couldn't give adequate directions. Or maybe his horse was in such a remote location, that following Mr. Filbert to the farm might not be such a bad idea. Following him might save me some time.

"Mr. Filbert, I'll meet you at your office at noon tomorrow."

In reality, Mr. Filbert's appointment was the only one I had that day, but I still did not want to get off on the wrong foot. Meeting him in town was setting a precedent.

Luckily, Mountain View is a small town, so parking places downtown are not hard to find. I parked and walked around the corner to his office.

I told his secretary, "I'm Dr. Thibeault, and I'm here to see Mr. Filbert."

"Oh my, I didn't realize Mr. Filbert was sick? What's wrong?"

Surely she doesn't think that physicians still make house calls!

"No, no. I'm a horse doctor, coming to give his horse an insurance physical."

"Oh, thank goodness. I'm glad Mr. Filbert is okay. He's on the phone and will be right with you. I'll tell him you're here."

As I waited in his office I was getting perplexed. I've spent hours waiting in the waiting room and exam room for a doctor's

117

I Make Horse Calls

appointment. Doctors never wait for their patients, but here I was, waiting for my next appointment.

I was grateful for the opportunity to gain a new client, but I'd have to find a way to be more efficient as my practice got busier.

Finally a tall, heavyset man in a business suit came out of the back office.

"Hello, I'm Tom Filbert. Glad you could come." he said as he grabbed his jacket.

"I'm Dr. Thibeault."

"I'm parked around back. Where'd you park your truck?"

"I'm on the side. Where are we going?"

"East on County Road 2."

"Okay, I'll meet you on Main Street. I've got a tan Chevy Suburban."

"I'll be in the red Ford pick-up."

As we drove out of town, we passed small farms whose owners were gradually becoming my clients. On the hill I could see Jack and Mary's house. We passed Carl and Vicky's new brick ranch house with the neat rows of evergreen trees lining the drive.

Mr. Filbert turned into the driveway a mile past Carol's house. We were on a major country road, with large address numbers on the pole. There had been no need to follow him - this pasture was easy to find.

Mr. Filbert had me follow him to his office because he simply didn't want to wait. By having me come to his office, he made me wait for him. I was mad. If I was going to continue to work for Mr. Filbert, he would have to be more respectful of my time. Now I knew why he didn't have a regular veterinarian.

As I waited for him to open the gate, unlock the tack room, find a halter and wander out into the pasture in search of his horse, my mind wandered as well.

I realize many veterinarians don't arrive on time for appointments in the field. While it's easy for clients to blame veterinarians, it is often their own fault. If clients don't catch their horses before I arrive, they often have difficulty catching them. Horses recognize the vet truck, and they don't look forward to a veterinary appointment any more than people look forward to a doctor's appointment, so they play hard to catch once they see my truck. While the owner says "He's never like this Doc. He's always easy to catch!" I know he's *always* like this once he's seen my truck. Horses aren't stupid. Smart owners catch their horses before they spot my truck.

I also have a number of spoiled horses that are kept as pets. Many of these horses have their owners trained to give up if the horse offers the least resistance. So when my job entails anything unpleasant, like filing down sharp points on their teeth, or giving injections, the horse puts up quite a fight because in the past that has allowed him to avoid an unpleasant situation. Once the horse realizes I won't give up, I can proceed quickly, but there is no way to know how long things will take on my first visit.

Once I even fell for a sob story of an owner who said she unknowingly hauled horses across state lines without the proper blood tests for Equine Infectious Anemia. To avoid disciplinary action from the Department of Agriculture, she begged me to Coggins' test her horses right away. As she had 15 horses, of course she wanted a discount.

I can't afford to own 15 horses, so why should I give a discount to someone who can? But of course I did. I was desperate for new clients.

The horses were a wild bunch of miniature foals that had never been haltered. They were loose in a five acre field, and they were all paints.

Coggins' testing requires detailed drawings of the horses' markings on official forms, which takes longer time when the horses are paints. While the owners ran around, tackling the foals reminiscent of a greased pig contest, I worked on the paperwork required to keep the owners out of hot water.

Once captured, the foals resented being stuck with needles, and their necks are so short and furry that jugular veins are hard to hit on miniatures foals. My syringes are longer than their necks, so their shoulders get in the way.

I finally collected the last blood sample, and in thanks for my hard work, they never called me again.

I Make Horse Calls

Mr. Filbert had finally captured his horse. The exam only took a few minutes, and his horse was fine. I charged him for one trip and the exam.

If Mr. Filbert called me again I would insist on meeting him at the farm.

There never was a next time, but I would soon learn that Mr. Filbert had a brother.

Chapter 10 Jet and the Heavy Rescue Unit

I first met Larry Whitley when he called me to treat his neighbor's mare. The neighbor was out of town at a horse show, and Larry was caring for her retired show jumper while she was away. The elderly mare was down with colic. She responded to my treatment and Larry asked me to care for his horses ever since.

Larry is an interesting character - a retired welder who decorated his ranch with sculptures he made out of broken pieces of old farm machinery. These sculptures resembled flamingos, bucking bulls, and various animals that sprung from Larry's imagination. Larry had made these art treasures some time ago, as they were rusting and tilting at odd angles alongside his driveway by the time I first saw them. The opposite side of the drive was a graveyard for rusting automobiles, or perhaps this was Larry's art supply warehouse.

Clancy never liked the sculptures. They appeared to be alive, as the wind tossed them menacingly on their flimsy legs. She barked furiously at them from the time I entered Larry's lane until we were well past the house. She kept guard over them from her post in my truck while I tended to Larry's horses.

Larry was a huge guy, weighing nearly 300 pounds, and I never saw him without a cigar in his mouth and a malodorous cloud of smoke encircling his head. His emphysema was so bad that he couldn't speak an entire sentence without stopping for air, and he coughed constantly.

His attire was predictable - sweatpants and a University of Nebraska t-shirt or sweatshirt, depending on the season. To me, a graduate of the University of Colorado, Nebraska's arch-rival, this was unforgivable.

Larry rarely bathed, and only shaved the top of his head,

never his face. He was the leader of a pack of huge dogs, a motley assortment of Great Dane and mastiff crosses that lived with him in the house. When Larry spoke, they listened. If the pack was in Larry's house when I arrived, they looked as if they might fall through the picture window in their barking frenzy to reach my truck. Their muddy paw prints coated the glass, so Larry didn't need curtains.

When Larry came out the back door, the dogs spilled out around him, swarming to the fence to check me out. The only way to get to the barn was through the yard, and I was apprehensive. The dogs weren't aggressive, but as they pushed each other aside to sniff me, I was carried along behind Larry on the tide of dogs.

I thought they might consider Clancy a tasty snack, so she always stayed in the truck.

Larry's house and yard were in shambles. The dogs had destroyed all of the grass in the yard, and the horses had done likewise in their small paddock.

Despite his attire and living conditions, Larry was intelligent, with a great sense of humor and a tremendous vocabulary. I don't know why he chose to live the way he did.

Jet Fighter and Ol' Red were quite a pair. After rather unsuccessful careers at the racetrack, they had equally unsuccessful occupations as dude ranch horses and carriage horses. Their hot-blooded temperaments did not make them suitable for inexperienced handlers, and they were repeatedly looking for new homes.

Larry stepped forward when he heard about them. He offered shelter, hay, room to exercise, and companionship, vowing to keep them together through their last years, "'til death do they part." It was the best offer these horses ever had. Their owner was glad to get rid of them, and so they came to live with Larry.

Larry's barns were made of sheet metal, and had not been mucked out since the horses arrived. He never groomed the horses. In the spring they shed their coats naturally, rolling in the sandy soil. Their coats glistened by mid summer, as they were well fed. Old grocery carts served as feed bunks, but somehow the horses never got tangled in them. Many horses would not survive in this environment, but Jet and Red thrived. Somehow they avoided the run-down fencing and sharp sheet metal.

I Make Horse Calls

I doubt that Larry ever rode a horse, preferring motorcycles, but Larry gave the horses a decent home. Larry had injured his knee in a motorcycle accident, so he couldn't do the upkeep around the barn, but he fed twice a day.

He adored Clancy, and always had a treat for her.

At first Larry's horses suffered from common preventable ailments - stomachaches and coughs, but a better vaccination and deworming program made my visits less frequent and less frantic. I now came for routine appointments, rather than emergencies. We both enjoyed the change.

But apparently Jet missed my frequent visits and attention.

Larry called me one summer afternoon.

"Jet's trapped in the barn. I don't know how he did it, but he dug a hole in his stall and fell into it, trapping his neck under the barn wall. I can't get him out. I've called the fire department for help, but I'm sure he'll need stitches. Please hurry!"

"I'll be right there."

Clancy heard the pager go off, and she could see we were going somewhere in a hurry. As I grabbed my keys and rushed out the door, I nearly tripped over Clancy in her exuberance. Being a Border collie, she thrived on excitement. She loved going with me every day, and emergencies kicked her into high gear. She raced ahead of me to the truck.

"Get in, Clancy!" I said as I opened the door. I could work better without her underfoot.

I always carry veterinary supplies, but today, under Clancy's impatient eye, I took a few minutes to load my truck with a saw, crow bar, sledge hammer, claw hammer, and tin snips. I didn't know what I'd need, so I took everything. If Jet stayed down long enough for me to get there, he might stay still long enough for me to demolish the wall.

But I knew I wasn't going to be able to drag Jet's 1200 pound frame out by myself, and Larry couldn't help. I hoped the fire department would come. If someone on the fire crew knew about horses, that would be even better. Many people in Mountain View had horses, so there was a chance.

My mind was spinning as I drove. How could I help Jet? I had untangled horses from fences before, and extricated a mare trapped under a fallen tree. In that case the fire department used chain saws to cut the tree. My job was to sedate the mare so she would tolerate the noise of the saw. Once the tree was off, the mare got up, and I treated her with IV fluids to stabilize her for the trip to the hospital for intensive care.

But in some jurisdictions fire departments aren't allowed to help with animal rescue, or sometimes they are too busy to come. While I hoped they'd come, I was prepared with my arsenal of tools.

As I turned onto the road to Larry's place, I gave a sigh of relief when I saw a huge fire truck in the road across from his driveway. The sign on the truck read "Heavy Rescue Unit." How appropriate!

I pulled into the driveway and Clancy went through her usual barking routine, trying to chase away the sculptures that lined the drive. She leapt from her seat, put her front feet on the console, and barked right in my ear.

"That'll do Clancy. You're making me deaf!"

When she saw Larry, she began wagging the tail end of her body. She loved him and his treats.

"They got him up." Larry gasped through the cloud of cigar smoke.

Larry held the gate for me as I waded through the waist deep sea of dogs, holding my tray of instruments high above my head. The dogs knew me now, but if they bumped into me, I would surely go tumbling. With the condition of the yard, I didn't want to go down in the muck and be trampled by the pack. I carefully made my way to the paddock.

The fire crew did have a horseman among its members, and with his expertise and their strong muscles and equipment they had gotten Jet out. Jet was standing by the barn and looked a bit worse for wear. He had cuts on his legs, scrapes on his hip and damage to his left ear.

Larry wasn't upset by the situation. He always stayed cool, which was a nice change. Many of my owners panic when they find their horses injured. Sometimes I think I should sedate the owner and then treat the horse. That wouldn't be necessary for Larry. Nothing fazed him.

124

I Make Horse Calls

"Larry, what was Jet thinking, to get himself in such a predicament?"

"Who knows?" wheezed Larry.

Jet could walk, so Larry put his dogs in the house and took Jet through the yard to my truck. Jet's wounds were minor.

Sometimes horses become trapped because they are suffering from colic. They throw themselves on the ground violently and may injure themselves rolling into fences or other hazards. I positioned myself upwind from Larry and checked Jet for colic. His pulse and gut sounds were normal. He was okay. There was no medical reason for Jet's pawing. Maybe he was just bored.

The barn where Jet was trapped wasn't really a barn. It was just a three-sided loafing shed, so Jet could walk in and out whenever he wanted. Why he dug the hole was a mystery to me. How he fell in the hole was another mystery.

And Jet wasn't talking.

Having ruled out other problems, I treated his wounds.

"His wounds need stitches, especially the ones on his legs. At his age, and after what he's been through, sedation is a little risky, so I'll keep the dose light. He's so gentle I'm sure he'll do fine."

I sedated Jet and began to clean his wounds. He was exhausted from his ordeal and let me go about my work without complaint. The difficult part of suturing wounds is injecting the local anesthetic, because it stings. Horses aren't very good at understanding that these injections are going to numb their pain. They only know the injections hurt and would prefer to avoid them. Jet was a big horse, and even at his age his legs could still do me considerable harm if he took offense at my actions. A dose of sedation given before the local took the edge off so I safely numbed the wounds and began suturing.

Open wounds on the lower legs of horses can be slow to heal. They can get infected or develop proud flesh, which is a non-healing, troublesome condition. Proud flesh can be prevented by sewing the wounds closed. Jet had enough healthy skin to pull across his wounds.

There were so many leg wounds that Jet had to be sedated again before I finished, and required many doses of local anesthetic. The sedative can slow a horse's heart rate, and the local anesthetic also has some affect on the heart. I was concerned for Jet. At his age, and with the stress of his ordeal, I did not want to harm him.

Before I sutured the ear wound, Jet was fully awake, and had finally lost patience with my doctoring.

Jet was a tall horse, and since horses instinctively raise their heads when upset, there would be no suturing this wound without more anesthetic. I couldn't block his ear without more sedation.

"Larry, I think we'd be better leave the ear wound alone. I've cleaned it up, but it'll take another dose of sedation to lower his head to suture it. I'm afraid to give him any more. Head wounds heal well, so it'll be okay, although the outcome might not be beautiful."

Jet was an old horse, with swollen joints from racing, arthritis twisting his limbs, and battle scars from a hard life. The years caused his muscles to sag, and his coat was graying. If he ever had been beautiful, it was a long time ago.

I knew Larry had a sense of humor so I kidded him

"You know though Larry, if I don't sew the wound, it may put his halter career in jeopardy. Is that okay with you?"

Larry burst out laughing.

Halter horses are the runway models of the equine world. The most beautiful, young horses are shown in halter competition, with the winners selected as the best animals for breeding. Jet was a gelding, with no breeding potential. Halter classes were never a part of his lifestyle.

"Doc, I guess it'd be okay," Larry coughed, "if he couldn't go in halter classes."

While I wrote the after-care instructions Larry went into the house. He came out with his checkbook and a treat for Clancy.

"Here you go, Clancy. You're such a good helper."

"Yeah, with her help I'll soon be deaf. I've got to convince her that your sculptures aren't in need of herding. She barks right in my ear as I come down the driveway."

"Hey Doc. She's just protectin' you."

"Yeah, I know."

"I'll be back in two weeks to take out the sutures."

As I drove home I still wondered, why Jet dug such a big hole in his stall.

But I'll never know.

Chapter 11 Nothing's Wrong

I had just settled down to supper after a full day of appointments when my pager let me know this was one meal that would get cold before I could eat it. The page was from Angie Palmer, and she was hysterical.

"Dr. Thibeault, you have to come right now!"

"Angie, calm down and tell me what's wrong."

Practically screaming into the phone she replied "It's Missy. She's foaling right now! Dr. Thibeault, I need you here *now*!"

Foaling problems are so serious that I'd have to drop what I was doing and get to Angie's right away. If I could get Angie to calm down and tell me exactly what was wrong, maybe there was something she could do to help the mare before I arrived.

If the foal had a leg in the wrong position Angie might be able to reposition it so Missy could deliver it. If the foal couldn't be repositioned, the leg might tear the mare's womb from the force of strong contractions. To help the mare, at least I could tell Angie to get Missy to her feet. This would drop the foal forward, out of the birth canal, making room for the foal to reposition itself. Maybe then Missy could deliver the foal unassisted.

I needed to know what was wrong so Angie could help her.

Again I asked "Angie, what's wrong?"

She screamed into the phone "*Nothing!*" and slammed down the receiver.

Okay...

I grabbed my keys and tripped over Clancy in the doorway. She and I jumped into the truck and she took her seat riding shotgun. She loved riding in the truck, and emergencies were the most fun. She fed on my adrenaline as I hurried to the Palmers' farm. Having delivered a few stuck foals, my confidence had grown since that snowy night at the Carsons' ranch.

It was early evening and the sun was barely peeking above the western sky. Emergencies didn't seem so bad if it wasn't pitch dark. I knew it wouldn't take long to get to the Palmer's ranch, but I was surprised by Angie's behavior. I'd never had an emergency call where the owner panicked and demanded immediate help while saying nothing was wrong.

I liked Angie and her husband, Todd, from the moment I met them. That day one of my clients was buying a horse from them. This should have put us into adversarial positions, as it was my job to find the horse's faults. But the Palmers were honest and straightforward. They disclosed the horse's imperfections to the best of their knowledge, and eagerly listened to my assessment so they could learn more about evaluating horses.

I was impressed by their knowledge of horses and by their honesty. They refused to sell a horse if they thought the buyer was unsuited for the horse. With the bad reputations that old time horse traders have, it was refreshing to meet people like the Palmers. After I did the pre-purchase exam on the horse they were selling, they hired me to do their farm's work. They appreciated my thoroughness.

Todd was a tall, lean redhead. He was very down-to-earth, and full of common sense. Todd never expected miracles. He just expected me to do my best - to find out what was wrong and tell him what could be done about it. He was prepared to handle the consequences, whatever they were.

Angie was a gorgeous brunette, and quite the joker. She loved to play tricks on her friends, and had a great sense of humor. She also had the most expressive eyebrows I've ever seen. If I did something to cause her to raise an eyebrow, she'd get a twinkle in her eye and burst out laughing.

Besides buying quality riding horses, the Palmers had a fine stallion, Glint of Gold, who was champion Missouri Foxtrotter at the regional shows. As a result, he had a full book of mares to breed each season. They also owned some well-bred broodmares and produced quality foals.

I had not been their vet for long, but having seen the well-managed stables and the well-bred horses, I was puzzled by Angie's behavior. They had owned horses for years. When I did some reproductive work for them last spring, I had seen young foals on their farm. I knew this wasn't their first foaling. But Angie sounded so panicked. I hurried to get there in time to save Missy and her foal.

Angie and Todd had two grown children, so birth was not a new experience for them. Angie and Todd were police officers and the horses were their hobby. Todd drove a patrol car at night, and Angie was a Crime Scene Investigator. They faced danger and horrific crime scenes as part of their daily routines. Angie told me about attending "Blood Spatter School" training. This made Angie's panic even more surprising. Oh well, I was nearly there, and soon should have all of this figured out.

As I approached their farm, I couldn't believe all of the cars parked in the Palmer's driveway and spilling out onto the road. I couldn't get my truck anywhere near the barn. Apparently Angie had called every one in town to report her mare was foaling!

I parked along the road and grabbed my obstetric kit as I rushed into the stable. There were people everywhere. I pushed through the crowd to the stall door. To my delight, the chestnut was mare standing over her newborn foal, licking him clean. All was well.

Now I was really confused!!

Todd, with a broad grin across his face, said calmly, "It's a colt."

Angie had her camera and was shooting photos of her new foal. She was a talented photographer and provided her services for other Foxtrotter owners, as well as produced some great brochures promoting Glint of Gold's stallion services.

I congratulated Angie, who was calm now, and I examined the mare and foal. Missy's heart rate was strong and steady, and her gums were pink, indicating no internal bleeding. Her udder was bulging with colostrum. The mare was relaxed, gently tending to her foal with no signs of distress. She accepted the crowd of onlookers.

The foal soon gained his feet. Angie held his unsteady body while I listened to his heart, which was beating strongly and rhythmically. His lungs had cleared the uterine fluids. I checked his eyes for cataracts. Both eyes were clear. His gums were pink and his temperature was normal. He was adapting normally to life outside the mare. I checked his navel - there were no signs of a hernia, and treated the cord with disinfectant. I administered an enema. Both mare and foal were fine.

As I joined the crowd of people observing the lovely scene of a healthy mare and her newborn foal, I was overwhelmed with a sense of happiness. At foaling time, when so many things can go wrong, from birth defects to premature foals, to difficult deliveries, I always consider it a miracle when everything goes perfectly.

In my work as an equine practitioner, I am called when things go wrong, not when things go right, so it was rare to see this happy scene.

A few months earlier Angie called me to check Special. Her favorite mare was overdue for delivery and Angie was worried. I had only known Angie a short while. After I examined the mare, I had to give her the bad news - the mare was no longer pregnant. Special had aborted her foal and there would be no cause for celebration. The long-awaited foal would never arrive. I remember the disappointment showing on Angie's face that day.

But today there was cause for celebration, and sharing the good fortune with friends and family. As I prepared to leave, I took Angie aside to talk privately to her. I didn't want to embarrass her in front of her friends, but I had to know why she panicked.

"Why were you so frantic on the phone? I know this isn't your first foal," I whispered.

"Well, Doc, with all of the other foals I just came out in the morning and the foal would be standing there beside the mare. I never saw one *born* before!"

Oh brother!

I left Angie and Todd to enjoy their friends and their new foal.

Two weeks later Angie's other mare foaled. She called me during my usual morning office hours and said calmly, "Tulsa has just foaled. Please come out at your convenience and check her new foal."

Clearly Tulsa had delivered her foal when Angie wasn't watching.

Chapter 12 A Holiday Tradition

It was another holiday, this time the 4th of July, when the call came from Sherry Orton. Destiny was colicking again.

"I'll be right out. Just keep her out of trouble."

"I know what to do this time. Just please hurry, Doc T.," Sherry's voice sounded a little less scared than last time.

As I grabbed my keys to go, Clancy was right by my side.

"Are you ready for another emergency run girl?"

Clancy was always ready. I opened the back door and she sprinted to the truck, bouncing in front of the truck door until I could get it open for her. She jumped in and I climbed in behind her. Off we went, windows open, Clancy's ears flapping in the breeze. Canine bliss!

When I arrived at the Ortons' young couples were playing volleyball in the front yard. They were having an Independence Day cookout. Sherry and George were tending to Destiny by the barn out back, leaving their guests to themselves.

As I climbed out of the truck George was quick to ask, "How come it's always a holiday when Destiny gets sick? We have to pay an extra emergency fee. I heard you charge triple for holidays."

"No, in fact I don't, but that's a great idea, George. Thanks for the suggestion! The emergency fee is only $20 for nights, weekends, or holidays. But then I'm sure if you could control the timing, you'd arrange not to have colic at all."

"You're right about that," said Sherry. I could see she was worried, but not as panicked as the last time Destiny colicked.

"It does seem like we're establishing a holiday tradition though, doesn't it - Memorial Day, Fourth of July...?"

I went to work, examining Destiny. It was gas colic again, and in less than 30 minutes we had Destiny's pain under control and her appetite returned. Sherry didn't need a long-winded explanation of Destiny's condition and how to care for her.

While waiting for the medications to help Destiny, I took a look at Spunky. He was finally adding some meat to his bones, and his legs looked much better since the farrier balanced his hooves. Spunky was becoming a character, tearing around the paddock bucking and tossing his mane. He was growing into his name. He was still incoordinated and looked like he might crash into the fence before he could stop his impulsive outbursts, but somehow he managed to veer away at the last second. I knew I would have to castrate him soon. He was becoming too much for the Ortons to handle. But castration is safer when done after the first frost, when the insects that might irritate the incisions have died. I hoped Spunky would behave himself until then.

As I prepared to figure the charges, George came out of the house with fresh bread, just as he had done at every appointment. His timing was impeccable.

"I have some of Dr. Mom's favorite cinnamon raisin bread, and some new variety hamburger rolls. Is there any other kind you'd like to try?"

"No, George, but this is great. Thanks. I'll tell Dr. Mom you sent the raisin bread. She really enjoyed the last batch."

"Why don't you let Clancy out?" asked Sherry.

I rarely let Clancy out of the truck when I'm working. I need to concentrate on my patients, and not be distracted keeping an eye on Clancy. She was easily frightened, and might run off, or more likely, she would begin herding the horses to me, which I might not appreciate at the time.

"Really, it's okay. King won't hurt a flea."

George had a huge male malamute named King, and Sherry had a female Australian shepherd cross named Tuffy.

"Really, King is fine. Oh please, let Clancy out! She can play with our dogs."

Reluctantly I let Clancy out. We were done treating Destiny, but the Ortons' farm was on a busy road, and I was afraid the dogs might chase each other into traffic.

King came over and sniffed Clancy wagging his tail. Tuffy raised her hackles and growled as she approached Clancy. Clancy was still a pup so she took a submissive posture, rolling onto her back, showing Tuffy that she was no threat. However, Tuffy was not fluent in dog communication and bit Clancy right in the stomach. Clancy howled, leapt to her feet, and jumped back into the truck.

Sherry looked horrified. "I'm so sorry Doc T. I really didn't expect Tuffy to be a problem," Sherry said apologetically. I could tell she was upset, and I wasn't so happy either. Clancy liked going on calls with me and liked my clients. I hoped being bitten wouldn't make her less eager to come.

I checked Clancy's wounds, but they were minor. She healed quickly and never held a grudge against Sherry. But Clancy never got out at Sherry's house again, unless Tuffy was locked up.

I took George's cinnamon bread and headed to the fireworks show at the Festival of the West.

In September I heard from the Ortons again. This time the call came in on my answering machine.

"This is Sherry Orton. George and I are having a Labor Day cookout and we'd like you to join us."

Sherry claimed she wasn't very smart. She and George had married young, right out of high school, and began working instead of going to college. She was very smart.

They thought Destiny might colic again, because it was a holiday, so she and George hoped to get out of paying an emergency fee and trip charge by inviting me to the cookout. She'd be exchanging a hamburger for part of her vet bill.

I saw right through their plan, but gladly accepted Sherry's invitation, and had a wonderful time at the party. I met their extended families and enjoyed the good food and camaraderie.

Destiny had a good time too. It seemed that in the three months since we'd improved her care, she'd made remarkable progress. She didn't colic at the Labor Day Party. In fact, she never had colic or any other illness for the rest of the time Sherry owned her.

Sherry thought she'd have the last laugh, ensuring that I would already be at her house when she might need me, but I had the last laugh. Since the filly had gone eight weeks without colicking, I thought there was a good chance she was cured. I was right, and bet my cookout dinner on it.

It was a win-win-win situation!

Chapter 13 Fort Fun

The old wooden screen door creaked as I opened it wide and pushed my bicycle through. Clinical rotations ran late, and with winter approaching I only had an hour of daylight to ride. I had to get moving.

I pedaled down the gravel lane toward Taft Hill Road, away from the small farmhouse I had called home for the past four years - the plain little house that I loved so much.

I had to leave my dog with my parents while living in the dorm in Boulder, so I searched for a house with a yard for my years in vet school in Fort Collins. Dogs' lives are so short that three years apart was already far too long.

I remembered the first time I laid eyes on Pischka.

A young, fresh face peered around the door frame as I sat in the tackroom recording the day's lesson income into the ledgers. It was my teenage employee, Debbie, and she looked distressed.

"What's wrong?"

"Oh Marcia, I took my litter of puppies to the pet store today. I had called ahead and they agreed to take them, but when I got there, they only took two, so I have two puppies with me, and I don't have time to go home before I start work. It's too hot to leave them in my truck. Can I bring the puppies in?"

Who could resist puppies?

"Go ahead."

"Are you sure?"

"Yes, bring them in."

"Oh, thank you," she said, her face washed by a look of relief.

I Make Horse Calls

She soon came back with two of the cutest puppies on the planet. They were tri-colored bundles of fluff, a large male and his little sister. They were marked like Bernese Mountain dogs, but were much smaller.

I had been waiting for an Australian Shepherd puppy from a friend of mine. She had a wonderful bitch, but she never produced a litter. Maybe I had found my puppy.

"What breed are they?" I asked Debbie.

"The mom is a cross between a Sheltie and a terrier, and the dad jumped over the backyard fence unseen."

"So I guess you could call them Sheltie/terrier/athletes?"

"Yeah, I guess you could."

The little female stole my heart, and that day she became mine. Debbie told me she was the runt of the litter, but she had a bountiful spirit. My Polish employee, Daniella, named my fur ball little Pupischka, and her brother big Pupischka, and the names stuck. Debbie's brother later adopted big Pupischka.

Life was great, until one day I heard Pupischka screaming. She had been sunbathing on the warm asphalt lane that dead ended shortly past the barn. Some ill-spirited person had run over her while she slept. I had thought she was safe, as there were only a couple of cars that went down that road each day, and she never chased cars. But I was wrong - nearly dead wrong.

I scooped her broken body up and ran to the vet, hoping she could be saved. I was so relieved that the vet found only one fracture - her femur - and he could fix it. But I felt so guilty because she was my responsibility, and I let her get hurt.

She was soon home, furry toes sticking out from under the plaster cast.

While she had been relegated to sleeping in the kitchen before her injury, I now set a soft cushion near my bed so I could keep a close eye on her. She could walk around well enough, so I let her walk out to the yard to do her business. There was only one step, and the grass was but a few feet from the door.

My Father pretended not to like dogs. He would occasionally pat the dogs I had as a child, but he acted like he didn't want to be bothered with them. The dogs were for my sister and me. When we went off to college and the last old dog died, there were no more dogs in the house. My parents wanted to travel, and dogs would make that more difficult.

But he melted when Pupischka looked at him.

My Father thought I was so cruel, making her walk outside to do her business. When she whimpered at him to go out, he would carry her, his strong hands cradling the tiny, and in his mind totally helpless pup, placing her gently on the grass. When she was finished he would gather her up and carry her back to her bed. Since Pupischka couldn't go to the stable with me until she was healed, my Father lovingly cared for her during her convalescence.

As she healed she got more active, but didn't realize her limitations. She used to crouch under the low coffee table when taking a shortcut across the den. One day she tried that with her cast on, and since she couldn't bend her leg, she became wedged under the coffee table, with its full weight on her injured leg. Her cries brought me running to lift the table off her leg.

She was smart enough never to try that again.

The surgeon did a fine job, and the pin and cast were soon removed. Still a puppy, she rebounded quickly, and regained her strength. It was time to begin her obedience training.

The first time I put her on a leash she fell to the ground on her back in complete disgust, refusing to offer any cooperation, and letting me drag her around the yard by her neck. My high school friend, Paulette, an accomplished dog trainer, called her a "pathetic collapser." But with Paulette's help, we got her on her feet.

I enrolled her in obedience school, where her Sheltie breeding shone through - she was a star. She willingly and quickly complied with my every request, following each exercise with a lick on my chin as I praised her.

At the end of the class was a final exam, and they awarded a loving cup to the best pup. She was sure to win it, but we practiced extra hard to ensure victory. My competitive side would not be denied.

One evening my Mom accompanied us to the training center for an extra practice session. I had Pupischka heeling off leash, performing circles and figure eights when I looked down and noticed I was alone. Pupischka was sitting in my Mom's lap in the third row of bleachers!

I Make Horse Calls

Mom would have to be out of sight during the final test.

Two weeks before the end of the course a Saint Bernard transferred into our class, and he was very obedient. He did not have Pupischka's quick reflexes. His huge size made his movements clumsy by comparison, but his willing nature matched hers. There was a chance he could win, so we practiced even harder.

When the day of the test arrived, we were ready. Pupischka went through all of the exercises flawlessly. I was so proud of her, and she so joyously responded to my praise.

Then the Saint took his turn. He completed the group exercises well and our scores were very close. Then his owner placed him at the end of the room, leaving him for the recall. The owner proceeded across the room to the far end, while the Saint waited patiently. When the owner called him, the Saint came running with unbridled enthusiasm - but he failed to stop. He leapt with both front feet onto his owners' shoulders, flattening him on the floor.

The loving cup was ours.

Pupischka always came running when I called, but she would never come for Dad. And it was a bit embarrassing. The cast had long since been removed, and she was completely healed, but when Dad called her to come in from the yard my prize-winning obedience dog would collapse helplessly onto the grass, not budging. Dad would obediently walk out and scoop her up, carrying her inside.

This had to stop. I made Dad take her leash out to the yard and snap it on her collar one day after she collapsed. One gentle tug and she was briskly trotting into the house ahead of him. He thought her behavior was exemplary, so he rewarded her with a biscuit.

She quickly invented a game - scratch at the door to go out. Get Dad to open the door, then scratch at the door to come in and walk straight to the biscuit cabinet. Stand by the biscuits looking cute until treats were forthcoming. Repeat at will.

She did this exercise as many times a day as Dad would allow, which was too many times, and soon my 18 pound dog weighed 23 pounds. And Dad was totally oblivious to the fact that she had trained him to give her a treat every time she asked.

I had to stop Pupischka from training my Dad before she became too fat to walk. Once I showed him how she had patterned his behavior, he quit rewarding her so often, but he spent his life adoring her, wrapped firmly around her little toe.

When Pupischka was a year old and no longer a puppy, I dropped the Pu and called her Pischka.

Pischka went everywhere with me as I earned my living as a riding instructor. She would sleep in the shade of a jump during my lessons, and curl up on the sofa in the office while I did the paperwork. All of the employees loved her, and Debbie got to see her every day.

But when I returned to college following our journey around the US on the way home from Florida, Pischka had to stay with my parents. Dogs were not allowed in the dorm, and it was the only housing I could afford. My parents adored her, and she had a great home, but I missed her so!

I went home on weekends to see my parents and take Pischka for walks and rides in the car. She loved sleeping on my tiny twin bed. I didn't mind curling around her warm body like a pretzel. Unconditional love was worth any price.

So when I went to vet school, I looked only at housing that would accept dogs, and was so fortunate to find the little farmhouse with the fenced yard, just two miles from the vet school.

I bicycled on Drake Road west to Foothills, and turned north, past houses lovingly landscaped by their owners. Because I was in class or clinics at least seven hours a day, my cycling route in Fort Collins was shorter than my favorite loop in Boulder.

I stayed close to town, so the route was less hilly, and lined with older houses and small farms. I had learned about gardening from my landlady, so I was keenly observant when the tulips and daffodils bloomed early each spring. In May I could smell the sweet fragrant lilacs. It seemed everyone in town had flowering trees and bulbs, but today was one of the last days of fall, and the autumn breeze scattered the dried, crunchy leaves on the roadway around me. It was cold. And as the sun was about to go down, it would be colder soon. I should have worn gloves.

I was so glad to find the old house. It wasn't pretty, and my Father thought I was crazy, giving up the modern conveniences of a condo with a dishwasher to live in a pea green wooden house that was 50 years old. It had shifted on its foundation, and not one window or door was straight, but I didn't care. It had a quiet country setting, ideal for studying. The fenced yard came with pet friendly owners. I could afford the rent and it was close enough to campus to commute by bicycle. It was perfect.

It felt like home from the moment I walked in. It shared seven acres with the landlord's house, so I had a close neighbor, but not too close. The huge back yard was grassy, and the fence would keep Pischka safe. It had a built-in security system, as the landlord's two German shorthair pointers kept watch over me as if I were family from the day I moved onto the farm.

My landlord, Dr. Will Aanes, was an equine surgeon who taught at the university. He and his wife, Barb, had a huge vegetable garden, and she tended pools of flowers that surrounded their log house. He raised a few head of beef cattle on the acres that ran down to Spring Creek at the back of the farm.

The front of my house was hidden from the lane by a huge stand of mature pine trees, and there was an old climbing rose at the entrance to the drive.

Beautiful plants were leftover from a time when the house had been a nursery - peonies, and poppies, French lilacs, and marvelous varieties of iris. A single cut peony released enough sweet fragrance to perfume the entire house for days. Mature fruit trees in the yard bore aromatic flowers in the spring and were heavy with fruit by summer's end. My interest in gardening flourished because Barb was an avid gardener. She taught me well, and they both loved that I cared for their house.

A pheasant left tracks in the snow by the towering brilliant "blue shiner" spruce tree in the side yard on Thanksgiving Day. I heard a pair of great horned owls hooting their courting calls back and forth from the pines as I studied by the open window on the first warm evening of spring. What a wonderful replacement for the fire truck sirens that sliced through my life when I lived in town.

I had come a long way since that foggy day in Florida, and for the next four years I lived my dream in the country. I spent all day with animals, or learning about their ailments, and had a life filled with compassionate students and professors who devoted their lives to helping animals. I didn't own the house, nor was I employed in the horse industry, but acceptance to vet school almost guaranteed graduation for any student willing to work hard, because the college had too much invested in us to let us fail.

I cycled over the Poudre River towards the small town of La Porte. The river was calmly confined within its banks today, but last summer had been raging out of control, flooding across the bridge which usually hung a dozen or more feet above the surface. Its nature changed with the seasons, swelled by melting snow in early summer, and shrinking to a lazy crawl by fall when students returned to campus.

The ecstasy of being accepted into the first year of vet school is balanced by a dread of the unknown.

On the Friday before classes began students had to purchase books, copies of lecture notes, and supplies. I reported to the dissection lab where mountains of heavy books weighed down the steel tables. I walked into the milling crowd of strangers with whom I would spend the next four years. I patiently went from station to station, checkbook in hand, doling out my savings for books, lecture notes, dissection kits, smocks, nametags…and a stethoscope…*a stethoscope* - the universal symbol of a doctor. How cool was that? I didn't think I'd need a stethoscope the first year!

Finally I was fully equipped with everything I needed, except maybe a wheelbarrow to lug it all home! It's a good thing someone warned me to drive my truck to campus today instead of riding my bike.

I got in line to have my picture taken. The faculty was making a book of photos of the entire student body, no doubt so they could keeps an eye on us.

Walking into the cafeteria my eyes landed on a picture of James Herriot taped to the wall, with "Our Hero" written underneath. I knew I was on the right road.

I was shocked the following Monday when the professors called us by name as we passed them in the hallway. In three years, only two of my professors at CU had ever bothered to learn my name, and they were professors who mentored my independent study projects. The vet school faculty had certainly done their homework, memorizing every freshman's name over the weekend! And we were handed copies of "The Green Book" - a directory of the names and pictures of the vet students in all four classes. It was an ice breaker. The names and faces became familiar - became friends.

The enthusiasm and dedication of both students and faculty were contagious. These were my soul mates, and although we came from different backgrounds and pursued our careers in different specialties, a common bond - the penchant for science and compassion for animals - drew us together.

I had done my homework as well. Before the first day of class I looked over my purchases and found a copy of each day's lecture notes. The courses were broken down into mini-courses - smaller units of cohesive information that were more manageable. I was so glad to be able to study information that would directly apply to my profession that I studied the first 20 mini-courses of Anatomy over the weekend. I would start the semester in great shape!

Agents of Disease began promptly at 8 AM with sections on immunology, bacteriology, virology, and parasitology. Each topic was taught by a different veterinarian, all specialists in their field. As many as 16 professors would collaborate on a single course. We were clearly getting expert instruction, although some professors were better at research and others excelled as teachers or clinicians.

Immunology lecture began as we were still rubbing the sleep from our eyes. The professor spoke in a monotone, and simply read his slides to us, boring us beyond belief since we had already read his notes. When the lights went out and the slide projector went on, we were subjected to slides with black backgrounds and fluorescent pink, green and yellow lettering. The contrast was so stark it brought tears to my eyes. Closing my eyes in self-defense soon returned me to slumber. His nickname - Dr. Sominex - was appropriate.

The anatomy professor covered 23 mini-courses before lunch on the first day of class, so my feeling of accomplishment was short-lived. At noon I sat in the lunchroom knowing that, after only four hours in vet school, I was already behind! I had smugly thought that since I held down three jobs when I was a full time student in Boulder and managed to earn grades good enough to graduate with honors, vet school would seem easy by comparison.

I was wrong.

I Make Horse Calls

When Bacteriology began, Dr. Tom Collins was so enthusiastic that no one slept. He was a young, energetic veterinarian with unbelievably curly blond hair and a passion for bacteriology. His vivacious demeanor and sense of humor were engaging, and I looked forward to his classes.

One of his introductory lectures covered the decision making process practitioners should use when deciding whether to set up a bacteriology department within their practices, or to rely on an outside lab for those services.

To this day I remember only his first words. "When you set up your own practice, you need to decide whether to purchase equipment and run tests in-house, or to contract with a local lab ... blah, blah, blah, blah, blah...."

Oh...my...gosh! He actually believed we would graduate! We would pass our board exams and become licensed practitioners. He even believed we would someday own practices. None of my professors at CU ever demonstrated such belief in my abilities.

From that moment on I believed my dream - to own an equine vet practice and live in the country - could actually come true some day.

In a few short weeks the first exam was upon us. You could cut the tension with a scalpel. And we had an unrelenting test schedule that continued all year long.

I had studied so hard, so many hours, but I still wasn't ready. Unlike my undergraduate classes, where I studied so much I begged to take the test just to put me out of my misery, the volume of information we were expected to cover in vet school was huge. I needed way more time to prepare! But there was no more time.

We began the first anatomy test at 9 AM, and the test was so long and detailed that by lunch time no one had finished. I was always a fast test taker, so the fact that no one else was done only eased my concerns a little. Because CSU had an honor code, we could go to lunch and talk, but not about the exam. After lunch we retrieved our exams and continued working for two more hours.

After the test we had immunology lab. It was a very long and stressful day, followed by a sleepless night.

The exam had been so hard.

We were expected to know such minute details.

I Make Horse Calls

Doubt crept in. Was I good enough to pass these courses?

The faculty was excellent at returning our grades promptly, and results were posted before the first student arrived the next morning. I was glad I was born in Maryland. Grades were posted by social security number, not by name, and being born in Maryland gave me a low number, so my name was at the top of the list. I looked over the heads of my curious classmates jostling for position in front of the list.

I couldn't believe it. I had passed my first exam in vet school!

Not only had I passed, but I got a B!

Life was good!

When anatomy class began Dr. Banks congratulated us, saying that we were 1/132 of the way towards completion of our veterinary degrees.

I had another 131 exams to take? The dread returned.

Freshman year continued at a hectic pace, but with every test we passed our confidence grew. Soon finals were over, and I threw a party at my house. We had plenty to celebrate - we were marching towards our destiny and making strong friendships along the way.

As I turned east out of La Porte, I cycled past the empty farmhouse where one of our sophomore professors, Dr. Wigton, used to live. I recalled how proud he had been when his red Angus cow gave birth at the end of the school year. He had named the cow Genuine Moo, in honor of Genuine Risk, the filly who won the Kentucky Derby on the day Moo was born. He invited students to see Moo's little heifer, so I visited his farm to compliment him on his fine calf.

Sophomore year brought a slightly lighter academic load, but the downside was that we would not touch an animal all year. The courses were only lecture and lab, no patients to treat.

With the stress of adjusting to life as a vet student, I had largely ignored my love of cycling the first year. So many hours spent sitting in lectures and studying made exercise more important than ever, so I tried to get at least an hour of cycling every day, rain or shine. If it was snowing, I played racquetball.

I Make Horse Calls

We sat through lectures seven hours a day, every day, as the professors droned on. The thrill of being accepted into vet school had worn off, and graduation seemed impossibly far away.

It was hard to stay focused on so many hours of class, and the lecturers went so fast. I bought a cassette recorder so I wouldn't miss a word. At the end of class, if my notes were complete, I'd re-use the tape. But if I missed something, I noted the place on the tape and that night I replayed the tape and filled in the blank spot in my notes.

When it came time to review my lectures for an exam, I found it hard to decipher the scrawled notes I had hurriedly taken only a few weeks before. My penmanship had always been horrible, making my old notes useless.

So I began to type complete transcripts of the lectures. I sat at the typewriter every night until 11 PM, and weekends were consumed with more course work, but it was a labor of love. I was learning so much. Reviewing each day's lectures the same day helped cement the concepts in my mind. My typed notes were invaluable - accurate enough to recall the professor's inflections ringing through the transcripts as I read and re-read them. I kept audio copies of the most difficult lectures and listened to them as I soaked in my bubble bath after working out.

As final exams drew near I was approached by a classmate who was struggling academically. She had heard about my transcripts and asked to buy a copy of my notes. I gave them to her. I couldn't charge her. We were all in this together.

I found out through the student grapevine that equine rounds were held early Friday morning, before our classes started. Even though sophomores and freshman were not invited, students who were brazen enough to come weren't asked to leave. So every Friday I bicycled down the worn path from campus to the hospital to attend rounds. I had to leave before they were over and hurry to class.

The cases discussed in rounds brought my course work to life. Hearing these marvelous veterinarians, highly trained specialists, discuss the intricacies of diagnosing and treating the more obscure referral cases heightened my attention to detail as I studied. I arranged my work schedule to continue attending rounds through the summer.

I Make Horse Calls

Sophomore year I worked at the saddlery in Boulder two Saturdays a month. It was as much time as I could spare, but the income kept my pantry full.

Sophomore courses included pathology, clinical pathology, and pharmacology. We were also beginning to learn about diseases that affected each body system - endocrine system, digestive system, etc. Each System's course would begin with a review of the anatomy of that system, and then infectious disease specialists would tell us about microbes that attacked those systems in each species. Then we would cover toxicology, genetic diseases, cancer, trauma, and so on.

My favorite course sophomore year was Dr. Wigton's class in clinical pathology, a discipline that involves making diagnoses based on blood work and other lab tests, done in the live animal. On the first day of class I couldn't even define clinical pathology, but I soon loved it. I much preferred it over pathology, which often entails post-mortem exams - the veterinary version of autopsies. I figured it was too late to have much success by the time the animal was dead, although I admit pathology is invaluable in containing disease outbreaks for animals that live in herds.

Dr. Wigton had true compassion for the welfare of his students, both in the classroom and in their personal lives. He helped students in need. But I was intimidated by him early on.

He brilliantly lectured, in minute detail, on how to interpret the myriad of tests we could run to diagnose our patients. I loved the involved thought processes he used to unravel the mysteries of each case he presented. The notes from his lectures were many pages long, and I read and re-read them, gleaning more information each time. There was so much material I doubted I could ever fully grasp it, but I kept working and it eventually got easier.

If I had to ask a question, I felt really stupid compared to him, but I felt that way with most of my professors, so I was getting used to it.

Professors did not give any homework assignments. Grades were based on test results. And who could blame them. With 130 students in each class, and patients to treat in the clinic, emergency duties, research, and families at home, they had little time for grading essays.

But Dr. Wigton took the time.

I Make Horse Calls

He assigned a case about a sick dog. Students had to decide, based on the clinical pathology test results he provided, what organs were affected and how serious the illness was. We needed to determine which results were abnormal, and make a list of reasons why the test results could be abnormal. We weren't yet far enough along in our studies to make a diagnosis or develop a treatment plan. He only wanted us to explain the test results based on our understanding of animal physiology and how it is altered by diseases. It was our first step toward becoming diagnosticians.

He allowed us a week to complete the exercise, and we had to limit our comments to one side of the sheet of paper he stapled to the lab report.

I looked over the case and made some notes during the week, but left the majority of the work until the weekend. I was working at the tack shop on Saturday, but set aside Sunday to work on the case.

Pischka was sick when I got home from work Saturday night, and despite staying up all night with her, she wasn't getting any better by Sunday morning.

When she was young, she had an illness no one could diagnose. She acted like a horse with colic, sitting with her head held low, her nose just hovering above her toes, refusing to eat. I took her to my regular vet seeking help.

He diagnosed an upset stomach from eating garbage. I knew he was wrong because Pischka didn't have access to garbage. He insisted. I followed his advice, giving her mineral oil for an upset stomach, the same treatment horse vets use for colic, but I know she got better on her own.

When the problem recurred, I took Pischka to a different clinic. The vet again diagnosed "garbage can gut." When I described her symptoms, he told me dogs don't get those kinds of symptoms. He implied that I was crazy, because dogs don't get colic. And he recommended mineral oil.

When the problem recurred the next time, I tried a third vet, who said Pischka wasn't sick.

I was frustrated that none of the vets tried to figure it out. The problem recurred several times a year, but remained undiagnosed until I became a vet student. The next time she was sick I took her to the teaching hospital. A senior vet student, in less than five minutes, using only her hands, diagnosed a rare liver condition based on the size of her liver. She just did a thorough physical exam, including palpating her abdomen, and lab tests later confirmed her diagnosis.

Pischka had a portal caval shunt - a rare blood vessel abnormality where a shunt running between two blood vessels is supposed to close down after birth, but it didn't. Her liver functioned normally, but remained small. It hadn't grown with her as she grew. So if she received a dose of medication based on her body weight, she was overdosed when compared to her liver size. Since the liver's job is to break down toxic compounds in the blood, including drugs, she would be under the influence of a normal dose of drugs for days beyond what was expected. And the liver removes excessive proteins in the diet, so when I lovingly bought her high protein dog food, I was unwittingly making her sicker.

Her condition was incurable. She was long past the age when a surgeon could put a suture around the shunt, closing it down. And so many puppies died when this procedure was done that I wouldn't risk her life. Knowing what was wrong helped me to avoid things that would aggravate her condition, keeping Pischka much more comfortable for the rest of her life.

I was so grateful for the care the gentle senior student took with Pischka that day. It was apparent the university hospital offered an unmatched level of care. I would not forget the thoroughness of that student, and would emulate her when I entered practice. I would never dismiss an owner's complaint, because I remembered how I felt when vets dismissed Pischka's illness, never trying to find out what made Pischka so sick.

But the disease continued to bother her from time to time.

All day Sunday Pischka continued to suffer. There was no medicine I could give her to ease her pain. The only place she was comfortable was sitting on my chest while I sprawled on the carpet. She was such a loving dog. I hated to push her away. She really felt terrible.

But that position did not lend itself to typing my paper.

By Sunday evening I decided to check her into the hospital. Breaking hospital policy, the attending veterinarian allowed me to walk Pischka back to her cage in the intensive care unit. It was important to me that she saw that I knew where she was. I did not want her to feel abandoned. There was little they could do, but they would monitor her while I did my assignment.

I worked furiously, spending nearly all night on the case. I couldn't sleep with Pischka so ill, so I didn't care if I went to bed.

After I interpreted the lab values, I typed my answer on the handout. Typing allowed me to fit more comments into the limited space and I'd get a better grade if Dr. Wigton could actually read my answer.

Before bedtime I called the ICU - they were open 24 hours - and checked on Pischka. She was no better.

I knew she was in good hands, but the little house seemed so empty without her joyous spirit floating around it.

I dropped into bed for a few hours, but sleep did not come as I worried about my little dog.

In the morning I called again, and she was feeling better. I couldn't pick her up until the doctors were finished rounds, so I went to my morning classes and picked her up at lunch.

She was overjoyed to see me, and licked my chin all the way home in the truck.

I hated to leave her alone while I went to class, but she was tired and I knew she would sleep on my bed for the rest of the day.

I turned in the assignment and wondered how Dr. Wigton would ever find time to grade all of those papers.

A week later, as I was sitting in my usual seat in the third row before class, Dr. Wigton was staring right at me - staring holes in me. His gaze was unnerving, and soon he started walking right toward me.

Oh my! What did I do?

He climbed the steps until he was standing right in front of me, with a stack of papers in his left hand.

I was terrified.

He stuck out his right hand, and I reflexively stuck out mine.

"I can't believe a sophomore student can be thinking so clearly when it comes to clinical pathology. Here's your paper."

There was a bold red A on the top. I was speechless. I mumbled something stupid and slid down in my chair, embarrassed, knowing that my classmates' eyes were on my back.

But inside I was ecstatic.

I Make Horse Calls

When my sister came to spend the weekend, I noticed a dark spot on her foot. I asked her about it, and she said it was just a freckle. I knew she was wrong and told her to go to the doctor right away.

The spot was a malignant melanoma, and surgery saved her life because we caught the rapidly spreading cancer early enough.

I credit Dr. Wigton's training for helping me notice the subtle abnormality so early in my career, while I was still a student. I had made my first diagnosis - and saved my first life.

As I pedaled back into town the traffic was growing heavy. It was rush hour, and I'd have to hurry to get home before dark. The Motobecane now had lights and reflectors - necessary for commuting to campus and the vet hospital, but drivers in Fort Collins didn't look out for bicycles like the Boulder drivers because cyclists were rare here. I shifted up a gear.

Junior year was the beginning of clinical rotations.

We were actually working with vets in the hospital half of the day, instead of attending class on campus. In the morning junior students were assigned to assist senior students with clinical cases. Afternoons were spent finishing the lecture courses, including a great class called Body as a Whole, which tied together the concepts taught in each systems course.

Every week our rotations changed. My first rotation was in food animal medicine, caring for all species of farm animals. I dragged myself out of bed unbelievably early to milk goats and cattle and assist the seniors with their treatments. As a girl born in the heart of the city, I had no experience handling farm animals, but I loved it.

I moved through my rotations, eagerly awaiting anything equine. I had a week of equine ambulatory, going from farm to farm treating horses. A week of equine medicine kept me in the hospital treating horses with infectious or metabolic diseases. Other rotations, like radiology and anesthesiology, served all species, so I might see an equine case or two, but my most anticipated rotation was equine surgery - the rotation that treated lame horses. Not all cases went to surgery, but all lamenesses were treated by the surgery rotation. My chance came right before Christmas.

I Make Horse Calls

Dr. Simon Turner, an Australian vet who had coordinated our musculoskeletal systems course - the lecture course that taught us about lameness - was an inspiration to me. He lived life with such intensity, whether it was teaching students, performing surgery, doing research, or running marathons. He moved at such a fast pace that he was accomplishing tremendous things in his life. I was humbled in his presence.

At the end of each section of the lameness course he supplied a list of references for further reading. I wanted to own the articles he cited, so I spent hours at the copy machine in the library, building a reference file for my practice, which I now believed would become a reality. I met with Dr. Turner to get more information on specific topics. He always had time to answer a question, but he was so focused that he didn't want to be distracted from his work for long. I learned to get to the point in a hurry, but he never made me feel like I was intruding.

The surgery department had two pairs of equine surgeons. Dr. Aanes wasn't on clinical duty that week so I hoped Dr. Turner was in clinics and I would be assigned to him. I knew him and I didn't know the other two surgeons on duty. There was comfort in a familiar face.

In the early hours of a cold December morning I milled around the equine barn with the other juniors, hands in our pockets, cold breath clouding the morning air, trying to dance the chill away from our toes. We were awaiting the arrival of our surgery instructors not knowing who would be teaching this week. When the first professor arrived, he told us half the group should stay with him, and the other half should go outside and meet with Dr. Turner.

Oh, joy!

I bolted for the door, making sure I was the first one outside, while trying not to appear too obvious or trampling anyone in my way.

I was finally, after so many years of study, going to be part of the veterinary team that treated lame horses! What a long journey it had been, and I was so pleased to have Dr. Turner as my instructor.

Being a junior meant being an observer and lowly go-for. The attending veterinarians made all of the clinical decisions. They were followed by the residents, then the interns, and then the seniors, with the juniors trailing behind. There were always at least four bodies between the patient and me for every procedure, but I didn't care. I was learning skills that would enable me to spend my life caring for horses.

I'd be a senior soon enough. The pace of student life was hectic. We were hurtling towards graduation and board exams.

Once finals were over and Christmas break arrived, it seemed to last forever. Juniors were free to go home, so I worked in the tack shop from finals until Christmas. I spent Christmas week with my family, but they went back to work and I was lost without anything to do until school resumed. There was no direction to guide my studies.

The hospital was at half staff for the two weeks around Christmas, so everyone had some time off, but in early January it was business as usual, but without the juniors. Maybe I could tag along on Dr. Turner's rotation. I had enjoyed his week so much, but I was too shy to ask.

It was time for me to grow up. I had been too shy to face the professors in Boulder when grad students ruined my grades. I needed to come out of my shell, and stand up for my future. It was long overdue.

I agonized over the choice.

Should I ask?

I hated being so shy.

Try to be rational.

Really, what was the worst thing that would happen?

Would Dr. Turner kill me?

Probably not. There had been no news reports of dead students at the vet hospital.

Although perhaps there'd been a cover-up.

Would he hit me?

Probably not. There were no reports of assaults either.

What would he say?

Would he be angry?

"How can you ask for three weeks of extra schooling without paying any more tuition?"

He probably wasn't paid a commission based on my tuition. He probably wouldn't care - but I couldn't be sure.

Would he be annoyed?

I Make Horse Calls

"Can't you see I have my hands full with all of these students - seniors who were *assigned* to me? And you want to tag along, too!"

What was the worst thing that was really likely to happen?

Would he scream at me?

Probably not.

When I concluded the worst thing that might happen would be he'd say no, and I knew not asking him would yield the same result, it was foolish not to ask. I had nothing to lose.

I was still as shy as ever, but I would force myself to ask. Tomorrow would be the day.

After a sleepless night tossing and turning, I found Dr. Turner in his office early the next morning and somehow summoned the courage to ask him.

He said yes.

He said yes!

I was welcome to join him.

I went on rounds all day, every day, for three weeks, and learned so much. The smaller group - just three students instead of six, let me participate in discussions. It did create a buzz around the hospital however, as the close-knit seniors whispered about this persistent junior who showed up for rounds every day when she should be on vacation. Who was she and why was she here?

I didn't care. I was challenged by the opportunity to learn more. Each junior was only assigned equine surgery for one week, and as a senior I would have another two weeks, so three bonus weeks would double the number of cases I would see.

I no longer was content to just become a vet - I wanted to be the best vet I could be.

Block tests were given to senior students at the end of a group of rotations. A glitch in the schedule had the senior students taking a block test from Dr. Turner at the same time he was supposed to be doing an arthroscopic knee surgery on a horse. The surgery went ahead, and I was asked to assist the resident, Dr. George Martin, when he performed the surgery. I jumped at the chance, and with only two of us in the operating room, Dr. Martin allowed me to operate the arthroscopic camera while he repaired the injury. He talked me through the procedure and made me feel much more competent than I really was.

I Make Horse Calls

Bessie, a Holstein cow that was part of the university research project studying digestive functions, was assigned to me when I was a junior. For research purposes, the cow had a fistula surgically implanted in her stomach. This Plexiglas window could be opened to retrieve the contents of her latest meal, and helped vets understand how cattle process feed and oral medications. She was an agreeable creature - easy for a novice like me to tend.

Bessie was content with her window. It didn't seem to bother her at all. I was amazed that she never scratched at this hole in her side that seemed more like science fiction than science fact to me.

Vesicular Stomatitis, or VS, a rare disease that resembled hoof and mouth, only occurred in Colorado about every 20 years, but an outbreak occurred while I was tending Bessie.

Cows stricken with VS get painful blisters in their mouths and on their udders. Dairy cows quit producing milk and refuse to let their calves nurse. Calves die without supplemental bottle feeding, and dairies can go bankrupt if the disease is widespread in their herds.

Bessie was the only cow in the hospital herd that got VS. The poor girl's mouth was full of blisters and she wouldn't eat. She was miserable.

Since the disease hadn't occurred in 17 years, any students who had graduated since the last outbreak had never seen it. I was fortunate to learn about VS while I was in school, seeing it first hand, but the animals that contracted VS weren't so fortunate.

The disease usually came through in late summer, and disappeared after the first frost, making it hard to study. By the time the outbreak was recognized, there was little time to gather samples and run tests. There was still so much we didn't know about it. No one could explain why only one animal in a herd might be affected, even though the herd shared the same water trough. The experts speculated that the disease was probably caused by a virus, but then why didn't it spread through the whole herd if all of the animals drank from a common water trough with open, infected sores in their mouths? Were there other factors, like oral trauma, that caused one animal to be affected while the next animal was fine? What caused the disease to remain dormant for so many years between outbreaks? Where was the virus in the years between outbreaks?

I Make Horse Calls

We did know that the disease could be spread to humans, and unfortunately, Dr. Johnson, the head of my rotation, was taken ill before we knew why Bessie was sick. In people the disease caused only flu-like symptoms, so Dr. Johnson would soon return. In the meantime, the resident was in charge of the rotation.

The senior students who shared the rotation with me were parents, and were afraid they might transmit the disease to their children since the mode of transmission was unknown. They soon made themselves scarce around the cow barn. The resident and I would have to tend to Bessie, and working one-on-one with him made it obvious to him that I had no skills handling cattle. Despite his experience with cattle, he never helped me improve my skills.

I tried everything to get Bessie to eat. I soaked her hay in water to soften it. I offered silage, corn, and oats to stimulate her appetite. I offered timothy hay, alfalfa, hay cubes and pellets, but she was too sick to care. Bessie was losing weight, and I feared we might be losing her. I was an attentive nurse, but I had no medicine to offer because the cause of VS was unknown. No virus had been isolated and few drugs killed viruses anyway. The medical advances made since the last outbreak might help epidemiologists learn more about VS from this outbreak, but it wouldn't be in time to help Bessie.

The resident decided we would feed Bessie by passing a tube through her mouth into her stomach. In horses the stomach tube must be placed through the nostril because of the horse's unique anatomy, so this would be a new procedure for me to observe. But Bessie was so sore. I knew the procedure would help her, but it would be painful. And she had a fistula. Couldn't we just pour the feed directly into her stomach through the window? It seemed so easy. Why was the resident intent on tubing her?

I was too intimidated to voice my opinion.

Like a sheep blindly following the flock off a cliff, I followed the resident's instructions. I loaded a bucket with pellets, and poured several liters of balanced electrolyte solution - fluid filled with the minerals Bessie would need to maintain her strength - over the pellets to soften them. I set the mixture aside to soak until evening rounds.

In my head I kept questioning why he overlooked her fistula. Some residents thought students should be seen and not heard, and

155

not to be seen might be even better. But I was growing bolder. I had to become more forceful if someday I would own a veterinary practice. I had found the courage to talk to Dr. Turner. It was time to step out of my comfort zone and challenge authority. I would go to bat for Bessie, confronting the resident about his treatment plan, hoping to help her without causing needless pain.

When the resident arrived, stomach tube in hand, to treat Bessie, he was clearly in a hurry to get on to the next case.

I made my suggestion. Couldn't we just pour the mash into her stomach directly through the fistula?

He reluctantly agreed, trying to hide the fact that he had missed the obvious, and that it had been pointed out by, of all people, a *junior* student.

Since it was my suggestion, it became my job.

I grabbed a handful of alfalfa and broke it into small pieces for scratch factor - something abrasive cattle require for proper digestion. The resident stood at her head while I opened the Plexiglas window. Bessie stood quietly. She was too sick to care and I wasn't hurting her.

I slowly poured the mash inside. When the bucket was empty, I dropped the alfalfa through the window, and it floated on top. I then donned a long plastic obstetric glove and inserted my hand into her stomach up to my shoulder, mixing the food inside her huge, bovine stomach. It was a warm, odd sensation, and I can only imagine what Bessie was thinking, but she didn't move. I withdrew my arm and closed the window.

I hoped we had helped her, but only time would tell.

I thought about Bessie that night as I drifted off to sleep. Was it too little, too late? Or had I actually helped her?

I was eager the next morning to see Bessie. I arrived at the barn early, and Bessie was on her feet, leaning against the front of the stall, watching me come down the aisle. She was holding her head a little higher. That could be a good sign.

I picked up a flake of the best alfalfa I could find and unlatched her gate. I walked into Bessie's stall, offering her the hay as I had done every morning all week. She had ignored me every day since she was taken ill. But not today. Today she snatched the hay out of my hand as soon as she saw it, almost sending me tumbling to the ground.

Watching Bessie's huge bovine jaws grinding the alfalfa, I knew Bessie must be feeling much better.

I had made a difference.

Life was good.

I cycled past the vet hospital as the last rays of sunshine were gone. The glow lit the undersides of the clouds, poised above the mountains ahead of me as I pedaled westward toward home. I had treated many animals while a student within the walls of the hospital, and it still seemed miraculous that we had saved most of them.

Senior year meant we all moved up a spot in the hierarchy as last year's seniors graduated and made room for us. We would get a better view of surgery and more opportunities for doing procedures. The juniors would now assist us as we accepted more responsibility.

As seniors we had to use what we'd learned in those countless hours of lecture, under the guidance of the attending vets. We took medical histories and gave patients physical exams. Then we would generate a list of possible causes for their problems. The list was called a differential diagnosis list. Then we made a plan of further tests to rule out the less likely causes and determine the final or definitive diagnosis. Based on the definitive diagnosis, we would develop a treatment regimen.

I felt a bit out of my element in small animal surgery, but it was here I would make my first diagnosis.

Mrs. Fister's young Pomeranian dog, Maxmillian, was my first patient.

Picking up the paperwork at the front office, I called for Mrs. Fister in the waiting room. She was easy to spot - the only lady in the room with the pointy nose of a Pomeranian peeking out from behind the crook of her right arm.

"Mrs. Fister, I'm Marcia, a fourth year vet student. What seems to be the problem with Maxmillian today?" I asked as we walked toward the exam room.

"He fell off my deck and broke his ribs."

Oh my, that sounded serious, but not much of a diagnostic challenge.

I Make Horse Calls

I closed the door as she placed the dog carefully on the exam table. I asked about Max's medical history as I gently felt through his thick golden fur for a swelling over his ribcage. Finding none, I then ran my fingers down each rib, and found no displacements. His ribs seemed fine, so I put a little pressure on his ribcage, moving it like a normal breath.

Max seemed to be pain free, not offering to bite, and breathing through his open mouth in a happy canine smile. If I had broken my ribs, I knew I wouldn't tolerate such manipulations without complaint, so I concluded Max's ribs were fine. I doubted the accuracy of Mrs. Fister's report, and needed more information to find out why she brought him in today.

"Did you see him fall off the deck?"

"Well, no, but he must have because that's the only place in the yard he could have hurt himself."

"Well, Mrs. Fister, his ribs seem fine to me. There's no swelling, and he's not painful to my touch. What makes you think his ribs hurt?"

"When I pick him up and tuck him under my arm, he cries out, so it must be his ribs."

I placed Max on the floor to watch him walk. His thick fur obscured his tiny limbs but I noticed something abnormal about his back legs - both of them. He had an odd, shuffling gait, marching like a stiff tin soldier.

I lifted little Max back onto the exam table and checked his hind legs closely. I soon found the problem - both of his kneecaps were dislocated. They were above and to the outside of the joint. I gently tried to reposition them, but they wouldn't budge. Max's legs were permanently locked in rigid extension.

When Mrs. Fister clutched Max tightly to her body, he couldn't bend his knees, and the pressure from her arm caused him to cry out in pain as his knees were pushed sideways.

My list of differential diagnoses was short - luxated patellas. My list of procedures to confirm my diagnosis was equally short - have the attending vet palpate the dog's hind legs and take x-rays. His treatment would require surgery to re-align his tiny patellas unless the attending vet's experienced hands had more success replacing them than I did.

I Make Horse Calls

I reported my finding to Mrs. Fister, and then spoke to the attending veterinarian. He raised an eyebrow when I said a dog presented to the college for broken ribs actually had knee problems, but his exam confirmed my findings and he praised me for my thoroughness. I was not led astray by an owner's kind-hearted but inaccurate report.

I had made my very first lameness diagnosis! My patient only weighed ten pounds, but I didn't care. I felt great!

Maxmillian was soon whisked off to surgery and had his limbs repaired by a surgeon on staff. I had to stand in the third row, behind the surgeon and resident, but I played a small part in restoring Max to good health.

He was soon home with Mrs. Fister, bouncing happily around her yard.

Food animal rotations brought patients of a different kind.

When I first saw Leroy he was standing on the parking lot, all 2300 pounds of him. The Limousine bull had been assigned to me. He loomed larger than my Suburban, and was undoubtedly a brown descendant of Paul Bunyan's giant blue ox, Babe. It seems that Leroy had a sore foot, and it was going to be my job figure out why.

I was feeling a little distressed that state law required veterinarians to be competent in all species before granting them a license. I only wanted to work with horses, and Leroy would test my minimal talents at handling cattle before his leg was healed. I doubted that this huge bull would be as kind-hearted as old Bessie.

If I vowed never to touch a bovine of any type again, could I get an equine-only vet license?

Please…

Unfortunately there was no such thing.

So I thanked my lucky stars for the cowboy attached to Leroy's lead rope. In his sage green down coat, faded Levis and chocolate brown felt hat, the cowboy urged Leroy into the exam room, which was quickly filled by Leroy's presence. The bull was in so much pain that he was limping badly, and his right hind fetlock joint was thickened. But in spite of his pain, he was cooperative. He had obviously been handled regularly and trusted his cowboy, whose name was Buck Jamison.

I Make Horse Calls

But I was no cowboy, and I had to examine Leroy's leg and Leroy was going to need x-rays.

A thorough history from Mr. Jamison revealed Leroy was a valuable bull, in the prime of his life, but he could not continue making calves because his leg was too painful to support him during breeding.

Leroy was not much of a diagnostic challenge. My short differential list included only fractured or infected fetlock, and I requested x-rays to supply the answer. If the joint was infected, sticking a needle in the swelling and withdrawing a fluid sample could lead to identification of the bacteria, and help us select the best antibiotic. It could also lead to someone getting their head kicked off trying to get the sample. I was afraid that someone might be me.

Dr. Knight checked my case work-up and ordered the x-rays and we waited Leroy's turn.

I was getting comfortable, actually enjoying, handling sheep and goats, and milking dairy cows was becoming a habit, but Leroy was no old milk cow. He had no horns, thankfully, but his massive head could have squashed me with a single butt, if he so desired. He seemed content with Mr. Jamison. I'd do anything to keep Leroy happy.

Mr. Jamison said he'd raised Leroy from a calf, and asked permission to restrain Leroy for us while the x-rays were being taken. I was only too happy to oblige and tried not to look unprofessional and jump for joy at the prospect of delaying taking control of Leroy as long as possible. If Leroy decided to make a break for it and go out the front gate to the road, my puny frame would be of no use slowing his escape. It had been known to happen.

To protect Mr. Jamison's breeding potential, we supplied him with a lead apron when he entered the x-ray room. Unfortunately, the only apron not in use at the time had pink cartoon characters on it, so here was Mr. Jamison, 6'4" of lean, Wyoming cowboy, dressed in an apron covered in Strawberry Shortcake dolls, controlling one of the most mammoth bovine creatures to walk the earth.

I wish I'd had a camera, but Mr. Jamison, good sport that he was to wear the apron, probably would have let Leroy kill me rather than let anyone in his cattlemen's association see him wearing that

I Make Horse Calls

apron. I didn't dare even smile. I had to maintain my professional demeanor, but it wasn't easy.

The x-rays revealed that Leroy had a severe joint infection which required flushing under general anesthesia. Leroy would sleep through the whole thing. Oh joy!

The surgical staff did the procedure while I observed, and soon Leroy was convalescing in his hospital stall. We sent Mr. Jamison home for a few weeks. Leroy's post-op care was up to me.

The food animal barn had some stalls with head gates to restrain our unruly patients, and some stalls without. For reasons unknown to me, Leroy was placed in a stall without a head gate.

Leroy was given a dose of injectable antibiotics while he was asleep during surgery, but he needed dosing every two days, and it was my job to give the injections. Because antibiotic doses are based on patient weight, it required two of our largest syringes filled to the brim to hold Leroy's dose. And the drug was thick, so I needed the largest needle to push the drug into Leroy's muscle.

After two days of feeding Leroy, trying to convince him that I was a nice person, worthy of continuing to live, I climbed over the stall gate with his medicine under the watchful eyes of my classmates standing in the aisle. No one offered to come in with me.

Leroy lay placidly in his stall, chewing his cud and resting his sore leg. I rudely stuck the huge needle through the tough hide over Leroy's backside and began injecting. Leroy quit chewing. I knew his focus was now on me. Luckily, Leroy's bulk and the fact that I surprised him allowed me complete my job before he got to his feet, but he made clear that he objected to my actions by threatening to butt me with his massive head.

I got out of Leroy's stall just as Leroy got to his feet and whirled to squash me.

I was already dreading his next treatment. Leroy would be ready for me.

When the next dose was due I recruited a classmate with cattle experience to assist me. We waited until Leroy was down, resting comfortably. When the time was right we climbed over the stall gate and my friend and lifesaver went to Leroy's head to try to restrain him. But he was barely able to slow Leroy at all, as Leroy knew what was coming and he was determined to retaliate against that annoying little human with the big needle. I managed to get the entire dose into Leroy's backside, and we both escaped with our limbs intact, but I knew a third dose would surely be fatal for me.

At rounds the next morning, Dr. Knight asked me to review for the benefit of all in attendance the virtues of the antibiotic that had been selected, and why an antibiotic might be changed in mid-course.

I listed the medical reasons - resistance of the organism to the current antibiotic or the animal might have an adverse reaction to the drug, and the financial reason - some drugs are too expensive.

Dr. Knight added a new reason to my list.

"We are going to change to a drug which can be given orally, and only needs to be dosed every five days, to ensure that Marcia lives to graduate."

I was soooo grateful.

Bless you, Dr. Knight.

We moved Leroy to a stall with a head gate, and with the help of my experienced classmate Leroy was encouraged to put his head through the bars. As the bars were tightened enough to prevent him from backing away, I loaded the first of many pills into the balling gun - a chrome rod with a chamber that held a pill. A plunger on the end would be depressed once the other end of the gun was over the base of the Leroy's tongue. That would ensure the pill was delivered to the back of the mouth and swallowed.

I stuck the gun in Leroy's mouth. His head was so huge that my entire hand had to be inside his mouth in order for the tip of the gun to reach its location. I was grateful that cattle have no upper incisor teeth. I gave Leroy his stack of pills with no complaints from Leroy. I would be on a new rotation before Leroy needed his next dose.

I silently thanked Dr. Knight again that I could live.

Finally the day arrived when I was a senior on equine surgery rotation. It had taken so long to get here - I was going to make the most of it.

Summer was a busy time at the university, with many lame performance horses to treat. Students were needed in the clinic year round. I asked to be assigned the summer equine rotation. There were no juniors on campus then; I would have more contact with both patients and professors.

The surgeons rotated throughout the year, with six months of research and six months of clinical work, so I was overjoyed to see Dr. Turner assigned to teaching duties during my rotation. We had become friends, so I fearlessly asked to be on his rotation, and he made me feel welcome. Over the course of senior year I would take as many electives as I could in equine disciplines, so I worked with three of the four surgeons on staff, but I felt most comfortable with Dr. Turner. I looked forward to easing into primary responsibility for equine cases under his tutelage.

We were standing around the barn on a hot summer afternoon conducting rounds, reviewing each case and making sure our patients would be comfortable for the night, when an emergency page came over the intercom. An injured horse had arrived, and a student from Dr. Turner's rotation needed to accept the case.

I jumped at the chance.

I had always been polite to my classmates, stepping aside for exercises like equine bandaging practice. I had wrapped so many legs as a show groom that I didn't need more practice, and I didn't need to show off in front of the faculty. I was secure that my grades were adequate to graduate, so I willingly helped my classmates perfect their technique. If a small animal case came in that was of special interest to one of my classmates, I stepped aside.

But when equine lameness cases presented themselves, all bets were off.

I had ridden jumpers in college, and most of them were ex-racehorses with orthopedic problems. No local breeders provided tall, athletic horses specifically for the jumping market. Jumping was not as strenuous as racing, so many of the horses could be successful in this second career. But they needed special attention to their old injuries to keep them performing comfortably. My interest in lameness was born then, and I needed all the experience I could get.

So when the call came over the intercom, I asked for the case.

Dr. Turner agreed.

I went to the business office to pick up the paperwork. A Mr. Wiggins, from Steamboat Springs, had a palomino mare named Gold

I Make Horse Calls

Nugget with a left hind leg injury. I proceeded across the parking lot where he had unloaded his horse and tied her to the trailer.

Mr. Wiggins was all of five feet tall, with a grizzled chin and hunched stance. He weighed about 90 pounds, and was about 90 years old.

"Good morning Mr. Wiggins, I'm Marcia, a senior student. Please bring your horse into the exam room."

He untied his horse and I walked beside him into the barn and began taking the horse's medical history.

"What's wrong with your mare?" I asked eagerly.

"He's mah stuud horse" he replied, in a low gravelly voice.

I was caught off guard. I checked the paperwork again and indeed it said mare. So now I looked really stupid. I hadn't looked closely at the horse yet. I'd assumed the paperwork was correct.

"Oh, the papers said it was a mare. Sorry for the mistake. I'll have the records corrected." I was a bit sheepish. This was not the start I'd hoped for if I was to win his confidence.

I could tell by the look on his face that Mr. Wiggins was not happy to have a female working on his horse, but there wasn't anything I could do about that.

"What happened to him?" I asked again.

In his deep, slow voice he told me "I turned 'im out in my arena with a mare to breed, but she didn't care for his attention, so the old sow kicked him in the stifle."

I could see he really didn't care much for female horses either.

But I would try to win him over.

Once we reached the exam room Nugget stood patiently while I asked Mr. Wiggins about Nugget's worming and vaccination history, breeding history, diet, housing, and any other injuries or problems we should know about.

Mr. Wiggins was impatient. He couldn't understand why I asked so many questions. Couldn't I see the mark on Nugget's leg where he'd been kicked?

I then set to work examining Nugget's heart and lungs, listening to his gut sounds, checking his eyes and his ears. I went over the horse meticulously - assessing each of Nugget's body systems in turn and filled out the medical record the university provided to guide our exams.

Mr. Wiggins was getting annoyed at the time I was spending, but CSU trained its students to be thorough. I had learned the value of being thorough, for things are not always as they seem.

I knew that once I looked at his leg, all other problems would be secondary, so I wanted to be sure the rest of Nugget was okay before I examined his leg. But finally I finished the history and physical and checked his leg. Sure enough, directly above his left knee was the perfect imprint of a horse shoe. The skin was intact, but the blow had removed the hair. My training in physics now kicked in. A blow to the lateral aspect of the stifle would unduly stress the medial side, so I must be certain to check there for injured ligaments.

I put my hands on the inside of the stud's stifle, but there was no swelling, and the ligaments were intact. He wasn't painful.

Because Nugget's injury might be serious, I didn't want to trot him until I knew it was safe. I wouldn't risk further injury.

"Mr. Wiggins, would you please walk him across the parking lot while I observe his gait."

He took the lead and begrudgingly began his journey.

I stood behind the stallion as Mr. Wiggins lead him away from me. Nugget's lower leg dangled backward from the hock, rather than bending forward, so Nugget had to raise his hip to swing his lower leg forward. It made the leg appear broken, but the horse could stand comfortably on the leg.

In a single stride I had my diagnosis!

Or did I?

Nugget had the characteristic gait of a horse with a ruptured Peroneus Tertius - a special ligament that runs from the hock to the stifle. This ligament forces the hock to flex when the stifle flexes, and the hock to extend when the stifle extends, and it allows horses to sleep standing up. This ligament must be torn if he didn't flex his hock normally when he walked. I had spent countless hours in the hospital's video room, reviewing tapes of lame horses trotting around the exam area, so I was sure of my diagnosis, but puzzled.

He must have a ruptured PT because of how he walked. But a ruptured PT was inconsistent with Mr. Wiggins' report, and it was inconsistent with the mark on the side of Nugget's stifle.

Nugget had to have a ruptured PT, but how did he get it? It wouldn't be torn by a kick from the side.

Nugget must have suffered another injury.

"Come back Mr. Wiggins. I know what's wrong with your stud."

The ligament may tear at the stifle, but usually the tears occur at the hock. I asked Mr. Wiggins to stop and I palpated Nugget's hock. I found a small swelling where the ligament attaches to the bone. Now I was confident in my diagnosis.

"Mr. Wiggins, your horse has ruptured a ligament in his hock. This usually occurs when the horse over-extends his leg. What else happened to him besides being kicked by the mare?"

"Well," Mr. Wiggins slowly drawled out his answer. "After the mare kicked 'im, he ran down the arena and kicked his back feet through the fence, and that leg got hung up."

Bingo! I now had the mechanism for Nugget's injury. When he struggled to free himself from the fence, he over-extended his leg, tearing the ligament.

"That's what caused the injury. It wasn't the mare's kick, but Nugget's own actions."

I could tell Mr. Wiggins wasn't pleased to hear that Nugget's injury was caused by the temper tantrum he threw when his amorous advances were rejected.

I made my diagnosis and reported to Dr. Turner.

He watched the horse move and extended his hand to me, smiling.

"Congratulations, Marcia. You were spot on," he said with his Aussie accent. I loved his accent, and his words were music to my ears. Praise was rare enough in vet school, but earning his respect meant the world to me.

"Let me show you the test that proves your diagnosis."

"No, Dr. Turner, let me show you."

I was so bold I even surprised myself, but I had prepared for this very moment.

I lifted Nugget's leg and gently pulled his hoof out behind him. The hock extended, but the stifle didn't, as it would have if the ligament was intact, and a characteristic dimple appeared in his Achilles' tendon. My diagnosis was confirmed by this painless test.

I Make Horse Calls

"All right DOCTOR Thibeault, how are you going to treat him?"

I wouldn't be a doctor for another six months, but I loved the sound of it. Dr. Thibeault!

Unfortunately, I couldn't remember any treatments. The videotapes only covered diagnostics. I had to think on my feet.

I stumbled quickly through some treatment options. I was still more comfortable repeating what I was taught, rather than actually thinking, but I was gradually making the transition.

"If the ligament has come off the bone, reattaching it with a screw and then immobilizing the limb in a cast will protect the repair until it heals."

Keep thinking....

"Or if the tear is in the ligament itself, suturing the ends together and immobilizing the limb should get it to heal."

Uh...

"Or perhaps simply immobilization of the limb could allow healing, as the lack of movement would prevent the ruptured ends from pulling apart during healing."

I really didn't have a clue. I was winging it. But I sounded so convincing that I almost believed myself.

"Well, Marcia, these horses usually heal quite well if they are simply confined to a box stall for a few months. As a matter of fact, encasing the hock in a full leg cast can cause this injury, if the horse should lose its footing and slip. So using a cast is a double edged sword in these cases, and surgery is usually not necessary."

I still felt pretty good. Nugget would be fine.

We sent Nugget and Mr. Wiggins on their way back to Steamboat for a few months of stall rest. Nugget should be ready to breed mares by next spring. Hopefully Mr. Wiggins would make sure his mares were in heat before putting them with Nugget next time.

But I was elated. I had correctly diagnosed my very first lame horse *and* earned praise from Dr. Turner, all on the same day!

Maybe I wouldn't *just* be a horse vet - maybe I'd be a *good* one!

Life was really good!

I Make Horse Calls

A few months later, I was in the horse barn early one morning, attending to my equine patients. I was on medicine rotation, not surgery, so I was assigned to one of the medical staff for this week. Dr. Turner scurried out of the darkness through the back door and stopped at the stall where I was examining one of my patients.

"Maaaarcia, I see that you're on equine surgery next week. I checked the student list and none of the other students have equine experience. You *are* planning to be on my rotation, aren't you?"

"Yes, I'll see you bright and early Monday morning!"

"Ta, Ta." And he was off in a flash down the breezeway, vanishing like an apparition.

I was stunned. He actually *asked* me to be on *his* rotation.

I'd come a long way in the months since I dreaded asking Dr. Turner for those few extra weeks.

Dismounting in total darkness I rolled my bike through the front door, collapsing onto the floor, panting and exhausted. I should know better. The days were getting shorter, and I should shorten my route. But instead I tried to go faster every time to complete the loop between the end of class and sunset. I was too stubborn to yield to the unrelenting cycles of nature.

In a matter of months, vet school was over. I was so happy to have made it through. My doubts about my ability to pass science classes were finally put to rest.

Graduation day found me grinning from ear to ear in the company of friends and family.

My studying partner, Tom Welsh, hit the nail on the head on graduation day when he said "I'll bet there's nothing that can wipe that smile off your face today." And Tom was right.

I had made it.

I was a vet. It felt good!

Chapter 14 Designated Fainters

The call was from Sherry Orton. "I think it's time to castrate Spunky. He's become a trick horse."

I knew Spunky was definitely not a trick horse. He was still an untrained boisterous colt in the hands of novice owners.

I wondered what was up.

"Spunky's a trick horse now? What do you mean, Sherry?"

"Well, George went down to the barn, and said how cute Spunky was. That Spunky offered to shake hands."

"Shake hands?"

I was puzzled.

"Yeah. Every time George goes down to the barn Spunky stands up on his hind legs and sticks out his hoof to shake hands."

Uh oh. No horse should be rearing and striking at his owners. I needed to castrate Spunky as soon as possible for Sherry and George's safety.

"Oh no. I'll get him scheduled right away. When are you available? We need to start early, on a warm day, and we need someone strong to be available in case anything goes wrong."

"How 'bout Wednesday? My brother, Jake, is off then, and George will be at work. George refuses to be there. He can't *stand* the thought of castrating Spunky."

"Okay. I'll see you Wednesday at 9 AM. Don't feed him any breakfast, and remove any hay he hasn't finished by 9 PM Tuesday."

"Great! See you then."

Very few amateur horse owners have the facilities or ability to handle a mature stallion, so castrations are done on most colts before they mature. Geldings are more tractable, and make excellent riding and driving horses. I prefer to geld colts as young as possible, as there is less bleeding, young animals handle the anesthesia well, and if they are unsteady on their feet waking up from the anesthesia, the smaller they are the more we can help them until they are fully awake.

Wednesday morning dawned bright and clear. The fall day was warmed by bright sunshine - Colorado's short Indian summer was in full swing. In the months Sherry had cared for Spunky he had grown strong enough to tolerate surgery.

When I got to Sherry's farm on Wednesday morning she and her brother were in the farmyard. She re-introduced me to Jake, her brother, whom I had met at the 4th of July cookout. Jake's curly blond hair fell to his shoulders, and his green t-shirt was stretched taut across his bulging chest and biceps. Jake's physique was the opposite of Sherry's - he reminded me of Sampson. I had asked Sherry for a strong assistant, and Jake seemed to be exactly "what the doctor ordered."

"Hi, Jake. Are you ready?" I asked our powerful assistant.

"Yeah," Jake replied, rather unenthusiastically, like he'd rather be somewhere else.

The sweet smell of pine shavings and hay greeted me as we walked into the dark barn to examine Spunky. Having not been fed breakfast, Spunky showed his displeasure by banging at the stall door. I had to push him back to keep him from bolting out the door as I entered the stall.

Spunky's health had shown tremendous improvement since I first saw him. He was taller, stronger, and his antics with George showed that he deserved his name. The weight tape I put around his girth measured 750 pounds. He'd be a handful if he gave us any trouble. It was a good thing I had a strong assistant today.

After examining Spunky I went over the procedure with Sherry and Jake, so they would know what was going to happen. Clients worry less if they know that what's happening to their horse is normal and expected.

"I'll have all of the medications and instruments I'll need for the procedure close at hand. I'll do the surgery in the grassy field behind your paddock. When everything is ready, I'll have Jake hold the lead rope while I give Spunky a sedative to relax him. After

Spunky drops his head to the level of his knees, I'll give him the anesthetic and take the rope from Jake.

"In about a minute Spunky will lose his balance and I'll ease him down gently, so he doesn't hurt himself. Then Jake can hold Spunky's upper leg out of the way while I do the surgery. Sherry, you'll sit by his head, talking to him to reassure him. I'll blindfold him to help him relax. He'll be stiff and jerk his legs at first, but he'll soon relax and lie still, in a deep sleep. His breathing will slow to only a few breaths a minute. You'll think he's dying, but that's a normal response to the anesthetic. For about ten minutes he'll be asleep enough to do the surgery, so I'll have to move quickly. We need to be quiet, so we don't disturb him or he may jump up too early. After the surgery is over, he'll sleep for another few minutes. When he starts trying to get up, we'll remove the blindfold and help him with his balance so he doesn't fall and hurt himself. Are you ready?"

Sherry said she was. Jake didn't respond and looked pale.

I led Spunky behind the barn and handed Jake the lead rope.

"Don't let him graze." I cautioned Jake.

Jake and Spunky soon engaged in a tug of war - Spunky trying to graze and Jake trying to keep his head up. Spunky was really mad. He was hungry, and was standing on what he thought should be his breakfast. Despite Spunky's protest, I managed to get a needle into his vein and inject the sedative. As soon as it took effect, Spunky would be easier to handle. I thought the rest of the procedure would go smoothly, that was, until I saw the look on Jake's face. He was as white as a sheet, and beginning to wobble.

I have had male clients faint from the sight of blood, and get distressed at the crunching sound the emasculator makes as the cord is cut, but I never had a client faint before the surgery even started.

As Spunky's head dropped, and his knees began to buckle, he and Jake seemed to be in the same condition. Soon Spunky had the full effect of the first drug, and was ready for the anesthetic. I injected the anesthetic quickly, and took the lead rope from Jake. Spunky began to wobble, then leaned back and sat down. I pulled hard against his body weight so he wouldn't go over backwards and hit his head. Spunky sat down on his rump and I eased him onto his left side. Jake began to wobble, squatted down, and grabbed his

171

knees. As I glanced over my shoulder, I saw that Jake looked like he'd had a dose of anesthetic as well.

Oh, brother!

I sprang into action blindfolding Spunky, and positioned Sherry behind his head. She would be close at hand, but safely out of harm's way.

"Just whisper sweet things in his ear" I advised Sherry as Spunky twitched and jerked on the ground.

I wound a soft cotton rope around Spunky's left rear leg, and handed the rope to Jake. Jake was still squatting down, with his forearm balanced across his knees, and his forehead resting on his forearm. He couldn't see anything, but he stuck out one trembling hand to hold the rope.

"Jake, keep this leg up and out of the way for the surgery." I raised Spunky's leg and Jake took up the slack on the rope. I quickly scrubbed the surgical site, sprayed it with antiseptic, and began scrubbing my hands. As I put on my surgical gloves, Spunky began to relax. As he got deeper under the anesthetic his muscles quit twitching and his breathing became slow and deep. Jake's white knuckles kept a firm grip on the rope without moving from his squatted position.

I picked up the scalpel to make the incision.

"Is this okay?" I heard Jake's trembling voice behind me. He was too wobbly to stand, and was making certain that he couldn't see what I was doing. Jake kept tension on the rope by leaning back keeping himself as far away from the surgery as possible.

"That's fine Jake. Keep up the good work," I mused.

Spunky was ready, so I made the incision.

I was used to young men fainting during castrations, but never had that problem with women. If women can't tolerate the sight of surgery, they stay home. Some men don't want to be present, like George, so they stay away. But for the last few castrations a young man who really didn't need to be there, like the owner's brother, or a neighbor's son, came eagerly to watch, and then passed out. At least Jake was asked to be there by Sherry, but I wasn't sure how much help he'd be if we really needed him. And during surgery, I am too busy to help these "designated fainters."

I Make Horse Calls

As I performed Spunky's routine surgery, my mind wandered to the first case of fainting boys I had seen. It occurred in Dr. Wight's practice where I assisted in surgery. There were three veterinarians in the practice, Dr. Wight and the Sinclair brothers, and surgery required two surgeons and an anesthesiologist. If an emergency occurred elsewhere in the practice during surgery, no one could leave. Dr. Wight asked me to assist him in surgery so one of the brothers could take emergencies. I was flattered when he asked, and accepted his offer, assisting as often as possible. It was a good opportunity to learn from experienced practitioners.

One day a junior high school class came to Dr. Wight's surgery for a career day field trip. The surgical procedure scheduled for that day was a cryptorchid castration - removal of a testicle that was lodged up in the horse's abdomen, rather than in the scrotum where it should be. Cryptorchid surgery requires a larger incision, and must be performed in a sterile operating room. It also takes longer than a routine castration, so for the horse's safety we used gas anesthesia, which requires specialized equipment and monitoring.

The colt was being prepared for anesthesia when the students arrived, and Dr. Wight and I were in the final stages of scrubbing ourselves for the surgery. Dr. Wight told the students that if they felt faint, they should sit down, rather than risk falling into the operation. I thought this was an odd remark. But I was a new graduate, unaware of the high incidence of fainting among young men during surgery.

Dr. Wight's operating room was only about ten feet by ten feet, barely big enough for two surgeons and our equine patient. When the horse was on its back, his neck extended through the only way out - the doorway which connected the operating room to pre-op. The anesthesia machine was in pre-op, where Dr. Sinclair would sit at the horse's head during surgery. Conditions were even more cramped when 17 observers were present, pressed against the walls of the operating room.

Most of the students seemed less than enthused about being there. As the surgery was about to begin, all of the female students and the female teacher left the operating room, before the horse's head blocked the way out.

All of the boys stayed.

I Make Horse Calls

The horse was draped for surgery. Dr. Wight began the surgery with a large incision in the horse's abdomen.

One of the boys fainted - hitting the floor with a thud.

Dr. Wight again urged the others to sit down if they felt faint.

Dr. David Sinclair was an older gentleman, with beautiful silver hair and a great laugh. He had a kind expression, a bit like Santa Claus. To get the boy out of harm's way, Dr. Sinclair crawled awkwardly through the doorway on his hands and knees, under the surgery table. The task was made more difficult because Dr. Sinclair's midsection was also a bit like Santa's. He grabbed the boy by his heels and dragged him on his back out of the operating room.

None of the other boys sat down, but as soon as Dr. Sinclair removed the first boy, another one collapsed in a heap in the corner.

Dr. Sinclair checked the horse, then got back on the floor and retrieved the second limp body.

Thump!

The third boy hit his head hard on the edge of the surgical table when he fainted. I was concerned he had split his head open, but Dr. Wight and I were scrubbed into surgery, with our sterile gloves and gowns, so we couldn't assist Dr. Sinclair without risking our patient's life.

Back on his knees again, Dr. Sinclair removed the third victim, and reported that his head was unscathed. Apparently the boy had hit his forehead on the top of the padded table, and just slid down across the edge. He wouldn't have to call 911.

The fourth boy fainted, gently sliding down the side wall and landing near my feet.

Dr. Sinclair checked our patient's vital signs, and then he crawled around under the table, dragging the unconscious observer past my feet to the door.

When the fifth boy fainted, I wondered whose idea it was to spend career day observing surgery.

Dr. Sinclair was now getting red-faced and beads of sweat were appearing on his brow. Dr. Wight stepped back from the table so the latest casualty could be slid past the table's legs.

The sixth boy fainted, and then the seventh. Dr. Sinclair was winded, but I heard an occasional chuckle coming from pre-op.

I Make Horse Calls

In contrast to his classmates, the only boy left standing was enthusiastic about the surgery. He kept leaning over the incision pointing and asking "What's that?"

I knew who suggested the trip.

The surgery was easier than anticipated, and we were soon closing the incision. Dr. Sinclair had to hurry to get the last bodies out. Soft moans were coming from pre-op as we closed the wound.

By the time Dr. Sinclair dragged the last oblivious student out of the surgery, we were done. It was a good thing, as this horse would be ready to get to his feet in a few minutes, and would need the entire operating room. Once the operating table was lowered into the floor, the padded floor and walls made a safe environment for a drowsy, unstable horse to recover from anesthesia.

Because horses are so heavy, their body weight impairs circulation to the legs on the downside even when lying on thick mats. Equine surgeons use the phrase "Time is trauma to a horse under anesthesia" so we had an obligation to get the horse up as soon as possible. We quickly lowered the surgery table, disconnected the gas anesthesia and gathered up our drapes and instruments. We couldn't leave anything in the room that could injure the horse as he tried to regain his feet.

When I walked into the pre-op room, I was startled to see the bodies of seven bewildered boys arranged along the edge of the room with their backs on the floor and their legs sticking straight up the walls. Dr. Sinclair had placed them in that position to assist the blood flow returning to their heads. They were moaning as they came to, still pale and a bit green around the gills.

"Where am I?"

"What happened?"

The sight of those dazed young men made me chuckle. Dr. Wight just smiled. He had seen it all before.

Back to reality. Spunky's surgery had gone like clockwork. I was done in no time and miraculously Jake managed to stay conscious, if not totally upright, the entire time. I put antiseptic powder in the incision and told Jake to let go of the rope, but that I'd need him again when Spunky tried to stand. I moved my surgical supplies out of Spunky's way and pulled off my sterile gloves.

I Make Horse Calls

"Sherry, the surgery went just fine. Now it will be your job to hand walk him ten minutes twice a day for two weeks, beginning tomorrow. That will help reduce swelling, and promote drainage, lessening the risk of infection."

"You're done already? That was fast!"

"Yeah, I had to be done before the anesthetic wore off."

I picked up Spunky's lead rope.

"Spunky will probably sleep a few more minutes. But be careful. He could jump up any time now, without warning. We'll leave the blindfold in place until he starts moving. Then take it off so he can get his bearings. When he begins to come around, we'll encourage him to roll onto his chest and stay there for a few seconds before he stands. When he is flat out, the blood flow to his brain is diminished. If he jumps rapidly to his feet, he may fall, injuring himself or us.

"We'll see if Spunky will take it easy and let us help him."

I was hoping Spunky would be sensible, but I didn't really expect him to cooperate. He was a hot-headed young Thoroughbred, with no training. He had proven dangerous to Sherry and George, but this surgery should change his attitude.

Jake was coming around, too, and just in time. It seemed that since Spunky's ordeal was over, Jake was feeling better.

As luck would have it, Spunky soon bolted straight to his feet without warning. There was no keeping him down. Sherry was able to grab the blindfold as he got up. As soon as he had his feet under him, Spunky began to sway. As he leaned to the left, Jake grabbed him. Jake's strong arms supported Spunky's head and neck, while I ran around to the opposite side to support Spunky's body.

A rough recovery could lead to serious injury, but there was little to do now but try to steady the colt. A hard fall can fracture a horse's leg, or injure the facial nerve, resulting in a paralyzed lip. Spunky was in a safe location, and with Jake's help everything would turn out okay. My professors in vet school repeatedly told us to "Hope for the best, but prepare for the worst."

I'm glad I listened.

At times like this I try not to let the owners hear any concern in my voice. If I sound concerned, they will magnify those feelings, sometimes into panic. I had done all I could, and Spunky would be okay. At least, I hoped so.

"You're doing a great job, Jake. Just keep him steady. He'll get stronger every minute."

For the next few minutes Spunky looked like a 750 pound fish out of water, staggering around the meadow, but we kept him from falling, and gradually he grew steadier on his feet. When he started nibbling at the grass I knew he was coming around. When he could stand without support I handed him over to Jake and I went to my truck to clean my instruments, keeping an eye on them in case Spunky got out of control.

Jake and Spunky were recovering nicely from their ordeals. By the time I had everything washed up Spunky could stand and walk without swaying. He let out a feeble whinny, and Destiny responded from the barn.

I called to Jake from across the paddock, "He looks like he's ready to go back to his stall now."

Jake slowly led Spunky back to his stall.

They went into the breezeway and I never saw Jake again.

"Boy, that was so quick and easy! You did a great job Doc T.!" Sherry said.

Quick yes, easy no. But Spunky was now a gelding.

"When you see Jake, thank him for his help. He really did a great job keeping Spunky from hurting himself," I said.

"Yeah, right," said Sherry sarcastically.

As I was packing away my surgical instruments, I asked Sherry what I should do with the Spunky's surgical "parts." I used to just dispose of them, but because of some rather bizarre requests my clients have made in the past, I never know just what to do with them any more. One client's young son had requested them for his "show and tell" project at school. Another client put them in a glass jar in the refrigerator next to her husband's beer. He had his wife schedule the surgery for a date when he would be out of town.

Sherry said to put them in the dumpster. I complied.

When I checked on Spunky in the barn, he had his head over the door, and looked awake. The bleeding was stopped.

"You can give him some grass hay, but just a little.

I Make Horse Calls

When Sherry tossed the hay in the manger, Spunky slowly went over and inspected it. He took a nibble.

"He's doing fine, Sherry."

As I was filling out the medical record and post-op care instructions, George came home from his delivery route.

He gave Sherry a big kiss, but stayed far away from my truck.

"How's Spunky?" George asked Sherry.

"He's fine, honey! The surgery went great! It was all over in ten minutes. He's back in the barn munching away on his hay," said Sherry.

"Where did you put his...uh...his...parts?" George asked sheepishly.

When Sherry said they were in the dumpster, I thought George would faint!

In the short time since I met the Ortons, Destiny and Spunky had needed so much veterinary care that I had gotten to know them well. I knew Sherry had a good sense of humor, and having had my fill of fainting men, I couldn't resist asking George, "Would you prefer a burial in the backyard and a short memorial service?"

Without replying, George headed up to the house.

As I drove out the lane I was more convinced than ever that some young men take castrations much too personally!

Chapter 15 Dead Man's Curve

It was 10:30 PM, and the weather outside was not fit for man or beast. On this winter's night the wind was howling, the temperature was hovering around zero, and the snow was flying. I had just finished watching the local weather report on television and the whole region was socked in with snow, although it would be tapering off, and the clouds would clear before sunrise. The good news is that winter is my slowest season of the year. Broodmare practitioners have to get up every night during foaling season, as the night watchmen check on their pregnant mares every hour throughout the long winter's nights. But I worked primarily on performance horses, not breeding animals. My clients rarely checked on their horses in the middle of the night.

I had set my electric blanket on simmer, so I could wrap up in warmth tonight. Clancy staked her claim on the foot of the bed. She loved the electric blanket as much as I did. I turned off the TV and headed to bed.

As I walked down the hall to my bedroom my pager went off, sending a chill up my spine. I knew I could soon find myself on the roads, risking life and fender, as required of veterinarians in rural practice. Clancy perked up a single ear, but did not budge from her warm roost.

Why hadn't I chosen a normal job?

I called my answering service, and was told I had a call from Cathie Ferrari. I didn't have a client named Cathie Ferrari. My practice was still small enough that I knew all of my clients. Maybe I could get her to use her regular vet, and I could spend the night snuggled in my warm bed.

"This is Dr. Thibeault. What can I do for you?" I tried to sound pleasant.

I Make Horse Calls

"You don't know me, but I adopted Goliath. You remember him. He was the stallion rescued by Horse Helpers after that truckload of horses turned over on the interstate. You treated him while he was at the shelter."

I did remember Goliath. He was a massive sorrel Quarter Horse stallion a rancher had used to breed horses for his cattle ranch. The ranch had fallen on hard times, and the stallion found himself on a truck bound for the slaughterhouse. The driver was speeding down the mountain, ignoring the flashing lights and warning signs at the approach to Dead Man's Curve. He lost control and rolled the semi off the hillside. Fortunately the stallion survived the accident and never made it to the slaughterhouse. Forty horses on the truck and several innocent people died in the accident. The four lucky equine survivors went to Horse Helpers' shelter for a new chance at life.

We found out later he had a fancy, registered name, but he was such a big, muscular horse that his nickname from the shelter stuck.

"What's the problem?" I asked Cathie.

"While I was at work he opened the door of the horse trailer and got into the feed. I bought two 50 pound sacks of grain yesterday, and most of it is gone. Because he's a stallion, and the dominant member of the herd, I can't believe he'd let the other horses eat anything. He is so sick now that he can't move. I can't even get him out of the storm into the barn."

"Where is he now?"

"He's pastured down the road from my house in Rocky Cliff."

Rocky Cliff? The small town was miles beyond the range of my practice, up a steep mountain canyon. It would be a dangerous drive tonight. Surely there was another vet closer to her. Please, let there be another vet closer to her!

"That's a long way from me. You are definitely out of my practice area. Can you find someone closer?" I tried to sound professional.

"I called Dr. Mount, but he has the flu. So I called the Johnson Valley Clinic, and they said they would be glad to treat him, but because I was so far away I would have to bring him in. The roads are too icy to risk pulling a trailer tonight."

I Make Horse Calls

That's crazy, I thought. Taking a four-wheel drive out tonight would be dangerous enough. No sane person would suggest pulling a horse trailer in this storm. But I really didn't want to go. There must be another vet closer...

"What about Dr. Jeffers? His practice is closer to you."

"I called him, too. His truck is broken down and in the repair shop. All of his equipment is in it, and the shop is locked for the night."

Why wasn't I smart enough to think up such excuses?!

I couldn't think of any other vets who could help Goliath. This horse could not wait until the roads were cleared in the morning. The next few hours were critical, like the "Golden Hour" in human trauma care. It was up to me.

"Okay, I'll come. Give me directions."

"Oh, thank you so much! I'd really appreciate your help tonight."

"Meet me at the Feedbag Restaurant at the corner of Highway 71 and High Mountain Road." Cathie requested.

"Can't you give me directions to the ranch? Goliath needs to be treated as soon as possible."

Here we go again. I had been through this with Mr. Filbert. Meeting at a location besides the farm would delay Goliath's treatment, and make my night even longer.

"It's such a hard place to find - no lights or sign at the turnoff, way back up the canyon. It would be best to meet you at the restaurant."

"Okay, I know the place. I've eaten there before. I'll meet you there in 40 minutes."

"Oh, the roads are so terrible. You'll never make it up the mountain in 40 minutes."

"Yes I will, and you'd better be there waiting."

"Okay. I'll be there!"

I hung up and put on as many clothes as I possible. This horse would need intensive treatment throughout the night, which would be somewhere between unbearable and impossible if I wasn't properly dressed. I might well be outside until dawn. Clancy continued to watch me, but thought I might just be dressing warmly for bed.

181

I Make Horse Calls

But when I grabbed my coat and keys, Clancy leapt off the bed and ran to the back door, where she began spinning and whining. She always knew when we were going out, and she loved to romp in the snow.

"Clancy, how can you be so eager to go out in the middle of the night in a snowstorm like this?" I grumbled under my breath.

Oh well, I should let her enthusiasm rub off on me. Border collies are known for their high energy, and I could use some more energy at this time of night. Besides, she was a warm body, willing to keep me company on this frigid night. My great-grandfather, Tom Hogan, had a Border collie named Pat, who was his constant companion. I was lucky Clancy had chosen me and would be my companion for tonight's adventure.

My Mother was now retired, and attended every appointment and emergency call, except when she and Dad were traveling. Tonight my parents were in Florida, so I would be tackling this job without Dr. Mom. The vision of my parents sunning themselves on the beach in the Gulf of Mexico only made me feel colder as I pulled my collar up to my ears.

My boots crunched on the snow as I walked to my truck. The sound always reminded me of ski trips. But those outings were during the day when the mountain sun was shining brightly. And I could come inside to sit by the fire and sip hot cocoa if I got cold. The crunching tonight meant that it was every bit as cold as the weatherman said, and I had a long night ahead of me. No lights. No barn. The poor horse is standing out in this fierce storm, unable to move. Soon we would be freezing beside him, trying to save his life.

I wondered how close I could get to him with my truck.

I wondered if I could save him. He was desperately ill.

I'd be lucky to be back before sunrise.

I wondered if I'd get frostbite.

"Get in Clancy. We have to hurry. Goliath needs help."

I was relieved when my truck started right up despite the frosty conditions. I had enough gas to make the trip, so at least I wouldn't be delayed trying to find a gas station open at this hour. I always bring the truck home with a tank full of gas because I know if I have to go out before morning, I'll be in a hurry.

182

I Make Horse Calls

The roads were snow packed and sanded, and slippery. As I climbed up the first canyon road, I passed Dead Man's Curve - the dangerous downhill stretch of road where unsuspecting drivers miscalculated the steepness of the hill and the tightness of the curve, and lost their lives. There were warning signs and flashing lights, but drivers disregard the warnings and continue to lose their lives there. Goliath nearly died there.

Oh well, I was going uphill. I wouldn't have to deal with Dead Man's Curve until I was coming home. The driving conditions were so bad I had no time to think about how I would treat Goliath. I had to concentrate on driving. Finding the lane and staying in it kept me busy. My first concern was just to get to Goliath as fast as possible without killing myself in the process.

As I started up the steepest stretch of the mountain I felt the rear wheels of my truck slide to the right. The roads must be extra slippery tonight, because my truck was normally sure-footed. With four-wheel drive, heavy duty tires, and the weight of my equipment, I rarely lost traction. My clients depend on me, so I keep my vehicle in top running order, but even that wouldn't keep me safe tonight. I had to slow down.

About halfway up the hill, my alternator gauge started to waver. Great! Now my car was going to be a problem! I turned off the heater, put my lights on low beam, and hoped the restaurant would appear out of the snow around the next bend. As it began to get colder in the truck, Clancy left her position riding shotgun, and pressed her furry body against my leg for warmth. I put on my heavy gloves. It felt awkward to drive in ski gloves, but I would need feeling in my fingers to examine Goliath.

I finally saw the light in the restaurant window through the blinding snow. The restaurant had long since closed for the evening, but the light represented some semblance of civilization. I was disheartened to see the parking lot was empty. Cathie was not there.

I had to keep the engine idling, because with the extreme cold and the malfunctioning alternator, I couldn't risk my truck not restarting. To come this close, but be unable to get my equipment to Goliath's side, was unthinkable.

Clancy looked around to see why we stopped, then pushed harder against me. We kept each other warm while we waited.

I Make Horse Calls

I checked my watch. I was right on time. If Cathie was as desperate as she sounded, why wasn't she here? Surely she would come soon. I hate to hurry up and wait.

Fifteen minutes crept by, feeling like an eternity. I kept checking my watch, and checking the gauges as the gas idled away. If my truck wouldn't start after I treated Goliath, maybe I could spend the night at Cathie's and call a mechanic in the morning.

I hoped it wouldn't come to that.

After 20 minutes I walked around the parking lot trying to stay warm. I found a pay phone and called Cathie's house, but there was no answer. Hopefully she was on her way.

Finally, headlights appeared out of the snow. The ancient yellow Chevy pick-up had obviously seen better days, but with four-wheel drive it churned through the deep snow. The passenger window rolled down. Below the hat and above the scarf, came out "Oh, you beat us here!" It was Cathie with her trainer Kris.

"Yes, and I almost left, I've been waiting so long." I was cold, stressed and mad.

I hate the cold, and to go out of my way for someone I don't even know, on dangerous roads, and then to be kept waiting - grrr.

Cathie climbed into my truck. Clancy jumped on her lap and began licking her chin. Clancy loved her right away. That softened my anger. If Clancy liked her, I probably would too.

"I really appreciate you coming, and I apologize for being late. I don't know how you made it up the mountain so fast in this storm," said Cathie.

"Well, I always drive like it's an emergency, and this time it is. My 'veterinary commute time' is shorter than most people think."

"Thank you so much for coming. He's really bad. I've never seen a horse so sore," she said as she removed her hat and pulled off her gloves.

I carefully followed Kris' truck to the pasture, about five miles down winding mountain roads to the junction, and then west up a narrow canyon.

Cathie filled me in on the details as I drove. The snow got deeper the further we went up the mountain.

"I'm a nurse, and worked a 12 hour shift today. He was fine when I checked the horses at 8 AM, before I left for work. I got home around 9 PM. When I found him in the pasture, he was too sore to move. I was on the phone for over an hour trying to get help before I found you. After you agreed to come, I called Kris. Thank goodness she came and together we got him inside. We don't really have a proper barn, but we have a portable stall set up in the field."

We drove and drove through the storm in total darkness. When the truck ahead of me finally turned and stopped, Kris got out and opened the gate. I followed her in. There was no way I would have found this place in the storm.

There was just a single stall - no breezeway with cross-ties, no electricity, and no heat, but at least we were out of the wind. It was pitch dark inside. There was no way to park with my headlights on the stall. I'd have to rely on a flashlight. Working in the dark always made a difficult situation worse.

Through their heroic efforts, Cathie and Kris had practically carried Goliath into the stall. He was wearing a thick, warm blanket but I could see he was miserable. The pain in his feet had him constantly shifting his weight from one leg to the other, trying to get his weight off one foot at a time. As I put the cold ends of the stethoscope into my ears, I feared I might be too late.

I'd never seen a horse that had eaten so much grain. He couldn't walk because he had absorbed too many carbohydrates. Grain overload usually causes abdominal pain before the horse's feet get sore. If I'm called right away, I can relieve the stomachache and prevent foot problems before they occur. Coating the horse's stomach with mineral oil, if done soon enough, helps prevent absorption of the toxic by-products.

But Goliath's condition was way past that point. The carbohydrates were already in his bloodstream, preventing blood from flowing to his feet. If a ruptured stomach didn't kill him, he was at risk of permanent damage to his feet, resulting in severe pain for the rest of his life. His prognosis was terrible. If he didn't die, he might be so crippled we would have to destroy him.

It was now nearly midnight. The feed had been in his system for hours.

Goliath's pulse was racing - three times normal.

"He's really bad, isn't he?"

"Yes, I'm afraid he is."

I Make Horse Calls

I put my stethoscope over his belly. His intestines were churning nonstop - the carbohydrates were wreaking havoc with his insides, producing enormous amounts of gas, stretching his intestines near the point of rupture. I pulled the stethoscope out of my ears.

I ran my fingers down Goliath's lower legs. My fingers were freezing, but I could feel the blood pounding in the small arteries above his hooves. Normally the digital pulse is too subtle to detect, but even the numbing cold couldn't hide Goliath's pulse. In these cases, blood goes through a shunt and returns to the heart without nourishing the hoof. I had to restore the blood flow now.

The pain in his feet was so bad Goliath just stood there, shifting his weight from foot to foot, trying to ease his pain.

"His pulse is way too fast, and his intestines are overactive. It's very bad, but he's alive, so he has a chance."

The sooner treatment is begun, the better. Cathie had called as soon as she found him. She had done her best, and had certainly been persistent in finding me. Now I had to give Goliath my best. He would die without aggressive treatment, and I hadn't come all this way to lose my patient.

I went to my truck for medications. The snow had stopped, and the moonlight peeking through the thinning clouds cast a silver glow on the fresh snow. As pretty as it was, I knew that as the clouds cleared, the temperature would continue to drop. It would become even colder.

Back in the dark stall, Kris pointed the flashlight at his neck. I injected two medications into Goliath's jugular vein, one to ease his pain, and one to open the capillaries in his feet. If blood flow resumed quickly the coffin bone might not come free from the hoof wall and rotate downward through the bottom of his hoof.

When I treated Goliath after the accident on Dead Man's Curve, I noticed a previous injury on one foreleg, but he was tough and managed to do his work anyway. That toughness would be called upon tonight, but he couldn't afford any more leg problems,

While the medications were coursing through his veins, I returned to the truck for some local anesthetic. By numbing his feet, I could relieve his foot pain and stop the spasms in his blood vessels that were hampering the blood flow even more. I usually raise the hoof, holding it between my knees while I inject the anesthetic, but

186

I Make Horse Calls

Goliath was in so much pain that he couldn't stand on one hoof long enough for me to hold the other one. I did the nerve blocks with him standing on both feet. The stoic stallion didn't flinch.

Even if the anesthetic was too late to save him, it would ease his suffering.

I tried to sound positive when I told Cathie "He should begin to feel better soon."

"Thank you," she said softly. She was duly concerned.

Cold weather also constricts the blood flow to the hooves, so I applied a thick layer of nitrofurazone ointment under plastic wrap and heavy bandages to increase the blood flow to Goliath's hooves and retain his body heat. Cathie had bedded the stall deeply in straw, but that wouldn't hold in his body heat as well as bandages. I also supported the soles of his feet with special bandages. It was hard to get the tape to stick in the cold weather, but it should last the night. Cathie's horseshoer could replace the wraps with special shoes the next morning.

Despite the pain, horses with founder rarely lie down. Goliath was tough. I knew he'd stay on his feet. He was a fighter.

I returned to the truck again for some warm water and my stomach tube. Because of a horse's unique anatomy, Goliath couldn't relieve the gas in his stomach by burping. But I could relieve it by passing a tube into Goliath's stomach.

The steam rose off the water as I carried the bucket into his stall. Its warmth softened the plastic tube, which had stiffened in the cold. It had to slide comfortably up Goliath's nose and into his stomach. Goliath put up no fight, which was unusual for him. When I treated him after the truck accident he was feisty and required sedation. He was too cooperative now. Either he knew we were trying to help him, or he was just too sick to care.

When the tube entered Goliath's stomach, gas came gushing out, easing his pain. He sighed and relaxed as the pressure was relieved.

"That helped. He looks a little better already," said Cathie.

I left the tube in place until no more gas was expelled. Then I put mineral oil down the tube to prevent absorption of any more of the carbohydrates. It was probably too late, but it was worth a try.

I Make Horse Calls

I needed x-rays to know how much damage his feet had already suffered, but there was no electricity to run my machine. Goliath couldn't be trailered on the roads tonight, and was too sore to walk anywhere. I needed to know if his coffin bones had already lost their attachments to the hoof wall and rotated towards his soles. If so, walking would make him worse. If they hadn't, walking would make him better by drawing blood to his feet.

Goliath's life depended on making the right decision, and without x-rays to tell me I'd have to rely on my intuition.

I was finished with my treatments, and it was time for Cathie and Kris to take over. Goliath was lucky that Cathie was a nurse.

The medications were working. Goliath's pulse was slower, and he stood quietly without shifting. If the medications did their job, blood should be returning to his feet, and walking was another way to encourage blood flow.

I made the decision to walk him.

"You have to walk him ten minutes out of every hour for the next 24 hours to stimulate the circulation in the feet. Also call your horseshoer and get some wedge shoes on him as soon as possible. Do it today! I'll leave you some medication for him."

"Can you give Goliath his medications by injection in the muscle?"

"Yes. I used to work as a vet tech in an equine practice. I can even give IVs if I need to."

"Excellent! That'll really help."

Goliath was due for some good luck.

I helped them get started. The three of us managed to push the stallion into the moonlit night for his first walk. He was barely creeping, but he was moving. He was better. It was a good sign.

I cleaned up my instruments as Goliath walked with Kris and Cathie.

When Cathie returned she said he was moving slowly, but he was much better than he was when she called me.

My truck started in spite of the alternator malfunction, and the three of us drove to Cathie's cabin to thaw out and discuss Goliath's care. I'd fill his prescriptions there.

Her steep driveway looked more like a ski jump than a road, but somehow we all climbed up safely.

188

I Make Horse Calls

A mountain cabin never looked so good. It was perched on the side of a mountain, surrounded by evergreen forest, and I'm sure when the sun came up the views would be spectacular. As Cathie opened the door, I could smell the smoke from the wood-burning fire and the heat bathed my frozen face in warmth.

Denis, Cathie's husband, greeted us warmly, as did the roaring fire he had going in the hearth. Her pack of dogs greeted us raucously at the door - a Yorkshire terrier named Tinkerbelle, a Borzoi named Bepoua, and a Boxer named Gretchen. In the corner was a large bird cage containing a gray, bald creature that kept squawking "I'm Wucky!"

Apparently Cathie had rescued a featherless cockatoo with a speech impediment.

Kris, Denis and I found chairs around the kitchen table and Cathie put some hot chocolate on the stove. Cathie's background as a horsewoman, a nurse, and a vet tech would help Goliath. If she had the dedication to follow my directions, his life might be saved. With the effort she put into finding me, she proved she was committed to getting Goliath through this ordeal.

As I laid out the medications on the kitchen table, I outlined the aftercare instructions. "Continue with the pain medication every four hours as needed. Give him the anti-inflammatory twice a day, IV or IM. Keep hand-walking him every hour for a full 24 hours, so you and Kris had better make a schedule.

"I need x-rays of his feet, so bring him to Green Meadow Farm on Wednesday. It's on this side of town, so you won't have to drive through Denver. He should be able to ride in a trailer by then."

Friends of mine owned Green Meadow Farm. The barn had electricity and was close to Cathie's farm, but within the boundaries of my practice. I wanted Goliath's trailer ride to be as short as possible, as it would be difficult to keep his balance in a moving trailer on sore feet.

I finished the most delicious cup of hot chocolate I thought I'd ever had. As I headed out into the frigid night, I was warmed by the compassion Cathie had for Goliath, and fueled by the optimism that we might win this battle.

The clouds had cleared and the moon and stars shone brightly. I knew the sun would soon be rising above the eastern plains. I stepped out into the clear mountain air, and wished Cathie "Good luck. You're going to need it."

Clancy had been attending to her duties as my personal canine seat warmer while I was inside, and she sniffed her way around the dog smells on my coveralls as she moved back to sit beside me. Luckily, my truck did not to have any more alternator problems, and got me safely down the mountain. I seemed to be blessed with ailing trucks that miraculously heal themselves.

When I got to Dead Man's Curve I crept around slowly. I didn't want to become another statistic here. In the pre-dawn hours I didn't have any traffic to concern me.

I fell into bed exhausted, knowing that Cathie, Kris, and Goliath would be freezing on the mountain all night, in a fight for his life.

He might just win. He'd rolled off the side of a mountain and made it. Maybe his luck would hold.

Cathie called me later that day. She had threatened her shoer with bodily harm until he rearranged his day's appointments so Goliath could have his prescription shoes by noon. The pain medication was working - Goliath stood on one front foot long enough for the shoer to work on the other.

The medications and shoes were helping.

"He's more alert and interested in eating." Cathie reported

The first milestone was passed. Goliath would not die of colic.

"That's great news! Now you need to come to my house for some nutritional supplements to help with his hoof growth. His hooves are damaged and we must strengthen them until the effects of the grain are gone."

"I'll be there after work tonight."

"Great! I'll leave the medications in the drop box behind my garden gate this afternoon."

I gave Cathie directions to my house.

Cathie arrived at my house just as I was returning from my day's calls. Her head appeared above the gate, and Clancy rushed over in excitement to greet her.

I Make Horse Calls

"She's some lousy watchdog. She'd let anyone in your yard."

"What do you mean? She's a great watchdog! Just ask the delivery men. She hates them. But she knows you. She sat on your lap last night and kissed you, so you're a friend for life."

I explained what the medications would do, and how to give them, and Cathie was off, up the mountain to treat Goliath.

Cathie followed my instructions exactly, Goliath cooperated, and things were going well. The true test would come when the x-rays were taken.

Wednesday dawned warm and sunny - quite a change from the last time I saw Goliath. I couldn't believe my eyes when he walked out of the trailer and into the barn at Green Meadows. The transformation was amazing. Most horses are still lame, despite corrective shoes and pain medication.

Kris had brought him down the mountain, as Cathie had to work. Goliath was walking well, and was even off most of his medications. That was a dramatic change from a few nights ago. When I picked up each hoof, the sole gave no indication that the coffin bone had rotated. The fact that he could stand comfortably on one hoof to let me examine the other hoof was very encouraging. I placed hoof testers over the tip of the coffin bone, and found remarkably little pain.

"Well, Kris, he looks so much better than I could even hope. You and Cathie have done a great job with him!"

Goliath was tough, and he had an excellent team providing his nursing care.

Kris told me of their adventures walking him that night on the mountain, while I set up the x-ray equipment.

"How come they never seem to get hurt in good weather? Cathie and I almost froze that night. She made a few runs to the house to replenish our thermos with coffee, and I kept the truck idling so we'd have a place to thaw out, but we both still nearly froze our fingers and toes. But that's the price we pay for living in paradise."

"I know. And if you could plan when they'd get hurt, you'd plan for it to be never."

"You're right about that!"

191

I Make Horse Calls

Goliath stood quietly, so Kris just dropped his lead rope and held the cassette containing the film. I aimed the x-ray machine. As I pressed the button, I said, "Smile."

Kris smiled, and then laughed out loud. "I can't believe I smiled."

I took several x-rays of each front hoof. As Kris loaded Goliath back in the trailer I promised to call later that day with the results of the radiographs.

Because I practice all over the countryside, I take my radiographs to any nearby human hospital, as they all have excellent equipment to process the films, resulting in high quality pictures. I don't take enough x-rays to justify the purchase of an automatic film processor that would need to be running every day. Today I would use Mountain View Community Hospital, as it was on my way home. The radiology technicians, Pat and Karol, look forward to my visits. The x-rays I take are a change from what they usually see. They always want to see my films, and get an explanation of the horse's problems. Veterinary medicine fascinates me, so I'm eager to share my enthusiasm.

Occasionally Karol will ask if I have any throwaways - pictures that aren't clear because the horse moves. She wants these films to play pranks on the radiologists on a slow day. If the radiologist has ordered an ankle x-ray, and the technicians put an x-ray of a horse's hock on the viewer, I can only imagine the response they get from the doctor. I oblige with films whenever I can.

As I unloaded the films and placed them in the processor, I was nervous. What would they show? Goliath looked really good when I took the films, considering how lame he had been only a few days before, but how much internal damage had been done? How much pain was being masked by the drugs? How stoic was he? I placed new film in my cassettes and left the darkroom.

By the time I got to the viewing room, the first films had already dropped out of the processor. The techs had gathered around, and the radiologist was curious too.

Flipping the first view on the light box, I could see that the front surface of the coffin bone was still parallel to the front surface of the hoof, meaning that there was absolutely no rotation - no permanent damage! How could that be? The view of Goliath's left

192

hoof was also normal. Goliath was unbelievably lucky! There was no permanent damage visible in either hoof.

However, the x-rays showed Goliath had previously fractured his pastern bone, the bone above the hoof. I noticed the bony thickening when I treated him for the trailer accident, but I thought it was just arthritis. Because it was an old injury and it didn't bother him, I hadn't taken x-rays when he was at Horse Helpers.

Happily, I explained the good news to the techs. But while human and equine medicine share many similarities, there really is no human counterpart for laminitis.

When I first saw Goliath on that snowy night, he was so sore he absolutely couldn't move. He had eaten a phenomenal amount of grain that would have killed most horses, yet he seemed to come through completely unscathed. It seemed miraculous.

I couldn't wait until I got home to give Cathie the good news.

"Karol. Can I use your phone?"

"Of course."

Karol led me to the waiting room and showed me the phone.

"Dial nine for an outside line."

"Thanks."

I was so excited, I was practically shouting into the phone.

"You won't believe it, Cathie, but Goliath's hoof x-rays are absolutely normal. There is no internal damage whatsoever!"

"That's tremendous. I'm so pleased. Doc, you really performed a miracle!"

"You and Kris did most of the hard work. And Goliath is one tough horse. You know that hard knot on his pastern? I thought it was just arthritis, but it's an old fracture, one that he had before the truck accident. Since it doesn't bother him, I'd leave it alone, but I thought you should know what it is. He's one lucky horse, surviving *three* accidents, any one of which would have killed a normal horse."

"Dr. Thibeault, thank you for all you've done."

"You are most welcome."

The good news is Goliath continued to do well, and now I care for all of Cathie's horses, and her friends' horses, and Kris's horses, and Kris's friends' horses...

I Make Horse Calls

And Cathie has never been late again. We've become good friends. Clancy was right.

The bad news is I am now driving up the mountain, around Dead Man's Curve, on a regular basis.

Chapter 16 Rocky's Championship Fight

It was a cold February morning. As I raised the blinds in my bedroom, my buckskin Quarter Horse, Rocky, tossed his head up and whinnied to me to hurry and feed him. If I had only peered between the slats of the closed blinds, I could have caught him dozing, standing in his paddock with his left side to the east, available to welcome the first rays of the morning sun and soak up its weak winter heat. But the moment the blinds went up, he knew breakfast was on its way and he sprang to life, stomping around his paddock, impatiently awaiting my arrival.

I loved living on this farm.

As my parents retired from work and began enjoying travel, my practice grew. I needed more space. While I wanted to spend my life living on a farm, my parents wanted someone to care for their home while they traveled, so it made sense to purchase a place together.

I grew up in the city and lived in college dorms until I entered vet school. Then I was lucky enough to find the small house in Fort Collins. I hated the tiny room in Los Angeles. It made me realize how important a country lifestyle was to me. I was eager now to find a place in the country where I could re-connect with the natural world, away from city noise and traffic.

While living in my parents' house had been a wonderful blessing because it helped me start my practice, it was time to have a place to call my own. Co-ownership was the best option for us all.

After a long search, we found the perfect farm. Ten acres felt like heaven for me, my family, and my animals. As a matter of fact, the realtor advertised the property as "Horse Heaven." But I knew that was not the best name for an equine veterinary clinic.

I Make Horse Calls

The farm was well laid out for conversion to a clinic, but it needed a lot of work. It had one six-stall barn which would become the clinic and several two stall barns in fenced paddocks. I could keep my horse separated from ill horses that came to the clinic. Although the fences were in disrepair, the farm had dozens of corral panels I could use for temporary fencing. And located only an hour's drive from the university, I could continue to refer difficult cases.

I would still do most of the work from my truck at the clients' farms, because my clients liked the convenience, but there were times when the clinic would be a lifesaver. There I could get my patients out of the wind, which contaminated open wounds, and a well-lit exam room would keep me from overlooking anything. It would shade me from the summer sun, and protect me from the winter chill. I could stay dry, and working out of the mud or dust was a welcome improvement over ambulatory practice. The barn doors could be closed, making it dark enough to do eye exams, which were impossible to do in the daylight. Once the improvements were made, it would be wonderful.

I cleaned and painted the barn, and put hiring an electrician on my list of things to do in the spring. The previous owner's teenage daughter had wired the barn, and it looked like it. Lightweight, poorly insulated indoor wire had been hooked into the control panel at the back of the house, run along the fence line and stapled in a few places to keep it off the ground. At the gate a tall stick on one side suspended the wire above the barn roof so the gate could open. The cable then ran under the front door through a tunnel in the ground, and up the inside wall to the rafters. Ten feet of excess wire was wrapped around the rafters a dozen or more times, and then a white porcelain fixture, dangling by a single, fraying strand of baling twine, held a bare light bulb.

We moved to the farm in August, so the long days meant I didn't need lights right away, and no patients would be invited until the facilities were ready. I removed the old wiring so the barn wouldn't burn down. Bringing the wiring up to code would keep my patients safe. In the spring I'd have lights everywhere and outlets for clippers and my x-ray machine.

The metal barn was well-built, and it was easy to disinfect its smooth interior walls. My parents and I went to work digging up the dirt floors to make room for new concrete floors and rubber mats. Although the native soil was sandy, the barn floor was packed as hard as granite by a decade of horses' hooves. The unyielding earth resisted the work of our maddux and pick axes.

We were elated when a neighbor offered the services of his strong son - a member of the high school football team - who would work for pay. We welcomed his strong back and hired him, but he lasted only two hours before quitting, saying the work was too hard at any cost.

When the young man gave up, it triggered a memory of my great-grandfather, Tom Hogan. He died decades before I was born, but he had such a strong influence on my Mother that she often repeats his favorite sayings.

Tom was a first generation American, born of Irish descent. He worked his whole life as a policeman in Baltimore, walking the beat with his nightstick before being promoted to detective. He was a tough guy with a soft heart.

Tom was fiercely determined. I inherited my determination from him. He continued to work at the police department after he was old enough to retire. His boss told him it was time, but Tom flatly refused, working several more years. Finally, his boss threw a retirement party for Tom. Tom politely went to the party, enjoyed the cake, and accepted his gold watch. But the following Monday morning Tom returned to his desk, rather gruffly evicting the young new detective seated in his chair. Tom continued to work until he was eighty. Then one day he fell ill. He went home from work and went to bed. Within a few days he was dead.

He was laid out in the front parlor of his house, as was the custom at the time. During the day the house was visited by officers and detectives on the police force, friends and neighbors, but at night a different crowd arrived. My Mother recalls, as a young child watching in the dim light from the top of the stairs, a motley array of Tom's former prisoners filing past, paying their respects. She overheard one of them telling the family that, even though Tom had arrested him many times, Tom always checked on his wife and kids while he was locked up, making sure they had enough to eat and were safe. Many of the people Tom arrested spoke kindly of him.

I Make Horse Calls

We remembered Tom's words: "The best place to find a helping hand is at the end of your own arm." And so we did.

With no one to help us, we finished digging up the barn floors by ourselves. My parents were in their late sixties, but they worked side by side with me. We laughed as we worked, thinking of how we did the job the strong young man had shunned.

It was a great day when the concrete floors were poured. The new surface was level, dust free and easy to clean. Rubber mats placed on top gave the horses cushioning and traction. New windows brightened the stalls and let in fresh air. I now had three clean stalls ready for my patients. Two had concrete floors, but one had fresh new sand for horses that might roll, and for foundered horses that needed sand to support their feet.

My attention turned to the landscape. The fields were so overgrown with weeds that I first named the farm "weed world" - at least until I got the tangled growth under control. We had prickly lettuce that towered six feet tall, blocking the view of the future clinic from the road. It took me two days, walking behind the old lawn mower, to level the front field. When I finished, the barn was once again visible to my neighbors who complimented me on painting the barn.

I had not painted the barn - I merely *found* it!

When I got around to repainting it the original colors, the building inspector stopped by, checking for a building permit for the new barn. I was flattered.

During my mowing I discovered not one single grass plant in the front field. The ground was covered with goatheads, low growing plants that produce thorns similar to thumbtacks - prone to puncturing skin and tires. I was plagued by flat tires on wheelbarrows and lawn mowers.

We also had sandburs which are small balls covered with barbs like fish hooks that skewer into everything they touch, including the hands that try to pull them off. I worked with the county extension agent and by necessity became an expert on agricultural weed control.

We took his advice and ordered grass seed - special variety of drought tolerate grass - for spring sowing. We planned flowers and sod for around the house, and shade trees and shrubs everywhere. We ordered 200 seedling trees which were to arrive at the fairgrounds in the spring. These trees were specifically adapted to the local climate and would grow to provide windbreaks and animal habitat. When I asked if I should bring the truck, or if I needed the horse trailer to get the trees home, the extension agent said that a shoe box would suffice. The seedlings were apparently a bit smaller than I had anticipated.

My Dad's talent lay in carpentry, which came in handy with farm repairs. He was so adept at wielding a handsaw that the tool virtually sang in his hands. He would lay his left thumb beside the blade, draw back on the handle to create a kerf, and then his long rhythmic strokes cut smoothly through the hardest of woods. He tried to teach me, but my strokes were always clumsy by comparison. The blade would chatter and jump out of the groove, leaving stray marks on the wood and endangering my left thumb. My skills with hand tools landed me in the emergency room for left thumb repairs.

I was safer with power tools that required both hands.

Dad learned his skills while a teenager, working as an apprentice carpenter. His job was to cut the wood along the lines the master carpenter laid out. The first day on the job he asked which side of the line he should cut on, and was told "The line goes in the sawdust." That phrase runs through my head every time I work in my wood shop.

Dad was exhausted by his day's work as an apprentice. He told me how easy his life became when the electric circular saw became available at the jobsite. Then he could work all day and not get tired. I cannot fathom hand-cutting each board to build an entire house. I inherited my Dad's love of woodworking, but I could never do it without power tools.

I was always fascinated by my Dad's woodworking projects. One of my earliest memories was when I was a toddler and watched him install tongue-and-groove maple hardwood floors in our upstairs bedrooms. I was mesmerized by the way the boards slid into each other and locked together. And the grain of the maple was beautifully smooth. The lumber was recycled from a bowling alley, and had a gorgeous golden patina.

In the hallway between the bedrooms Dad laid out a floor medallion, hand cutting each board from different wood species to create an intricate star pattern. He punctuated the point of each star with a circle sliced smoothly from a dowel. How he figured out the sizes and shapes of each board for a perfect fit was beyond my comprehension. My set of building blocks no longer held my interest. I wanted to do what he could do.

When I was a little older, Dad had a small workroom tucked into the corner of the basement. I was still small enough to be in danger of being hurt by the tools, but I wanted to be with him. He kept me safe and amused by sitting me on the floor with a two-by-four and a hand-operated drill, called an egg-beater drill because it had a wheel just like an old-fashioned hand operated egg beater. Turning the wheel made the drill bit turn. I couldn't hurt my fingers, because both hands had to be on the drill - one to hold it straight and one to turn the wheel. A soft piece of pine would keep me amused for hours. I would sit by his feet, watching him hand plane beautiful aromatic pieces of wood with the curls falling to the floor around me, soothed by the rhythm of his strokes.

I progressed to using a hammer and nails. He started the nails for me so I wouldn't bash my tiny fingers, and because I needed two hands to lift his hammer. Soon I was helping on real projects around the house. I learned so much at his side.

When I was in high school Dad built a garage so he had more room for his tools and work. He then finished the basement, making a living room, bedroom, and a built-in desk with an entire wall of bookshelves. He installed a fireplace and patio, and the trees he planted shaded the entire yard. While he always tinkered with cars, he turned his interest to restoring classic cars, focusing on the 1957 Thunderbird. By the time we bought the farm he had restored over 30 of them.

His career began as a carpenter's apprentice but after he and Mom were married he worked as a traveling salesman selling auto parts to dealerships. His mechanical inclination suited him to the job.

I vividly recall the sunny day he came home for lunch and took me for a ride in his company's red pick-up truck. Being a small child, I could barely see out the back window of our aging sedan, but riding in the truck's high seat made me feel ten feet tall. I could see over everything. Since the day I got my driver's license I have only owned pick-ups and Chevy Suburbans because of that one ride.

I Make Horse Calls

Dad later worked in the aircraft industry, for Glenn L. Martin Co. He ran a yoder-hammer - a machine that stamped out airplane wings. Standing at that machine for hours contributed to his later hearing loss, but he helped the war effort before being drafted.

When he returned from Germany after World War II he continued at Martin and went to college at night. When Martin made the move from airplanes to aerospace, Dad worked on the rockets. He coordinated work between the Denver and Baltimore plants that were building the rocket for Project Gemini - the two-man space flight. He reviewed contract specifications, assuring quality control. His job wasn't to send men into space; it was to return them safely to earth.

I smile when I hear "it's not rocket science" because for Dad, it always was.

After landing a man on the moon, the government cut back funding on aerospace research, and Martin laid off employees, including my Father. Dad went to work for Ball Aerospace in Boulder while I was in college there and he would treat me to lunch once a week. The change from dorm food was delightful and I looked forward to our meeting all week.

Over lunch one day I asked him about his job. He was a man of few words when it came to his own accomplishments. He told me that he was working on a telescope that would be launched into space and orbit the earth to observe the stars. It had to turn on at night, and turn off during the day, as it circled the earth, and transmit pictures back to earth. It was beyond my comprehension that such a marvelous instrument could be built. I didn't realize until years later that he helped build the Hubble Telescope.

When the project ended Dad was out of work again, but was nearing retirement age, so he went to work for a local home improvement store and rode his bike to work every day in his 60s. His career in aerospace no longer existed when the government withdrew funding. Seeing him struggle, I decided to choose a career in medicine - a field that would not disappear due to changing economic or political whims.

Dad loved working with his hands, but at our house in town he had done every imaginable home-improvement project. There was nothing left to do. He would walk around the property, but it really seemed like a part of him was missing until we bought the farm.

Working on projects at the farm filled him with renewed energy. He now had more projects than he could ever finish, and he jumped right in. One of our first projects was to build a big garage and workshop, our headquarters for farm improvements. A builder did the framing and roofing, but Dad and I worked together insulating and hanging drywall. He put in lights and heat, and a refrigerator for my medical supplies. It was good to work by his side again, as we had grown apart during the years when I was in high school, away on the horse show circuit and in college.

He had always helped me purchase and maintain my trucks, although I could tell I had disappointed him by buying Chevys. He was a Ford man - an expert around a Ford. But at the time Ford did not make an SUV, which was the perfect vehicle for me.

My first vehicle was a 19 year old, $200 pick-up truck, which I used to haul hay to my horse. The steering was so bad I couldn't go over 50 without the wheel shaking too hard to hold. I'm sure my Dad planned it that way - for my safety. Plus it was as heavy as a tank - slow and clumsy, but almost indestructible. I never had an accident in it, but I'm sure if I did, whatever hit me would have been the loser. It had mechanical problems so I learned about master cylinders and transmissions. And Dad made sure I could change a tire before he'd let me drive, although I found replacing a new tire on an old wheel to be strenuous work.

I bought my first Suburban when I was a riding instructor. It allowed me to take students and their horses to shows. When I became a veterinarian, my old suburban was outfitted with the custom cabinet Dad and I built. It was ideal for carrying medical supplies and better than any commercial unit available.

It was difficult to maintain the farm with equipment made for home use. The lawn mower was soon replaced with a riding model, and Dad found a 9-N Ford tractor. I thought it was for me - for farm chores, but soon learned it was for him - another restoration project. The end result was the most beautiful, fully restored 50-year-old tractor with fresh paint, new Ford decals, and a bright red, white, and blue umbrella to protect me from the damaging summer sun.

I Make Horse Calls

In honor of his hard work keeping my vehicles running I had a custom jacket embroidered for him with the practice logo, his name and his title - "Fleet Maintenance." Dr. Mom also got a jacket embroidered with "Veterinary Assistant." They wore them proudly.

Dr. Mom liked to paint, so she repainted every room in the house while Dad and I replaced and repaired fences. Dr. Mom then painted the fences while I painted the barns. Between the mowing, repairing and painting, the farm was beginning to look good. I looked forward to the day when I would proudly hang my shingle out front.

Our old yard in town was small and shaded by an ancient cottonwood, so few flowers would bloom, and the soil was hard clay. The new farm had no shade, and sandy soil - ideal for flowering plants. The soil was rich enough, but the lack of rain in this region meant only drought tolerant plants thrived here.

With the growing demands of practice I could no longer take long bicycle rides which would take me away from my truck. I had to find a hobby that I could drop in an instant if an emergency call came in. So I switched my energies to gardening. I was eager to dress this barren land in trees and flowers.

The farm soil grew healthy day lilies and iris, and red climbing roses soon draped across the new cedar picket fence. But most species of plants suffered from the severe climate and pests. The late freezes damaged the tulips, daffodils and lilacs in the spring, and a horde of hungry rabbits consumed the pansies as soon as they were planted. I found Dr. Mom laughing one day after watching a beautiful red tulip get sucked into the ground and disappear. Apparently pocket gophers loved bulbs, and took them through their tunnels to their nest. We found the nest's location when the tulips bloomed in the front pasture the following spring.

One of the farm's best features was an unobstructed view of the mountains, and the farmhouse was built to enjoy those views. Wide windows in the kitchen overlooked the horses grazing in the fields beneath the mountain backdrop. The sunsets were so gorgeous that each night we would stop what we were doing for a sunset alert - to enjoy and score each sunset. The living room window had five panes of glass spanning the wall from floor to ceiling, bowing out above the flower bed bursting with petunias. The old Boston rocker provided a front row seat to watch enormous thunderheads build above the Eastern prairie on a summer's eve. The golden and orange reflection of the last rays of day was offset by the dark sky and flashes of lightning beyond. The displays were still as spectacular as my childhood memories from the campfire site on the hillside.

I moved Rocky to the farm as soon as the fencing was safe. He was my only horse, but my neighbor had two mares, so he enjoyed their company over the fence. While I was outside gardening or doing chores, Clancy would be in Rocky's paddock keeping her watchful eye on him.

We all loved the farm.

Rocky kept up his impatient calling as I threw on my insulated coveralls. Clancy bolted through the doorway as soon as I told her it was okay and ran ahead of me to the barn. The sun was just coming up. The air was cold and clear, and I had a short book of appointments today, glad my work load was lighter in the winter.

All winter long the low grasses made it easier to see coyotes and foxes as they passed through the fields on hunting forays. Great Blue Herons flew to their nests at the nearby reservoir. Soon the silence would be broken by the meadowlark's call. By midsummer the killdeer would do their broken wing dances when I would unknowingly threaten their nests hidden on the ground. They foolishly nested in the most dangerous places - the riding arena or the driveway.

When I walked into Rocky's stall, I knew immediately that something was wrong. He hadn't finished his hay from the night before. He was in the paddock, and nickered to me as usual, but when he came into the stall for breakfast, he walked away without eating. He had left half of his dinner hay from yesterday. I always bought beautiful timothy hay, with no weeds or dust, and Rocky cleaned up every last bit. The saying "eats like a horse" is true. If a horse stops eating, it means he is in trouble. And Rocky really loved to eat.

I checked the hay he had left. It was fine - fresh and green, not moldy and it smelled sweet, like newly cut grass. I got my stethoscope and thermometer. Rocky stood motionless while I examined him. Temperature, pulse, respiration rate, gum color, gut sounds – everything was normal. The manure in his paddock was normal, although there wasn't as much as usual, which would be expected if he wasn't eating. My paddocks were sandy and dry, with no flattened places indicating Rocky had been rolling. He showed no signs of stress or pain, so it didn't look like an average colic. I checked the water trough. Occasionally a bird will drown in the tank trying to get a drink or a bath. No birds today - the water tank was sparkling clean. I scrubbed it twice a week.

Rocky had eaten some of his hay, and most horses with colic go off feed entirely. His manure was normal, so his intestines seemed to be functioning. He had been vaccinated and dewormed on schedule and no sick horses had been in my clinic recently, plus his normal temperature ruled out infection. The soil was sandy, so sand colic was possible, but I treated him regularly with psyllium to remove sand from his intestines, and always fed his hay over rubber mats that I swept free of sand daily.

Because he didn't seem painful and he was still eating some hay, I gave him a mild pain reliever and went about my regular schedule of appointments. As I drew up the medication I wished I didn't have to travel so far from the farm on my rounds today. Dr. Mom and Dad were at the beach in Florida, so no one would be around to keep an eye on him. Rocky would be in the back of my mind all day, but surely he would be alright.

I returned my clients' calls as usual at 8 AM, and then checked on Rocky again before Clancy and I began our rounds. His condition hadn't changed.

As I drove, I kept thinking about Rocky. What could be causing him not to eat? The hay was beautiful. His vital signs were all normal, but something was wrong.

I hurried through my day's appointments, not shortchanging anyone, but leaving promptly at the end of each appointment without stopping to chat.

When I arrived home that night, Rocky was standing in the paddock and whinnied to me as I drove in. I was glad to see he was standing and showed no signs of distress or pain. Maybe he was better.

I went to his stall right away to check on him. He was no better. There was hay left in his manger. He had eaten half of his breakfast, and produced half of his normal amount of manure. The water level in the tank had dropped slightly, so he was drinking. He still had not been rolling in the paddock, and showed no signs of sweating or distress. I repeated my exam with the same results.

I couldn't wait any longer, not knowing the cause. It might be something serious, but what? When the physical examination doesn't lead to a diagnosis, blood tests may give the answer. If the results come back normal, there may not have been a serious problem. I drew blood right away. If the sample was ready by 7 PM, the lab would pick it up and run the tests tonight. I would have results when I awoke in the morning.

I checked on Rocky again before I turned in for the night, but there was no change. He seemed fairly bright and aware of his surroundings, but he just picked at his hay. Something was wrong, and by morning maybe I would know what it was and how to help him.

I couldn't sleep well that night, worrying about Rocky. Vets, at least my female colleagues, admit they fall apart when their own animals are sick. We know all the complications that can occur and envision our animals suffering every one. We lose our objectivity when the patient is our own.

And I'm one of the worst for worrying.

In my insomnia I reflected on the circumstances that brought Rocky into my life.

Rocky was a tall, handsome buckskin gelding. He stood just over 16 hands high, with four white stockings and a blaze, and a lovely temperament. His registered name was Leo Lorenz, but everyone called him Rocky. He had big, expressive brown eyes and a broad forehead, which horsemen think indicates intelligence. He was smart enough to win my heart. He was big boned. Quarter Horse judges don't like horses with big feet, but veterinarians know that small feet may mean lameness problems. Rocky had huge feet, and never had any lameness problems arising from his feet.

When I first laid eyes on Rocky, he was standing in a large open pasture where I boarded a mare I had leased. I was told his owners no longer wanted him because he had frightened his young owner so badly she refused to ride him. Several buyers tried him, but none got along with him. They were too forceful and he wouldn't tolerate their rough handling. His huge size belied his gentle nature.

I Make Horse Calls

They tried him at barrel racing and polo, but his bulk made him handle more like a limousine than a sports car, so his test rides were brief. Tipping the scale at 1550 pounds, agility was definitely not his middle name.

The first time I rode him I foolishly broke the rule of safe horsemanship, but he never put me in danger. I walked into the pasture, threw a halter on him, and took him to my truck. I dropped the lead rope and he stood ground-tied while I groomed him, tacked him up and climbed on.

I rode to the arena, reached down and opened the gate from his back, and he moved obediently away from the slight pressure of my leg so we could pass through and close the gate. He walked, jogged and loped smoothly, backed through rails laid on the ground, and walked willingly over the bridge. Considering that he hadn't been ridden in months, and that his last rides were by strangers interested in buying him, I was impressed by his willingness to please. And he seemed happy to be getting attention.

Now that I am older and wiser, I always have the seller ride first to demonstrate that their horse is trained before I climb on. Rocky's owner wouldn't ride him, or even come to the farm any more, but Rocky was a perfect gentleman.

I couldn't afford to buy a horse at the time, so I talked a client of mine, Dave, into buying him. Dave's daughter outgrew her horse, so he was looking for another horse. He rode Rocky and bought him on the spot because of his good looks. His riding buddies would be impressed when they saw him astride such a powerful and attractive mount.

Dave took him home but soon had second thoughts. He purchased Rocky in the fall, and his daughter would be involved with school activities until spring, so Rocky sat in his field unused.

I had the perfect solution. I liked Rocky, but couldn't afford the purchase price. I could probably afford board, but if I leased him and ran into financial difficulties, I could just return him to his owner at the end of the month before the next board bill was due.

Winter was my slow season, and if I found an affordable stable with an indoor arena, I could ride all winter. So we struck a deal and I returned the mare I had leased. Rocky became mine, almost.

I Make Horse Calls

We had a great winter together. He loved going on the trails, but didn't care for the indoor arena, and jumping was not his forte, especially jumps with plastic flowers.

Rocky had a lovely temperament, and would do anything I asked, but if I got demanding, he would object, giving me a gentle warning by rearing up a few inches to show his displeasure. I would ease off. Then he would agreeably do what I wanted, if I asked politely. We quickly developed a kind relationship and I safely rode him everywhere. He trained me to be a gentle rider.

We crossed deep water in cool mountain streams, and ran with the deer and the coyotes in mountain parks. He was fearless, surefooted and cooperative. He was calm, and careful. We were a perfect match. He was the horse I'd been looking for all my life. He never betrayed my trust.

Come spring, Dave gathered him up after we watched his daughter ride him. I gave her some pointers on what I'd learned about his personality and they hit it off great. She loved him.

I was getting busier with a growing book of appointments, so I had little time to miss him, and knew he had a good home.

A few days later I got a call Rocky was for sale - he was a terrible horse! Dave threatened to sell him to Gene, a beginner rider who weighed 300 pounds, just because Rocky was big enough to carry the weight. I knew Rocky would object to Gene's handling, as I had seen him bouncing around on his horse's back, jerking on the reins and nearly falling off whenever the horse responded to his commands.

Dave put a high price on the horse and offered him to me, knowing I couldn't watch Rocky be abused. Gene was a roughneck with no riding skill, and I feared Rocky might hurt him and wind up at an auction being sold for horse meat if he got a bad reputation.

In the time I'd had him he'd been a delight, so I had to find out what was wrong.

Dave was vague about why he was selling Rocky, but another of my clients, Alex, later told me the story of the events that had Rocky looking for a new home.

Alex had been riding his horse alongside Rocky the day he caused so much trouble. It seems that Dave rode him in the Easter parade to show off his beautiful new horse to his buddies. He wore

I Make Horse Calls

large, Mexican rowel spurs and used a severe western curb bit because it matched his image of a cowboy, but he didn't know how to use this tack properly. He couldn't ride well enough to sit still, so he kept unintentionally gouging his sharp spurs into Rocky's sensitive sides. But Dave didn't want to go faster, so he kept pulling on the bit.

Rocky didn't know what to do. The conflicting messages of the cruel spur - go forward, and the painful bit - stay here, gave him no way to please this rider, so he went up, rearing on his hind legs and, as Alex tells the story "hopping down the road like a 1500 pound rabbit."

Dave was embarrassed that he couldn't control his new horse in front of his friends, especially since his twelve-year-old daughter could ride him safely, and he was the laughing stock of his riding club. He was so embarrassed that Rocky had to go.

And he went to me. I couldn't let this wonderful horse go to someone who didn't understand him, and it seemed like no one else did. My practice was now generating a little extra income, and I knew that if I needed some cash to get through a tough spot, Dr. Mom would help me. She had quickly grown to love Rocky too.

I never had the problems Dave had, probably because I never rode him in spurs. He didn't need them. In fact, he didn't even need the stiff heel of leather riding boots. While I usually ride in proper boots, one day I rode him in running shoes, and found him totally responsive to the light touch of my soft rubber shoes.

And I always used just a plain snaffle bit, the gentlest of bits. Despite his enormous size, it was all he needed - he was so gentle by nature. One day I trail rode him with the Palmers, who had heard through the grapevine the story of his awful behavior on Easter Sunday, but had never seen Rocky before. I asked Angie what she thought of my horse as Rocky's trot matched strides with their Foxtrotters across the grassy fields of Chatfield Reservoir. Angie described him as "a prince." I couldn't agree more.

Rocky never displayed any dangerous maneuvers when I rode him. We understood each other.

We were soul mates. I was so lucky to have him!

After I bought Rocky, my horseshoer told me horror stories about what a rogue he was as she shod him. I heard he would throw his head up trying to hit the rider in the face, and rear straight up to

209

throw his rider off. He never showed any such behavior with me. How could this be true?

I was really glad that I hadn't known about this behavior before I tried Rocky, or I might have missed an opportunity to enjoy this wonderful horse. But I needed to investigate her report.

I learned that the young girl who used to own him was not strong enough to control him when she rode him in gymkhana events - horseback games that are races against the clock. To control such a powerful horse when excited by the prospect of racing, her father put a mechanical hackamore on Rocky. This severe bit, in the hands of a child, undoubtedly caused pain. The bit was placed low over his nostrils, interfering with his breathing. Rocky reacted by tossing his head in an effort to flip the bit off his nostrils. In response to his head tossing, they used a tight tie-down to keep his head low. Between the pain and difficulty breathing Rocky felt trapped, so he reared up, trying to free himself of the confining tack.

I realized he could have done all these things they told me, and yet never showed me this behavior because I rode him in a snaffle and let him carry his head wherever it was comfortable for him.

I brought Rocky home after checking the fields and fences for hazards. Dr. Mom loved to feed him carrots about as much as he loved eating them. She volunteered to clean his paddock. She was always safe around him.

One rainy day right after we moved to the farm, Rocky was out in the pasture when a severe storm bore down on the farm. Summer squalls usually blew over quickly, and I wasn't sure whether I should brave the elements to bring him in, as the storm would probably subside by the time I got him in and I'd be drenched. But the rain was heavy and large hail was pelting him, so I decided to catch him.

Horses are too smart to put their faces into a storm. They put their tails to the wind and drop their heads into the protected zone below their shoulders. Rocky was far out in the field when I started out. He would usually trot to the gate when called, but he would have to face into the storm today. He was so willing to please that each time I called he took one step backward, toward the gate. He must have thought I was crazy when I forced him to face into the storm coming up to the barn. He hated the sound of the pounding rain on the metal roof, but kindly obliged when I asked.

About a minute after we reached the barn the storm let up. I was thoroughly soaked, but Dr. Mom, watching from the kitchen window, got a laugh out of Rocky stepping backwards toward the gate each time I called him.

He showed more horse sense that day than I did.

In the time I had owned him we'd had some wonderful rides. I hoped those good times weren't over.

I tossed and turned all night, worried about Rocky. As soon as the sky started to get light, I called the lab. The test results were shocking! His creatinine and BUN were extremely high. Rocky was in kidney failure! Kidney failure? That's so rare in horses. How could he get kidney failure?

I immediately called the university. He needed a complete work-up to determine the cause of the problem and see if treatment was an option. I waited for an equine medicine specialist to come on the line.

Kidney failure is most commonly caused by an overdose of anti-inflammatory pain killers like bute, but Rocky hadn't been given any drugs.

Poisonous plants were another possible cause, but Rocky's hay was free of weeds. We had recently purchased the farm, but I cared for the mares of the previous owner, and they were healthy and produced vigorous foals, so the pasture grasses must be safe.

Water was another source of toxins, and that did worry me. Our water tasted sweet, and was from a very deep well. But there was a government facility nearby that produced chemicals that contaminated the water table when mixed with run off from hard rains.

I was aware of the problem before we bought the farm, so I checked into the situation. The contamination drained into the creek west of our farm, not our creek system, and had only been found in shallow wells - wells that were less than 50 feet deep. Our well was nearly 300 feet deep. Prior to purchasing the farm the well water tested negative for bacterial contamination, but we hadn't tested for toxins. If our well was contaminated, then my family and Clancy would be at risk.

The University connected me with Dr. Traub. She could see Rocky right away. I told them I was 75 miles away, and had to hitch the trailer and load up, but I'd try to be there in 90 minutes. I took a few minutes re-scheduling my day's appointments. I couldn't leave clients wondering where I was.

As sick as he was, Rocky climbed right into the trailer, and soon we were on our way, with Clancy riding shotgun. Clancy clearly considered herself responsible for Rocky, keeping a close eye on him, no matter what the circumstances.

Every morning, Clancy went straight to Rocky's paddock where she could watch him. If he moved too far from his hay, she would run up and bark at him to keep him by the feeder. He tolerated her and quit trying to kick her. She was so fast, and he was so slow that Clancy was in no danger. Clancy was polite enough not to nip, as some Border collies do. Her herding instinct was so strong that I had to call her repeatedly when it was time to come inside. She didn't want to leave him.

There was no snow on the road today, so as I sped to the hospital I searched my brain to find the source of the Rocky's problem by going over his medical history.

The farm was seeded in tall fescue grass, which can be a problem on breeding farms, because it may contain a fungus that interferes with the delivery of foals or the production of mare's milk. But the mares on this farm had no problem delivering or providing milk for their foals, so the fescue probably didn't harbor the fungus.

I inspected the pastures before bringing Rocky home. We purchased the farm in August, so the weeds were fully grown with seed heads, which makes identification easy. I took my copy of Weeds of the West as I walked through the fields, and although I found almost every species of weed listed in the book grew on my farm, none of them were on my list of toxic plants. Horses rarely eat poisonous plants unless they are starving, and Rocky certainly wasn't starving.

The miles flew by, and I was getting closer to the university, but no closer to a diagnosis. Perhaps Rocky had a kidney stone from minerals in his diet. That's rare in horses. Perhaps he had kidney cancer. That was even rarer. If he had an infection, he should have had a fever.

Now that I knew the kidneys were the problem, his urine would be tested. Crystals in the urine indicate kidney or bladder stones. Red blood cells are present in infections. Cancer cells indicate a tumor. White blood cells or bacteria indicate infection. One test could yield a lot of information.

As I pulled into the parking lot, it was empty, so the entire group of students on Large Animal Medicine rotation would be looking at Rocky. I was certain that these young, curious minds, working with the expertise of the vets mentoring them, would solve Rocky's problem.

I got out of the truck and headed to the office.

"Clancy, you stay here. Rocky will be in good hands."

I walked across the parking lot to hospital admissions.

"Hey, Dr. Thibeault! What have you brought us today?" Mindy, the receptionist called out to me as I entered the office. At least I thought it was Mindy. She and her twin sister, Robin, shared the receptionist duties, so I was never certain until I could read the name tags. Thank goodness for name tags. It was Mindy.

"I brought Dr. Traub a horse suffering from kidney failure."

"Kidney failure? In a horse? We don't see that very often."

"I know. I wanted to make your life and mine more interesting, so it's my own horse that's sick today."

"Uh oh. That's not good."

"No, it's not, but I know he'll get the best care here."

I had confidence in the vet school's ability to treat my horse as well as they had treated my Sheltie years earlier. The respect the college earned from me that day grew stronger as I completed each year of training, and saw the successes they had treating desperately ill animals.

Mindy gave me the paperwork and I headed out to unload Rocky. Dr. Josie Traub and her group of students followed me to the trailer. As I got Rocky out of the trailer, the students' eyes got bigger and bigger when they saw how huge he was.

"Don't worry. He's as gentle as he is big." I assured them.

In every class some of the students had experience with horses before they started vet school, while others were interested in small animal practice, and simply wished to get through their large animal rotations alive, and as quickly as possible. These future small animal vets were amazed at his size, but just like when I was in school, the future equine practitioners came forward to examine him, while the other students stood by observing.

The vet students asked for a complete medical history, even though we knew his kidneys were the problem. I appreciated their thoroughness and was not annoyed at the time it took. Rocky stood in the stocks, waiting patiently.

In emergency cases, I found CSU to be faster and more efficient than other university hospitals I had visited since graduation.

Some of my clients complained that they didn't like to deal with the students when I referred their horses here. They only wanted the specialists touching their horses. I explained that the students were the reason the Teaching Hospital existed, and that tomorrow's specialists were working on their horses under the supervision of some of the best experienced practitioners in the profession.

I handed Dr. Traub the test results from Rocky's blood work. While she looked them over, she ordered an ultrasound exam of Rocky's kidneys. If there was cancer, or an inoperable kidney stone, there would be no treatment. I would have to euthanize him so he wouldn't suffer. If they found anything treatable, we'd try to save him.

The ultrasound arrived and the technician specialist could not find any problems, but really couldn't get a very clear look at Rocky's kidneys because his body wall was so thick. Dr. Traub ordered another scan with a newer machine. The results of the scan from the second machine were not much better. She then ordered their most powerful machine, primarily used for research, to be delivered, and asked the head of the radiology department to assist. A few minutes later, an ultrasound machine about the size of a compact car appeared in the large doorway. Soon I had a specialist in radiology, two ultrasound techs, one specialist in internal medicine, one resident in large animal medicine, three fourth year students and four third year students all examining the images from the ultrasound machine. When Rocky was confidently declared free of tumors and stones, I was relieved - treatment would be an option.

I Make Horse Calls

Dr. Traub repeated the lab work I had done yesterday to see if Rocky was getting better or worse. Rocky patiently let a struggling, nervous student poke him for a blood sample. A urine sample was also taken to evaluate kidney function, and to culture for bacterial infection.

I walked Rocky to the hospital scale. Patients were weighed at admission to accurately determine drug dosages. He had been 1525 pounds last summer, but was down to 1450 because he had not been eating. I wasn't concerned because horses often weigh more when the grass is lush in the summer, and he had some fat reserves, so 1450 was okay.

Rocky went to the intensive care ward. An IV was placed in his jugular vein to give him fluids which would help flush out any toxins that might be poisoning his kidneys. His kidneys were too sick to do it on their own.

"We'll have the results of the blood and urine tests later today and the culture results in 24 to 48 hours. Until we know what we're treating, we'll support him with IV fluids. Any other medications might make him worse. I'll keep you posted," said Dr. Traub.

I said good-bye and stopped at the business office to get an estimate. The costs were very reasonable, considering I would have to shut down my practice and go without any income if I were to do his intensive care by myself. And I couldn't really offer the expertise of the specialists - veterinarians like Dr. Traub who spent years getting specialty training in internal medicine. Plus, I couldn't offer the manpower of an entire college of eager students. Rocky was where he needed to be if he was going to recover.

Still, in ten days my savings would be gone. I didn't have a better reason to spend those savings than to help Rocky, so I signed the forms.

For his sake, I hoped he would recover. And for my sake - the sooner the better.

I climbed back in the truck to Clancy's warm greeting. She put her head in my lap as I drove home. Rocky was in good hands, but I still worried about him. The news certainly could have been worse. He didn't have a kidney stone or cancer, but what caused his kidneys to fail? We could treat the symptoms, but how could we eliminate the cause if we couldn't identify it? Was it something on the farm?

I treated a few patients that afternoon, and I concentrate so much on my work that it took my mind off Rocky for a while. But seeing his paddock empty when I came home made my heart ache. Clancy ran to look for him in the barn, but soon returned to my side. I tried to assure her.

"Sorry girl. He's not home right now. He'll be home soon," I hoped.

That evening I called Dr. Traub, and there was no change. Rocky was still picking at his hay, and not showing signs of severe pain. The tests didn't give us any new information, but did rule out some other ailments.

In the morning, Clancy was jumping at the door, anxious to go out, as always.

"There's no need to go out this morning, Clancy. Rocky's not here to feed."

She couldn't understand why today's routine was different, but eventually she curled up on the rug by the door awaiting our day's rounds.

I called Dr. Traub before picking up the calls for my clinic.

"The blood tests are a slight bit better, and the culture has shown no growth yet, so we're not dealing with a blood infection. When are you coming back?"

I still had to run my practice, and the round trip to the college was 150 miles, so I decided to visit him every other day. He would be okay without me.

"I have a full book of appointments today, but can come tomorrow afternoon."

"Bring hay, feed, and water samples so we can check for toxins. There may be something poisonous in his diet."

"Will do. See you tomorrow. Please call me if anything changes."

"I will."

I remember when I was a student there was a mysterious ailment found on only the best breeding farms, and the problem occurred all across the country one year. Foals were dying of liver failure, for unknown reasons. Tests done on the foals found the cause was a toxin and not an infection, but the disease ran its course so quickly that the cause was not determined before the disease disappeared. Some breeders allowed their mares to undergo liver biopsies to determine the cause. But the mares' biopsies were all normal.

The following year the disease recurred. In the meantime, epidemiologists, veterinarians who study how diseases occur, looked into the problem and asked the farms' managers every conceivable question regarding the management of these foals. Their diagnostic work revealed a supplemental feed had been improperly manufactured with the level of iron ten times higher than it should be. Only the best run farms - farms that gave their newborn foals this supplement, had the problem. As soon as the product was identified, it was pulled from the market and the problem was over. As a result of these fatalities I never feed anything a horse doesn't need.

Rocky ate only pasture, hay and water, with alfalfa or soybean meal added to his diet for extra protein, and a mineral salt lick.

The next day my appointments dragged on and on. I couldn't get Rocky out of my mind. Every client seemed to have a "while you're here, Doc" extra problem to solve, but finally I was finished and could go see him. I gathered up the hay and water samples. Dr. Hamar, the college's toxicologist, looked at the hay samples, and sent the water to an outside lab. Dr. Knight was an expert on poisonous plants, and would examine the hay as well.

Clancy kept me company on the drive, and my mind was now free to worry non-stop.

When I got to his stall, I could instantly see he was worse. Rocky was standing with his face in the corner, his head down. He didn't even look at me when I called his name. He was depressed and disinterested in his surroundings. He looked much thinner. It's hard to see the loss of a few pounds on such a large frame, but I thought he had lost weight. I walked him to the scale. He was down to 1375 pounds. Now I really was scared! He had lost 75 pounds in less than 48 hours. Losing nearly 2 pounds an hour, could I expect to cure him from an undiagnosed ailment before he was too weak to save?

I took him back to the stall and offered him fresh carrots from home.

I Make Horse Calls

"Here boy. Wanna carrot?"

He looked at it, but then looked away. I was heartbroken. He must feel awful to refuse carrots. When I rubbed the favorite spot in his chest, he moved away. He didn't want to be touched. He just wanted to be left alone.

His blood tests results weren't worse, but *he* certainly was. And vets don't treat the test results - we treat the patient.

Rocky felt terrible. We were losing him.

I gave the hay and water samples to the students and left. I would call Dr. Traub in the morning.

It was a sad drive home. Thank goodness for Clancy's companionship.

After another sleepless night, I called Dr. Traub first thing the next morning.

"The lab found no growth in the urine sample, so both the blood and urine are clear of infection," said Dr. Traub.

She had received the samples from the students. The hay was examined by Dr. Knight, who said it looked so good that he wanted the name of my farmer so he could order some for the vet hospital. Dr. Hamar, the toxicologist, said fungal toxins are common in grain, but Rocky wasn't fed grain. The water tests were still pending.

I was relieved that Rocky was not suffering as a result of a lapse in my management, but we were no closer to an answer.

Again I drove to CSU, but there was no change in Rocky's behavior. I hand walked him outside in the sunshine, but he was really dragging. I didn't have the courage to weigh him again. He looked weaker and thinner. He was still miserable. He had been in the hospital for four days, but wasn't responding to treatment. I stopped by the business office on my way home, and the total so far was approaching the value of my savings account. I was still willing to spend all of my money, but it did not look like we were going to win the battle at any cost.

I had another sleepless night, trying to decide if it was humane to continue treating Rocky. He was not sweating and in agony, like horses with colic, but those horses die quickly. Could I let Rocky waste away until he was too weak to stand? He had been such a strong, massive horse when he was healthy. With his desire to be left alone, discomfort at being touched, and lack of interest in his beloved carrots, I knew he was dreadfully sick. I would call Dr. Traub late the next morning, after she had run another set of blood tests. If there was no improvement, perhaps it was time to end his suffering.

I had no early appointments this morning, and no need to go outside and feed, so the hours dragged by from dawn until I could call Dr. Traub. My parents were still in Florida, so the house was somberly quiet.

I sat on the side of my bed, Clancy beside me, while I gathered the courage to make the call. Could I make the right decision - the one that was right for Rocky?

I called the hospital and waited for Dr. Traub to answer her page. The wait was agonizing, but finally she came on the line.

"This is Dr. Traub."

"This is Dr. Thibeault. How's Rocky doing this morning?"

"We drew blood this morning and I just got the results back from the lab. His creatinine is coming down, so I think he's turning the corner…blah,blah,blah."

I didn't hear anything she said after that. I was so happy!

I never cried tears of joy before, but the flow couldn't be stopped as I turned and hugged Clancy so tightly I almost crushed her.

My big, beautiful, Rocky was going to be okay!

You can order **More Horse Calls** by visiting our website at **www.imakehorsecalls.com** or send payment of $14.95 plus $4.95 S&H to I Make Horse Calls P O Box 1702 Georgetown, KY 40324